MONTH-BY-MONTH GARDENING

ROCKY MOUNTAIN

Brimming with creative inspiration, how-to projects, and useful information to enrich your everyday life, Quarto Knows is a favorite destination for those pursuing their interests and passions. Visit our site and dig deeper with our books into your area of interest: Quarto Creates, Quarto Cooks, Quarto Homes, Quarto Lives, Quarto Drives, Quarto Explores, Quarto Gifts, or Quarto Kids.

First published in 2015 by Cool Springs Press, an imprint of The Quarto Group, 401 Second Avenue North, Suite 310, Minneapolis, MN 55401 USA. Telephone: (612) 344-8100 Fax: (612) 344-8692 www.QuartoKnows.com

Cool Springs Press titles are also available at discount for retail, wholesale, promotional, and bulk purchase. For details, contact the Special Sales Manager by email at specialsales@quarto.com or by mail at The Quarto Group, Attn: Special Sales Manager, 401 Second Avenue North, Suite 310, Minneapolis, MN 55401 USA.

ISBN: 978-1-59186-434-9

Library of Congress Control Number: 2015937651

Acquisitions Editor: Billie Brownell
Senior Art Director: Brad Springer
Layout: S.E. Anglin

Printed in USA

MONTH-BY-MONTH GARDENING

ROCKY MOUNTAIN

**What to Do Each Month to Have
a Beautiful Garden All Year**

JOHN CRETTI

COOL
SPRINGS
PRESS

Dedication

For Gloria; you have enriched my life, my living, and my faith.

Acknowledgments

Thanks to all gardeners throughout the Rocky Mountain region! Your enthusiasm for gardening, following me for over thirty years on radio, television, and other media outreach, and encouraging me to continue writing have inspired me to keep sharing my passion for growing plants in our beautiful and unique region.

Thanks to the many horticulture professionals throughout Colorado, Wyoming, Montana, Idaho, and Utah, and across the country. You have generously shared your knowledge and enthusiasm that inspires new and experienced gardeners throughout the nation.

Thanks to the volunteer Master Gardeners who donate their time and talents answering questions and helping newbies garden with a greater measure of success.

The process of compiling this book was an inspiring journey. I want to thank my friends for their patience and support during the process. Thanks to Debbie for your tolerance and patience, and for reminding me of what is most important in life.

I want to thank Billie Brownell, my editor, for persisting and fine-tuning the manuscript into a more readable and understandable form. Thanks to everyone at Cool Springs Press (Quarto Publishing) for this opportunity.

Contents

Introduction

Gardening throughout the Rocky Mountain region is an adventure. The climate in the Rockies is perhaps more varied than any other climate in the United States. Elevation often dictates much of the climate in this region. Mountain communities have cold winters and short summers. Lower elevation river valley areas are milder and often wetter. Rainfall averages less than 10 to 20 inches a year in desert areas to 40 to 50 inches a year in the mountains and valleys of Colorado and Idaho. The Rocky Mountain region features extreme and rapid fluctuations of temperature, wind, hail, drought, and light intensity. Snowfall may stay around for only a day, a week, or all winter long. Winters can be dry or very snowy, and very cold. However, in some of the warmer, more protected microclimates (against sides of buildings, boulders, or areas with consistent winter snow cover) and in lowland valley areas, less hardy plants can be successfully grown. Spring can appear suddenly, but so can a late spring snowfall and frost. All this will put your gardening skills and patience to the test each year.

The Rockies feature garden styles that are as distinctive as the land itself. You'll find more naturalistic styles where the beauty of rocks and streams are designed to reflect the local area. Other cultures have also played a part in shaping our landscapes, including the French, Dutch, Irish, German, Italian, and Japanese. An overview of the natural ecology and cultural influences is useful, but it does not take into account our American ingenuity to create innovative gardens that reflect our modern living style.

Knowing the "when and how" of gardening will help you to be successful. This book is designed to help you eliminate some of the guesswork. It is a guide to help, not restrict, your gardening efforts and hopefully save you time and money.

A nicely landscaped yard can include a number of elements, including shrubs, perennials, trees, and lawn areas.

KEEP A GARDEN JOURNAL

Though you can write notes in this book and add bookmarks, I strongly encourage you to keep a separate gardening notebook or journal. One of the best reasons for keeping records may not be obvious at first, but sooner or later, the information you jot down can keep your memories fresh and help you avoid repeating the same gardening mistakes. It can help you plan what will work best in specific areas of your landscape, since there may be various microclimates just in your own garden.

Despite our best intentions, humans forget. Remember when you planted that beautiful peony last year and then sliced into the shoots during the autumn while planting hardy spring-flowering bulbs? Placing labels in the garden can help identify spots where perennials are located to avoid this mishap. You can even sketch a simple drawing to mark plant locations.

Keeping tabs on where you bought what, how much you spent, and how the plants performed will help develop a personal reference source. In a sense, simple record keeping is like writing your own garden book, specific to your property, your needs, and your gardening style. Over the years, as your garden matures and your gardening skills improve, you will know predictably the succession of bloom in your garden, when pests and diseases arrive, and how to be ready to cope with specific problems.

Don't forget to take pictures, either conventional or digital photos, to show the "before and after" of what's happening in your landscape. You don't need to be a rocket scientist to maintain a journal or garden notebook. I often use a 100-page, college-ruled composition notebook to record specific information such as weather conditions, the first and last freezes of the gardening year, the dates plants were installed, and names and varieties of vegetables, herbs, flowers, shrubs, trees, vines, groundcovers, and other plants that I'm attempting to grow. Keep notes about fertilizer applications and pest problems. When you visit other gardeners in your area, jot down interesting techniques or tips that may help you become more successful with your gardening endeavors. A journal is a tool, just like a spading fork or a good set of hand pruners.

PLANNING AND IMPROVING YOUR GARDEN

Whether you are creating an entirely new landscape or renovating an existing one, plan the landscape or garden area on paper first. It does not have to be a fancy design, unless that's what you desire. You will need a pencil, ruled graph paper, and tracing paper. If you have house plans or a plat map in your files, get them out too.

- Create a base map. This is simply a plan of your property drawn to scale on graph paper. It shows the placement of the house, its orientation to the sun, other buildings and structures on the site, and existing plants. A base map helps you visualize your ideas and plan for the kinds of plants and hardscaping you will add.

- Using the graph paper, trace the outline of the house from a plat map, or simply measure the house and grounds. Next, measure the landscape area. Measure at right angles from a house corner to the property lines, and from the corner of the road to establish where your house sits within your property. Also, measure from fixed points of the house to the driveway, deck, patio, and any walkways. Draw in any existing trees, shrubs, retaining walls, boulders, and flowerbeds. Identify north on the plan. Plot all these measurements to scale on a large sheet of graph paper (¼-inch grid allows for a scale of 1 inch = 4 feet).

- Analyze the land to familiarize yourself with the growing conditions within your property.

Sketch the landscape features you're considering on a photo-copy or tracing paper copy of your site map.

Lay a sheet of tracing paper over the base map, and title it "Site Analysis." Make notes about sun exposure, shade patterns (morning sun, afternoon sun, full sun, full shade), wind exposure, topography, and water drainage.

- Look for and identify any microclimates—areas with atypical environmental conditions. For example, a microclimate could exist on a south-facing slope protected between two large boulders, which may be warmer in winter and hotter in summer than the open area surrounding it. A microclimate could also exist where water drains from the roof or collects in low spots.

- Examine drainage patterns and mark them on your map. Also take note of structural limitations such as overhead power lines and underground utilities.

- Consider which plants you want to keep, and list factors that will affect the selection of new plants. Does your site require plants that will tolerate the cold temperatures, full sun, shade, dry conditions, occasional flooding, or browsing from deer and other critters?

- Use another sheet of tracing paper over the base plan and site analysis to sketch out a landscape plan. Draw in trees where you want them and add shrubs, groundcovers, or flowering plants. Remember to keep plants about 4 to 5 feet from the foundation to allow for growth and to make house maintenance easier. Be aware of the ultimate height and spread of the plants in various areas. Note whether you want plants that attract wildlife, birds, hummingbirds, or butterflies. Group the plants based on their watering needs so you can water more efficiently.

- If you are planning to irrigate, add an automatic sprinkler or drip system to your plan. In-ground watering systems are not always needed in every landscape, particularly if you choose to create a water-thrifty or "xeric" garden (see the glossary). While plants are becoming established in the first growing season, however, it is very desirable to have a drip system or soaker hoses.

SOIL

Soil, like the weather, will present challenges to gardening success. We often get caught up in the beauty of plants in magazines and books without remembering that the foundation for any healthy and pest-free garden, landscape, or lawn is the soil. A good soil allows air, water, and nutrients to be absorbed by plant roots and lets the root system roam freely.

How do you build a healthy soil? Begin with a soil test through your State University or local county Cooperative Extension Service. The test will tell you the pH level of the soil and the level of nutrients available to plants.

Stated in numbers, pH is a measurement of acidity or alkalinity of the soil. On a scale of 0 to 14, a pH of 7 is neutral. Numbers below 7 indicate acidic conditions and readings above 7 are basic or alkaline. Soil pH affects not only plant health but also the availability of nutrients. If the soil is too acidic or too alkaline, minerals such as nitrogen, phosphorus, potassium, calcium, and magnesium can be "tied-up" and unavailable to plants. Adding more fertilizer *will not* help. You can lower the pH by adding organic matter such as compost or sulfur (in moderation or as recommended by a soil test). You can raise soil pH by adding agricultural lime, calcium, or wood ashes (in moderation), but this is rarely needed in our region.

Organic matter such as compost, sphagnum peat moss, and aged manure is an important component to soil building. It improves the soil tilth—the physical condition or structure of the soil. When added to clay soils, organic amendments hold the clay particles apart, improving air and water movement in the soil. This is essential for healthy root growth and translates to deeper, more extensive root development as well as drought endurance.

Cover crops or "green manure" such as crimson clover or annual ryegrass are relatively inexpensive sources of organic matter. Sow these crops in the early fall, and then turn them under in the spring to enrich the soil.

Organic fertilizers derived from naturally occurring sources are my favorite alternative to synthetic plant fertilizers. They include composted animal manures, cottonseed meal, alfalfa meal, and bloodmeal, among many others. Although they contain relatively low concentrations of actual nutrients compared to synthetic fertilizers, they help to increase the organic content of the soil and ultimately improve the soil structure.

To avoid damaging soil structure, never dig or cultivate when the soil is too wet or too dry. Follow this simple test: if the soil sticks to your shovel or spading fork, the soil is too wet. Postpone digging until the soil dries out.

Coarse-textured, sandy, or granite soils have excellent drainage but hold little water. Add organic matter to them to increase fertility and water retention.

Sand has often been touted as the perfect fix for improving drainage in clay soils. Unless you add it at the rate of at least 6 inches of sand per 8 inches of clay soil, your soil will be better suited for making adobe bricks than growing plants.

PLANT

Proper planting is important to establishing healthy, long-lived plants. Be mindful of their maintenance requirements under the conditions at your site. Write the common name and the scientific name

■ *Take a handful of soil and dampen it with water until it is moldable, almost like moist putty, then squeeze it into a ribbon. If a ribbon of greater than 2 inches forms before it breaks, you have very heavy and poorly drained soil. It will not be suitable for a garden without some major amendments.*

(genus and species) on your plan. Common names are less specific than scientific names and can be confusing when you are shopping for plants. At this step you should also consider landscape materials for pathways, mulch, edging, and borders.

Purchase quality plants from reputable sources and follow proper planting techniques to ensure rapid and healthy establishment and long-term survival. Preparing the site, digging the hole, and planting at the proper depth and time will help ensure your transplanting and gardening success.

If you were overly ambitious and planned for an incredible design, remember you don't have to build it all at one time. Break the project into phases as your time and budget allow.

WATER

Anyone can water a garden; what's more challenging is to meet the water demands of the plants while conserving water. This requires attention to detail. The goal is to avoid the common mistakes of over- or underwatering, the two practices most often associated with injuring or killing plants.

Water needs depend on both the plant and the soil. Moisture-loving plants require more frequent watering than plants adapted to dry conditions. New plants, even drought-tolerant ones, will need more water at first to become established. Generally, after the first growing season, they may not require supplemental watering even during the hot, dry summer months. Mulching will help conserve moisture and suppress weed invasions that compete for moisture. Some trees, shrubs, and groundcovers are quite drought-tolerant and can withstand long periods without rain or irrigation.

Use shredded leaves, evergreen needles, cedar shavings, or wood mulches to reduce watering frequency. A thin layer of these materials over the soil surface will not only conserve moisture, but also suppress annual weeds, moderate soil temperature fluctuations, and gradually improve the soil.

Soil also affects watering in several ways. For instance, plants growing in moisture-retentive

clay soils need less frequent watering than plants growing in faster-draining sandy soils.

FERTILIZE

Fertilizers add minerals to soil, minerals that plants take up as nutrients. The three most important are nitrogen, phosphorus, and potassium. Three numbers on the fertilizer bag or package represent them. For example, 5-10-5 gives the percentage by weight of nitrogen (N), phosphate (P), and potash (K). In this case, nitrogen makes up 5 percent of the total weight, phosphate, which supplies phosphorus, accounts for 10 percent, and potash, a source of potassium, makes up 5 percent. The remaining weight (the total must add up to 100 percent) comprises a nutrient carrier.

In addition to the primary elements (N-P-K), the fertilizer may contain secondary plant nutrients such as calcium, magnesium, sulfur, or minor nutrients such as manganese, zinc, copper, iron, or molybdenum. Apply these nutrients if dictated by soil test results or plant appearance.

My favorite fertilizers are slow-release types. They are available to the plants for an extended period up to six months (follow label recommendations). While more expensive than conventional granular forms, they reduce the need for supplemental applications and the likelihood of fertilizer burn.

A slow-release fertilizer is a good choice especially in sandy soils or crushed granite that tend to leach, or for heavy clay soils where runoff can be a problem. If the soil has been properly prepared at the onset of gardening, supplemental fertilization may not be necessary for several years after planting.

When fertilizing your plants, let their growth rate and leaf coloration guide you. Rely on soil tests to make the right choices if you are not familiar with the plant symptoms of nutrient deficiencies.

CARE

There is an art and a science to pruning. Pruning helps improve the health and appearance of plants.

It is helpful for training young plants, developing a strong framework in trees and shrubs, encouraging flowers and fruiting, and preventing and reducing damage. You should prune carefully and selectively with a purpose in mind.

It can be as simple as pinching the spent or faded flowers from your annuals and perennials, called "deadheading." This process will encourage repeat bloom and discourage seed development. You can prune young perennials to control height and bloom time.

Pruning becomes more involved especially when removing a large limb or smaller branches from deciduous trees or evergreens. Understand why you are pruning before you make the first cut.

PROBLEM-SOLVE

You are *bound* to encounter insects, diseases, and weeds while trying to grow a healthy landscape. Deer, elk, voles, pocket gophers, meadow mice, squirrels, and rabbits can also be viewed as pests or critters.

Deal with pests sensibly. Just because you see one aphid on your rose bush, you don't have to get out the pesticide to kill the bug. There are many beneficial insects in the garden that will help keep insect pests at bay.

I like to recommend the Integrated Pest Management (IPM) program. It is a common-sense approach to managing and dealing with pests that brings nature into the battle on the gardener's side. It combines smart plant selection with good planting and maintenance practices, and an understanding of pests and their life cycles. It starts with planning and proper planting to produce strong, healthy plants that, by themselves can grow and prosper with minimal help from you. As in nature, an acceptable level of pests is accommodated. Control is the goal, rather than elimination. Several techniques can be used in the garden and landscape IPM approach.

IPM CULTURAL PRACTICES
- **Proper soil management:** Maintain the appropriate soil pH for plants by having your

soil tested every three years. Add generous amounts of organic matter to build and maintain soil fertility.

- **Plant selection:** Match plants suited to the soil and climate of your area and select species and cultivars that are resistant to pests. These plants are resistant—not immune—to damage. Expect them to exhibit less insect or disease injury than susceptible varieties growing in the same environment.

- **Watering:** Water late at night or early in the morning. Avoid watering in early evening because the leaves may remain wet for an extended period of time. This often favors fungus and other disease infections.

- **Mulching:** Apply a shallow layer of mulch such as compost, shredded leaves, bark shavings, pole peelings, pine needles, or other organic materials to conserve moisture, suppress weed growth, and supply nutrients as they decompose.

- **Sanitation:** Remove dead, damaged, diseased, or insect-infested leaves, shoots, stems, or branches whenever you spot them.

IPM MECHANICAL CONTROLS
- **Handpicking:** Remove insect pests by hand, or knock them off with a strong spray of water from the hose.

- **Exclusion:** Physically block insects from attacking your plants. Aluminum foil collars can be placed around seedlings to prevent cutworms from attacking the tender plant stems. Plants can be covered with cheesecloth or spun-bonded polyester products to keep out the insects.

IPM BIOLOGICAL CONTROLS
- **Predators and parasites:** Some bugs and spiders are on our side. Known as beneficial insects or natural enemies of the "bad bugs," they fall into two main categories: predators and parasites. Predators hunt and feed on other insects. They include spiders, praying mantises, lady beetles, and green lacewings. Parasites, such as braconid wasps and *Trichogramma* wasps, hatch from eggs

deposited on or in another insect, and eat their host insect as they develop.

Releasing beneficial insects into your garden may offer some benefit, but it is better to conserve the beneficial insects already there. Learn to identify the beneficial insects in your yard. Avoid broad-spectrum insecticides that will kill beneficial insects.

- **Botanical pesticides and insecticidal soap sprays**: These naturally occurring pesticides are derived from plants. Two common botanicals include pyrethrins, insecticidal chemicals extracted from the pyrethrum flower (*Tanacetum cinerarifoliium*), and Neem, a botanical insecticide from the tropical Neem tree (*Azadirachta indica*), which contains the active ingredient azadirachtin. Insecticidal soaps have been formulated specifically for their ability to control insects. Soaps are effective only against those insects that come into direct contact with sprays before they dry. These natural pesticides break down rapidly when exposed to sunlight, air, heat, and moisture. They are less likely to kill beneficial insects than insecticides that have longer residual activity, and they are not as harmful to birds and other wildlife.

- **Microbial insecticides:** These are microscopic living organisms such as viruses, bacteria, fungi, protozoa, or nematodes, that combat insects. Although they may seem out of the ordinary, they can be applied in ordinary ways such as sprays, dusts, or granules. The bacterium *Bacillus thuringiensis* (B.t.) is the most popular pathogen. Formulations from *Bacillus thuringiensis* var. *Kurstaki* (B.t. K) are the most widely used to control caterpillars, the larvae of butterflies and moths.

- **Horticultural oils:** When applied to plants, these highly refined oils smother insects, mites, and their eggs. Typically, horticultural oils are derived from highly refined petroleum products that are specifically manufactured to control pests on plants. Studies have shown that horticultural oils derived from vegetable oils such as cottonseed and soybean oil also exhibit insecticidal properties. Dormant applications generally control aphid

eggs, the egg stages of mites, scale insects, and caterpillars such as leafrollers and tent caterpillars. Summer applications control adelgids, aphids, mealybugs, scale insects, spider mites, and whiteflies. Oils have limited effects on beneficial insects, especially when applied during the dormant season. Insects and mites have not been reported to develop resistance to petroleum and vegetable oils.

- **Pesticides.** Always read and follow label directions before using any product—whether synthetic, natural, or organic—in your landscape and garden. Make sure it is labeled to control the target pest on the plant you want to treat. Wear any protective clothing recommended or required by the label. Wear long sleeves, pants, goggles, and gloves as a regular part of your pesticide application gear.

WINTER CARE

Non-native plants often need a little help surviving our winters. Snow is the best mulch, but it often arrives late, melts too rapidly, or comes and goes throughout the winter.

You can protect new plantings, borderline hardy plants, or those subject to winterkill and frost heaving with winter mulch. Apply winter mulches of cedar shavings, wheat straw, or evergreen boughs over the plants after the ground freezes. The goal is to keep the soil consistently cold throughout the winter. Fluctuating soil temperatures often cause early sprouting and frost heaving. Plants that emerge too early can be damaged and flowers terminated when normal cold temperatures return. Frost heaving causes the soil to shift, damaging roots and may push perennials and bulbs right out of the ground.

One of the greatest enemies of landscape plants in the Rockies is lack of late fall and winter watering. Lack of soil moisture, drying winds, low precipitation, and fluctuating temperatures are common in fall and winter. In many areas, there is little or no snow cover to provide soil moisture from October through March. Landscape plants and lawns growing under these conditions are often stressed and damaged if they don't receive supplemental water periodically. Winterkill is often the result.

INTRODUCTION

Water when air and soil temperatures are above 45 degrees Fahrenheit with no snow cover. Water early in the day so water soaks into the ground before freezing nighttime temperatures. Landscape plants receiving reflected heat from buildings, fences, and walls are prone to winter damage. Windy locations result in faster drying of lawns and plants. This predisposes lawns to later winter mite damage. Watering is the best way to prevent lawn damage. Monitor weather and soil conditions and water during extended dry periods without snow or rain, once to twice a month.

My preferred way to water trees is a frog-eye lawn sprinkler. The most important area is halfway between the trunk and several feet beyond the "drip line" or the branch extremities. Let the sprinkler run twenty to thirty minutes at each setting.

LEARNING MORE

Use the *Rocky Mountain Getting Started Garden Guide* as a companion to this book. It features more complete details on individual plant selections and additional gardening techniques suited to our region.

Contact your local state University or county Cooperative Extension Service. They have many publications as well as volunteer Master Gardeners to help answer some of your gardening questions.

Take time to visit local public gardens, botanical gardens, and arboreta to gather more gardening and landscaping ideas. The local library has a plethora of garden books, magazines, and videos. It is a great place to spend spare time in the winter months, planning for the upcoming season.

HOW TO USE THIS BOOK

Rocky Mountain Month-by-Month Gardening is a resource written to be the when-to and how-to guide of caring for and maintaining our beautiful and unique region through the seasons. It's a great companion to my other book, *Rocky Mountain Getting Started Garden Guide*.

Each monthly chapter is a schedule to keep track of what needs doing, and when, covering the major reminders to keep your plants growing and maintaining a healthy and attractive landscape. Whether you garden in a small lot or a sprawling

country retreat, you'll find this book is just what you need to get started and to sharpen your gardening skills.

I've tried to pack plenty of practical information and how-tos to take you through the basic techniques involved in all aspects of gardening. These include: Plan, Plant, Care, Water, Fertilize, and Problem-Solve. Plus, I've added tips for "gardening with an altitude." It is presented to help you become a more responsible and sustainable gardener so you will be complementing our natural surroundings. My mantra is to first choose the right plant for the right place, and you're on your way to successful gardening in the Rockies!

Though you can write in the margins of this book and add bookmarks, I strongly encourage you to keep a gardening notebook or journal. One of the best reasons for keeping records may not be obvious at first, but sooner or later, the information you jot down can keep your memories fresh and help you avoid repeating the same gardening mistakes. It can help you plan on what will work best in specific areas of *your* landscape, since there may be various microclimates just in your own landscape.

Gardening in our region will need some fine-tuning. The seasons do not always arrive here when expected. There are drought years (some droughts last for several years), water restrictions, and pest or disease problems. As your landscape matures, "microclimates" develop—areas that are more or less protected from the open parts of the landscape—that will allow you to grow more unusual plants or to experiment with plants not in your hardiness zone. Soils can vary from acidic in the High Country to extreme alkaline in the lower elevations. Soil structure can range from crushed granite to sand or heavy clay. Rapid temperature fluctuations are the norm in winter and early spring.

You'll discover many benefits from tending your home garden and landscape. Not only will you add beauty to your landscape and neighborhood, you are increasing the value of your property while improving your quality of life. Now, go forth and dig in!

USDA COLD HARDINESS ZONES FOR THE ROCKY MOUNTAINS

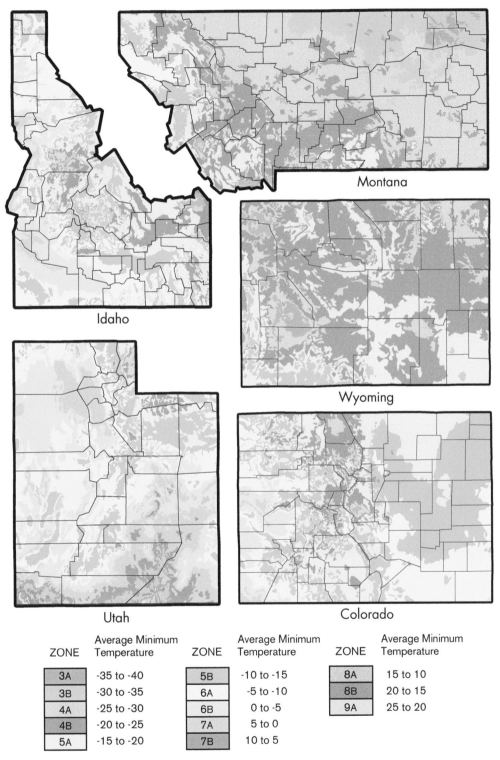

ZONE	Average Minimum Temperature	ZONE	Average Minimum Temperature	ZONE	Average Minimum Temperature
3A	-35 to -40	5B	-10 to -15	8A	15 to 10
3B	-30 to -35	6A	-5 to -10	8B	20 to 15
4A	-25 to -30	6B	0 to -5	9A	25 to 20
4B	-20 to -25	7A	5 to 0		
5A	-15 to -20	7B	10 to 5		

January

January is a time for resolutions. Is your landscape too much to maintain? Maybe you'd like to hire a lawncare professional. Maybe it's time to evaluate and re-design to make it more manageable. Check your garden notebook to see which plants didn't perform as expected. Maybe it's best to replace the undesirable ones.

Relax and enjoy your winter landscape. Look out your windows to see the view beyond—do your shrubs have eye-catching features including berries, interesting bark, evergreen foliage, or colorful stems that add form and structure to the winter landscape? Or are most of them planted too near the house, able to be viewed and appreciated only by passersby?

This month, browse through garden catalogs to discover new plants that may have potential in your area. Though the wonderful photographs may not be realistic for how the plants will fare in your garden, information about their cultural requirements will help determine if you want to try them. Place orders as early as possible, especially if you want new or unusual perennials. Note their hardiness before making definite plans to order. Some can be very costly; shop wisely to make sure they're hardy for your area.

Avoid excessive de-icing salts on paths, driveways, and sidewalks. As the salts accumulate in the soil around perennials, they cause harm and kill the roots. Instead, use an inexpensive fertilizer such as ammonium sulfate or wood ashes to de-ice if you must.

If you get an urge to prune, only remove injured or broken branches. Make clean cuts where a branch joins a larger branch or the main stem. Take care not to cut into the main branch or trunk, as this will cause further dieback. You don't need to apply any wound dressing to pruning cuts.

Winter watering of the landscape may be necessary if there are extended periods of dry weather without rain or snow. As long as the ground is unfrozen, you can water trees, shrubs, and, turf areas every four to five weeks when daytime temperatures are above freezing. Don't forget to drain the hose and return it to storage when you're finished.

PLAN

ANNUALS

January is the time to begin planning your annuals garden. Most mail-order catalogs and websites will offer you lots of help with plant selection and planning too. Even if you don't order via mail, these seed and nursery catalogs provide helpful information. Use them as a resource to learn about new varieties being introduced. The All-America Selections (AAS) are highlighted by the companies that offer them. These are good plants to try since they have been grown in various trial gardens throughout the country, but their success depends upon your particular garden site and area.

Some things to do for January planning:

1. Once your list is complete, place your order early to beat the rush and to guarantee that you get the choices you selected.

2. Consider growing your own seedlings indoors if you have the space and time.

HERE'S HOW

TO ORDER BY MAIL AND ONLINE

Mail-order and online shopping is convenient and provides you with a larger selection of plants. Here are some tips for success:

1. Order from reputable seed companies and nurseries that have a refund or replacement policy.

2. With perennial plants, order from a nursery with the same climate as you have.

3. Order early for a better selection.

4. Specify a shipping date so plants don't arrive before you are ready to plant them.

5. Unpack plants as soon as they arrive and examine them carefully for any problems.

6. Plant as soon as possible after receiving plants. The exception is a bare-root plant, which should be soaked in a bucket of water for a few hours before planting.

3. Plan to build a plant stand to start seeds indoors, particularly if you lack adequate bright light to grow strong seedlings.

4. Consult your garden notebook, calendar, or journal to refresh your memory of the annuals that performed best in your landscape last season. Note specific varieties you'd like to grow again, and experiment by growing some new ones.

5. Sterilize old containers and pots by scrubbing off old soil and debris with a scouring pad. Soak in a solution of bleach and warm water (1 part liquid chlorine bleach to 9 parts water) for a half-hour or so. Then rinse with clear water.

BULBS

For winter color in a short time, plan to plant paper-white narcissus bulbs indoors. They are usually available at garden stores now and require no chill period. Just plant them in a pot of moist pebbles, and enjoy the show in a few weeks.

Unpack plants as soon as possible to inspect them and rehydrate them.

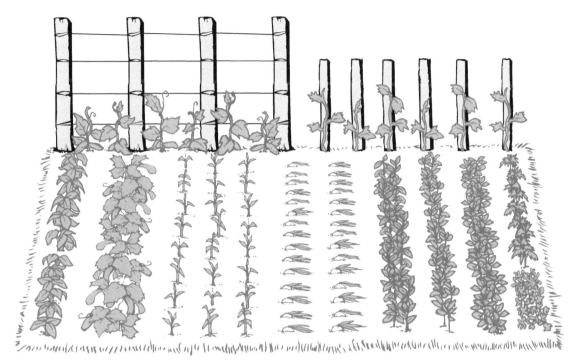

■ *Construct a trellis or use stakes to train vining plants up, leaving more space in the garden.*

January is good time to select flowering bulbs, corms, rhizomes, and tubers to provide accents in your summer garden. For example, summer-blooming gladiolus are sure to invite hummingbirds to your yard. Study mail-order catalogs to learn more about the various kinds and how they can be used in your landscape.

EDIBLES
As you plan your vegetable garden, your local garden retailer or state university can provide a list of recommended varieties suited to your area. Draw a garden plan to scale, and browse through mail-order catalogs. Check out the newest All-America Selections, and give them a try if you have space in your garden plot.

With limited space, consider growing vining plants such as cucumbers, melons, pole beans, garden peas, and others on supports. You can construct a fence or put up garden netting to support plants that like to climb.

If you live in an area where deer, elk, and other creatures will share your garden, now is the time to plan a fence for the vegetable garden. Your local Division of Wildlife can help you with information on deer fencing and strategies to thwart wildlife. Lower fencing can be placed around the garden to keep out rabbits, dogs, cats, and other critters. If your municipality permits, a low-voltage electric fence can repel many animals.

If you are new to vegetable gardening, start with a small plan. Preparing and maintaining a large area can take a lot of time for novice veggie gardeners, so ease in to it first.

LAWNS
You normally wouldn't be thinking about lawns now, but during these quiet times, it's good to evaluate *why* you have a lawn, how manageable it is, and the kind of grass or grass mixtures you have in your lawn. If your lawn has become a "pain in the grass," now is the time to think about making changes.

It is a good idea to check the air filter of your lawn mower once a month or so to make sure it looks clean and doesn't need to be replaced midseason. You can remove the air filter and tap it on the ground to dislodge some of the dust to extend its life.

■ *You should replace the air filter at the beginning of every season.*

■ *Most lawn mowers have a dipstick as part of the oil cap. Remove the dipstick and look at the oil on the end, which should be clear to light brown. If it is any darker, you'll need to change the oil. Consult your owner's manual about how to change the oil, and recycle the old oil by taking it to a local mower or engine repair shop. Refill the oil by using the right weight and type of oil for your mower. Your owner's manual will have information about whether to add two-stroke or four-stroke oil.*

This is a good time to have your lawn mower blade sharpened during the slow period at local hardware and fix-it shops. Be sure the gasoline is drained from gas-powered engines, the oil has been changed, and the spark plug has been replaced, if needed.

Consider investing in a new lawn mower to replace an older model; maybe you can upgrade to a mulching mower that recycles the grass clippings.

If you want to be more ecological, consider a push mower or battery-rechargeable electric mower.

PERENNIALS

Wouldn't it be nice to have a perennial garden that provides color throughout the seasons? Now is the time to plan such a garden. You can even have "winter roses" (*Helleborus)* in February. If you have kept a garden notebook or journal, get it out during the dreary, cold days and evaluate last season's garden. You may have made notes on which plants need to go and other plants you would like to add.

ROSES

Roses can be planted as garden focal points or integrated into other facets of your landscape. Take time to consider placement of roses carefully. Assess your site. Do you need a colorful hedge to screen an unsightly view? Will you use roses as a border or fill, or will you add a formal rose garden?

Browse garden catalogs and study the new introductions. Ask local rose gardeners about the most reliable roses for your area. A great resource is the "Handbook for Selecting Roses," a booklet published annually by the American Rose Society (American Rose Society, P.O. Box 30,000, Shreveport, LA 71130-0030; www.ars.org). It covers everything from old garden to modern roses. Check with local rosarians, garden clubs, your County Extension office, or state University for varieties best suited to your area.

SHRUBS

Examine nursery and garden catalogs arriving in the mail. As you pore over photographs of attractive shrubs, learn about their adaptability and hardiness to our region. Before you buy new shrubs, draw a sketch or design to help you in spacing and selecting the right kinds of shrubs for a particular site. If you don't feel comfortable doing this, consult a landscape designer, contractor, or certified landscape architect.

TREES

This is a month to enjoy your winter landscape and your favorite trees. Look out your windows to see which trees are in view. Deciduous trees are showing off their attractive bark, architectural trunk, and branch structure now. Enjoy!

If you're keeping a garden journal or notebook, check it now to see if pests plagued any trees last season. It may be time to plan to replace certain trees that have become problems. You can have them removed and replaced when spring arrives.

Plan to place orders for bare-root fruit trees and ornamentals if you want to get a bargain early in the season. Mail-order catalogs offer many bare-root trees, and your local nurseries may stock some. Check to see what's available in your area. Before you shop, do your homework. Be familiar with the growing conditions required for the trees you want. In addition to full sun and well-drained soils, fruit trees need regular pruning, watering, and pest control if you want to reap a bountiful crop.

VINES, GROUNDCOVERS & ORNAMENTAL GRASSES

Gardening catalogs are arriving almost daily in the mail. Think about problem areas in your garden, and browse your catalogs for unique and interesting vines, groundcovers, and ornamental grasses to fill in these areas with background effects and accents. Utilitarian vines, groundcovers, and grasses will serve many purposes, so consider which ornamental characteristics you desire. The foliage of evergreen types provides year-round color. Deciduous plants offer attractive leaves and handsome fall colors to enhance the architectural features of a trellis or latticework. Some vines have fragrant flowers that attract hummingbirds, while others have colorful and edible fruit or unique seedpods.

Observe the winter landscape from the windows in various rooms to see what kinds of plants might add beauty. Maybe the vertical lift of a tall ornamental grass would accent an area or border. Perhaps woody vines wrapped around arbors or posts might add compelling texture.

Is there a need to replace an expansive lawn with an attractive and drought-enduring groundcover? Imagine the sound and movement of the wind stirring ornamental grass stems and seedheads. Where horizontal space is limited, vines can offer architectural interest, colorful foliage, flowers, berries for wildlife, seedpods, and shelter for birds. As you compile your list of favorites, remember to match the vine, groundcover, or ornamental grass to the site where it will be planted.

PLANT

ANNUALS
Seeds of cool-tolerant annuals such as pansies, primroses, and violas need a longer growing period and can be started toward the end of the month. Read the instructions on seed packets to determine how far in advance to start seeds indoors before you intend to transplant them outdoors. Look up the average last spring frost in your area to aid in your decision. Then count back, and mark your calendar.

BULBS
When the ground is frozen, it's not appropriate to plant bulbs. However, if you have spring-flowering bulbs in storage, plant them in pots *now* rather than leaving them in their bags to dry out. Use a good potting mixture, and water after setting them in their containers. Store them in a cool garage where they can undergo their chilling requirements.

On a day when the soil outdoors is not frozen, work some compost into the area, and plant the spring-blooming bulbs directly outside. Then water in well, and mulch with compost, shredded leaves, or wood shavings.

EDIBLES
It's still a bit too early to start seeds indoors, but now is a good time to build a seed-starting system. Place seed orders as early as possible. Some seed varieties will sell out fast.

If you decide to start seeds indoors in the latter part of the month, organize your seed packets to create a sowing schedule for specific varieties. Follow the step-by-step information on the packets for suggested starting dates indoors. This can give you a head start on the short growing season.

PERENNIALS
While it remains too early to plant perennials outdoors, it is not too early to start some from seed. If you have a space and good light, maybe a cold frame, perennials can be started early to assure their germination and give them a head start on the season.

TO BUILD A PLANT LIGHT STAND

Before planting seeds indoors, you will need to purchase or construct a sturdy plant stand to ensure success. The plant stand can be placed in a basement or unused room and will free up valuable counter space elsewhere. To build a stand:

1. Use a workbench or secure boards over sawhorses to make a stand that is about 4 feet long and 20 inches wide. This can accommodate several flats or pots.

2. Construct a frame to hold simple lighting fixtures above the growing shelf. An inexpensive shop light that holds two 40-watt fluorescent shop lights will work well. Use two light fixtures to provide enough light to the growing surface. Use one cool white tube and one warm white tube in each light fixture.

3. Hang the lighting setup so that the light fixtures can be suspended over the shelf or growing bench. The fixtures can be attached to chains that can be easily adjusted for height with pulleys. Most seedlings do best with the light source 2 to 3 inches above the tips of the young seedlings as they grow.

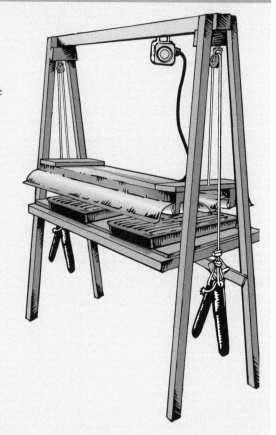

If you are rooting cuttings from last year's annuals, transplant them into a sterilized growing mixture for healthy, vigorous root growth. Place in bright light for optimum growth.

Sow those varieties that need twelve to fourteen weeks indoors before they can be transplanted outside.

Thoroughly clean any pots or flats for starting seedlings. Unwashed flats or pots can harbor pests and diseases. Sterilize the containers in a 10 percent solution of liquid bleach (1 part bleach to 10 parts water). Rinse after thirty minutes or so.

Unlike annuals, most perennials are fussy about their cultural requirements for germination. Follow the label directions carefully to provide proper growing conditions and temperature requirements. Unless you have the time or want to start a new hobby, let the professional growers do the complicated propagation.

Select perennials that will come true from seed. Some perennials are hybrids, so if you have collected seed, you often end up with offspring that will resemble one of their grandparents rather than the hybrid plant. Buy fresh seed of specific varieties you wish to grow and try in your garden.

ROSES

Although it's still too early to plant, this is a good time to make sure you have the space in your landscape, plus the time to tend roses. Order plants early to ensure that they arrive at the proper planting time for your area.

SHRUBS

This is not the time to plant shrubs, even if the soil is not frozen. Temperature fluctuations, prolonged periods of drought, wind, and other variables can make it a challenge for transplants.

TREES

This is not the best time to plant new trees, even though some may be showing up at garden retailers.

The one exception would be the living Christmas tree if you chose one in December. Rather than trying to maintain and grow it indoors, it is much better to plant or heel it in outdoors. For a week or so, acclimate the plant in an unheated garage before moving it directly outdoors.

After the acclimation process, check the weather forecast and plant outdoors when temperatures are above freezing. Ideally, you would have already chosen the proper locations, dug the planting hole in November, and covered and marked it for the tree. Use the stockpiled backfill soil to cover the rootball. Then water thoroughly and apply a 2- to 3-inch layer of mulch over the root zone.

VINES, GROUNDCOVERS &

■ *If you have live Christmas trees, you can plant in January if the ground is not frozen.*

ORNAMENTAL GRASSES

This is not the time of year to plant vines, groundcovers, and ornamental grasses. Be patient.

CARE

ANNUALS

Annuals that have been growing indoors as transplants need bright light in the winter months to grow healthy, pest-free foliage and to set flower buds. Since the days are shorter, you may want to supplement natural light with artificial lights. Use fluorescent lights that are specially designed as plant lights. Suspend artificial lights within a few inches of the seedlings and leave the lights on for sixteen to eighteen hours out of every twenty-four. To save time, plug in a timer to regulate the duration of lighting time.

Indoor annuals naturally stretch to reach for more light. This leggy growth can be limited by pinching back the terminal bud to encourage more lateral buds and compact growth. Place plants that need lots of light in a southern exposure or underneath artificial light sources.

BULBS

If you received or planted an amaryllis bulb for the holiday season, cut off the faded bloom and stalk this month. Leave the narrow, straplike foliage. This grows and stores energy for the bulb. Keep the pot in a bright location. Water the potting mixture as you would a houseplant; when the soil begins to feel dry to the touch, give the plant a good drink. Fertilize with a soluble plant fertilizer mixed at half strength every other watering.

If you planted bulbs in containers for forcing indoors, their chill period has most likely been met. Green shoots will begin to emerge from the potting soil. The bulbs will have developed roots that may be nudging the crowded bulbs up out of the pot or gravel. This is normal and not to be of concern. What you should do:

• Move the potted bulbs first to a warmer area that is about 45 to 50 degrees Fahrenheit for a week, then indoors to warmer quarters. Water the potting mixture as needed.

• Bring the potted bulbs indoors to a bright window (not direct sun) as the buds start to swell. Avoid really warm areas, as this will cause the stems to grow leggy and buds to bloom quickly and fade.

Once paperwhite narcissus has finished blooming, discard the bulbs since it is almost impossible to force them to bloom again.

Deadhead or cut off faded flowers of potted bulbs once they finish blooming. Yellow leaves should also be trimmed away. Droopy leaves indicate insufficient light and may need to be propped up with bamboo stakes.

EDIBLES

If you have a cold frame to overwinter herbs, be sure the plants get proper ventilation. Heat can build up on sunny days, so prop up the glass cover slightly during the day, but close it at night. Snow on the cold frame cover is good insulation, so leave it in place. If there is no snow cover, you can cover the top with an old rug at night to buffer extremely cold temperatures.

LAWNS

Lawns are dormant. You can enjoy the peace and quiet!

PERENNIALS

Periodically check the soil conditions in your perennial garden. It's that time of year when temperature fluctuations can cause some perennials to suffer from frost heave. Press soil around heaved plants, and cut off broken or damaged stems. If mulch has blown away from the base of your perennials, top or renew mulch in those areas. If you have leftover evergreen boughs from the holidays, use them to mulch beds. This can provide additional protection to plants with shallow roots (including coral bells, vinca minor, scabiosa, strawberries, and minor bulbs).

Inspect plants for damage from rodents in your perennial bed. Look for gnawing on the bark and stems, raised soil mounds around perennials, and rodent droppings. Walk on pathways where possible (to reduce soil compaction over roots).

If some of your perennials are beginning to lose their winter interest, it's okay to cut back the dried and broken stems from fall-blooming perennials including asters, hardy chrysanthemums, and goldenrod. Leave the ornamental grasses standing as long as possible. Their seedheads continue to provide structure and form for winter garden interest.

ROSES

Outdoors, check your rose bushes for broken or damaged stems or canes from wind or the weight of snow. It may be necessary to do some periodic cleanup as the weather permits. Determine whether protective mulches are still in place. If the weather has been dry and windy, you may need to replace protective mulch that has been blown away by the wind.

Miniature roses moved indoors need to be kept tidy during their stay inside the home. Pinch or prune off spent blooms. This not only improves appearance, but will encourage more flower buds to form. Remove yellow leaves from the plant to prevent the onset of pests and diseases. Fallen leaves on the potting soil should be picked up and disposed of to keep fungus gnats from becoming a problem.

■ *If roses or other shrubs have damaged stems, it's okay to prune them off now.*

SHRUBS

You may need to protect new shrubs planted last fall from winterburn by shading them with burlap screens or snow fencing on their south and southwest exposures. Temperamental evergreens like Alberta spruce may also require similar sun and wind protection to prevent the foliage from turning brown and getting scorched.

Ice and snow can bend and break weak-wooded shrubs. Gently brush wet, heavy snow off the shrubs as it falls, before it weighs down the branches. Use a broom to lift the stems upward, *not downward*, to allow the snow to slide off the branches. A light accumulation of snow is not

■ *Protect shrubs with burlap screens.*

harmful and will actually insulate the plant, so don't get carried away about brushing off the snow. In some areas, snow protects the lower parts or stems that will produce blooms in the spring.

Protect shrubs planted near the street from salt sprays. Salts accumulate in the soil and will stunt or kill shrubs. Set up burlap screens or other barriers to protect vulnerable shrubs.

TREES

Check trees planted last fall for signs of wind damage or winter desiccation. If they were staked for wind protection, make sure the rubber or nylon straps are secured to the lowest point on the trunk to give the tree a little room to move back and forth. This encourages the development of a stronger, thicker trunk.

If the tree stakes have started to heave out of the ground due to frost, hammer them back down. Make a note in your garden notebook or journal to remove the tree straps in the spring after growth has started.

VINES, GROUNDCOVERS & ORNAMENTAL GRASSES

Most vines, groundcovers, and ornamental grasses are self-reliant. They can tolerate the cold of winter. Check the list of vines, groundcovers, and ornamental grasses in the *Rocky Mountain Getting Started Garden Guide* for a selection that is hardy in your growing zone.

WATER

ANNUALS

Routinely check potted annual cuttings for moisture. If your home is warm and dry, the potting mix may dry out more rapidly. Water when the growing mix feels dry to the touch, or when the seedlings look droopy. Newly sown seed will need proper moisture to ensure good germination. Do not waterlog the growing mixture, however. Use a mister or watering can. It is better to underwater than to overwater, as the former reduces the onset of diseases. Cover the plant trays with plastic, but as soon as the seeds have germinated, remove the plastic cover to prevent the seedlings from damping-off disease (which is caused by a pathogen in soil and is aggravated by keeping the growing mix too wet).

BULBS

Indoors, potted bulbs will need to be watered as the potting soil dries out. Do not waterlog the potting mixture as this will cause root rot.

If there is a prolonged period of warm weather without snow or rain, water bulb beds on sunny exposures outdoors. Water when the soil is unfrozen, and apply water early in the day so it has time to soak in. Winter watering will sustain the root system and keep the soil cool to delay early emergence.

HERE'S HOW

TO PRUNE A TREE

1. Make the first cut on the underside of the branch, about 6 inches from the tree trunk. You'll only cut one-fourth to one-third of the way through the branch.

2. Make the second cut farther out on the branch from the first cut. Cut the branch all the way off. The branch will probably break off while you're cutting it. That is why you made the first cut on the underside of the tree—to help the branch break in the direction you want without stripping the bark off the branch.

3. You can see the finished second cut here. At the very bottom of the cut edge, you can see where part of the branch ripped. Heavy branches will rip further, often down to the cut on the underside of the tree. The cut on the underside of the limb keeps the branch from ripping all the way down the tree trunk and causing more damage. You never want to make a cut that strips the

bark off of a tree branch, because all of the water and food in the tree travels up and down the tree right under the bark.

4. Cut off the branch stub remaining on the tree. Place the pruning saw just outside of the branch collar, which is the bark swelling between the branch and the main trunk. Saw all the way through to remove the stub. Do not cut the branch flush with the tree trunk, or you'll hurt the tree's chances of healing itself.

5. In this picture, you can see that there's still about ¼ to ½ inch of branch left to allow the branch collar to heal. Never cover pruning cuts with tar, concrete, or sealant. The tree will heal itself if left alone. Sealant or tar creates a dark, moist environment that is perfect for bacteria to grow. Sealing a cut can actually hurt the tree, so resist the urge to "help" the tree heal. If you follow this pruning technique, the tree will heal itself.

If you're planning on pruning your trees in winter, have a purpose in mind so you will maintain the tree's natural growth habit and health. If you are uncomfortable doing the pruning yourself, have a certified and experienced arborist examine your trees. An arborist can make an assessment of needs and provide a bid for services.

Pruning is both an art and a science. Studying trees and appreciating their natural growth patterns will develop your skill. January is a good time to see the framework of deciduous trees. Since they are without leaves, you can determine which branches need removing and mark them with a bright orange or red spray paint.

When temperatures outdoors are comfortable, thin out any dying, dead, or pest-infested twigs and branches by cutting them where they join the limb or trunk. Thinning opens up the center of deciduous trees to more sunlight and reduces the number of water sprouts that may grow along the branches. Proper thinning will not dramatically change the tree's natural appearance or growth habit, or give it the "just-pruned" look.

Never "top" or head back the limbs of maturing trees. You are likely to weaken their structure by causing the growth of numerous fast-growing water sprouts. The remaining stubs will be exposed to attacks from insects and disease.

January is a good time to remove a branch if it is rubbing or crossing another. Wounds that create entryways for invading insects and diseases will develop on rubbing branches.

Remove branches that form narrow, V-shaped angles to the trunk. These are weak points that may split with the weight of snow and ice. Branches that form at an angle of less than 45 degrees from the trunk or point of attachment (10 and 2 o'clock) are best removed. Also prune out upright side limbs or suckers that tend to grow taller than the main trunk.

You don't need to apply tree paints or wound dressing to the cut ends. There is no scientific evidence that dressing wounds prevents decay. Paint can actually retain moisture and encourage disease organisms to enter the wound. If you start pruning after the coldest part of winter has passed, this will allow the tree wounds to heal and will reduce dehydration of the cut ends.

Check seedlings carefully and often to make sure the potting mix does not dry out. Covering the seed-starting trays will help maintain humidity.

EDIBLES

Carefully water indoor vegetable plants and herbs that have been salvaged from the garden. Avoid daily watering because this may keep the soil too moist and lead to root rot. Check the soil moisture with your finger. When it feels dry to the touch, give the soil a good drink, and let the water drain out. Remove excess water with a turkey baster, or carefully pour into the sink or a plastic tub.

Outdoors, if we experience a prolonged dry period and the soil is unfrozen, perennial edibles (rhubarb, asparagus, chives, strawberries, raspberries, for example) may need water. Apply water early in the day when temperatures are above 45 degrees Fahrenheit. When finished, disconnect the garden hose, drain, and return to storage.

LAWNS

Even though turfgrasses are dormant at this time of year, they may need attention to check moisture availability in the subsoil. Hot, windy, dry exposures can dry out quickly, thereby exposing the crown of the grass plants to desiccation. Additionally, the root system will begin to dry out, resulting in the so-called "winter kill."

If snow or rain is scarce for over a month, pick a warm, mild day for "winter watering." Choose a day when temperatures are above freezing (45 to 50 degrees Fahrenheit) and apply water to areas where the ground in not frozen solid. You do not have to turn on your automatic sprinkler system to water, since you had it winterized last fall. Bring out the garden hose and a frog-eye sprinkler to spot-water areas that are most vulnerable to drying out. Water each section ten to fifteen minutes, or to the point of runoff, and then move the sprinkler to the next area or zone.

Water early enough in the day to permit the water to percolate into the subsoil so the roots can use it. Remember to disconnect the garden hose, drain it, and store in the garage or garden shed. Winter watering can be done every four to five weeks, depending upon weather conditions.

PERENNIALS

If the weather has been unseasonably dry for an extended period, check the soil moisture around your perennials. Pay particular attention to southern and southwestern exposures, or those areas that are subject to continual wind. Water on a warm day when temperatures are above freezing. Apply water early in the day so it can percolate down to the root system. Disconnect and drain the garden hose, and return to storage for future "winter watering" as needed.

ROSES

Inspect outdoor roses for soil moisture. On warm, sunny days and during dry periods without snow, it may be necessary to "winter water" your roses. Pick a warm day when temperatures are above 50 degrees Fahrenheit and the ground is not frozen, and give your roses a deep drink of water. Bring the garden hose or frog-eye sprinkler out of storage, and soak the root zone for fifteen to twenty minutes. Water early in the day, and allow the water to soak in before freezing temperatures at nightfall. During extended periods of drought, wind, and warm temperatures, water the soil monthly to maintain moisture to the roots.

Indoor miniature roses should be watered carefully. Avoid overwatering because this often results in root rot or stress to the plant. A stressed plant is more prone to insect and disease invasions.

Water thoroughly to saturate the soil, but discard excess water in the drainage saucer after an hour

deciduous types. Established trees may need supplemental water as well. Use a frog-eye sprinkler; set over the root zone, and water each area for ten to fifteen minutes. Allow the water to soak in before nightfall.

Trees planted on southern and western exposures, and those subject to drying winter winds, are more susceptible to winter desiccation. The subsoil needs to be charged with adequate moisture that will be available to the trees even during winter. "Winterkill" is not apparent until the summer, although root damage occurs in the dry winter months.

Miniature roses, or other plants being overwintered indoors, benefit from being placed on top of gravel or other stones to increase humidity. Keep the gravel layer watered.

or so. Allow the soil to dry out slightly between waterings to allow the root zone to receive oxygen. Simply poke a finger into the potting mixture to check; when it begins to feel dry to the touch an inch down, it's time to water again.

Because of our low humidity indoors, place potted roses on waterproof pebble trays. Simply fill a shallow plastic saucer with 1 to 2 inches of gravel. Keep the gravel layer moist so it can consistently promote humidity around the miniature rose plants. Maintain moisture in pebble trays by keeping the gravel damp, but not so full that the bottom of the container sits in a pool of water. Grouping plants together also creates more humidity.

SHRUBS
Check underneath the mulch around your shrubs to see if the soil is moist. If it is not, winter watering is in order. Choose a warm day when temperatures are above freezing. Set out a frog-eye sprinkler at the drip line of the shrub, and let it run for fifteen to thirty minutes. Do this early in the day to allow the water to soak in. Don't forget to disconnect and drain the garden hose after winter watering; otherwise, you may end up with a very expensive plumbing repair.

TREES
During dry winter spells, when temperatures are above freezing and the ground is unfrozen, water fall-planted trees including evergreens and

VINES, GROUNDCOVERS & ORNAMENTAL GRASSES
In dry winters, fall-planted vines, groundcovers, and ornamental grasses need supplemental watering. Choose a day when temperatures are above freezing and the ground is not frozen. Water for ten to fifteen minutes using a frog-eye sprinkler. Apply water early in the day so it can percolate to the roots. Don't forget to disconnect the hose, drain it, and put it back in storage for future use.

Mulched plants will not need to be watered as often. Evergreens continue to transpire through their foliage, and they can lose moisture even though it is winter.

FERTILIZE

ANNUALS
If you did not use a slow-release granular fertilizer in the potting mixture of overwintering annuals or new cuttings, apply a water-soluble plant fertilizer at half strength at every other watering. Plants that are not forming flower buds or those not blooming do not require very much fertilizer.

BULBS
If you have amaryllis and other forced bulbs, fertilize them at half strength with a soluble houseplant fertilizer. This helps restore some of their depleted energy.

EDIBLES
Indoor herbs should be fertilized minimally because too much will cause them to grow spindly and to

develop rapid succulent growth that dilutes flavor in the leaves. Some gardeners recommend seaweed (kelp) and fish emulsion for feeding indoor herbs and vegetable transplants. These organic fertilizers often contain other trace elements as well as the three major nutrients. Read and follow label directions for dilution rates and application.

LAWNS

There is no point in fertilizing dormant lawns now. If you fertilized in the autumn, a granular, slow-release fertilizer will last for many weeks over the autumn and kick back into gear in the spring.

PERENNIALS

No fertilizing is needed this month.

ROSES

Roses growing and blooming indoors will need an occasional application of fertilizer. I prefer to mix time-released fertilizer into the soil at planting so it can sustain the plants for several months. Otherwise, you can use a water-soluble rose fertilizer. Apply to a *moist*—never dry—potting mixture. Follow label directions for dilution rates and frequency of application.

If plants are not vigorously blooming, use fertilizer diluted to half strength.

Miniature roses that are not blooming can be repotted into fresh potting soil, if needed. Check the roots and carefully root prune potbound plants. Move into a container one size larger than the old pot. After replanting, water in thoroughly.

SHRUBS, TREES, VINES, GROUNDCOVERS & ORNAMENTAL GRASSES

This is not the time to fertilize shrubs, trees, vines, groundcovers, or ornamental grasses. Wait until at least budbreak (as the buds begin to expand in the spring).

PROBLEM-SOLVE

ANNUALS

Hot, dry air from the furnace can lower the humidity in the house, a condition that favors spider mites. Be on the watch for aphids and spider mites on indoor annuals. When you detect pests and their eggs, wash them off with tepid water. Look for mottled or yellowing foliage, and fine webs between stems and leaves. Washing the foliage with water or applying a homemade soap spray can control many indoor pests. A safe and easy spray is to mix 1 tablespoon liquid Castile soap into 1 quart of water. Transfer to a spray bottle and treat infested plants, both upper and lower foliage.

Fungus gnat larvae live in the potting soil of indoor plants and overwintering annuals. Keep the soil surface clean of debris and let the potting mixture dry out between waterings. Place gnat traps near plants that are infested.

Whiteflies and fungus gnats can be easily controlled by trapping them with yellow sticky traps available at garden centers and nurseries.

BULBS

Insect pests may find their way from your houseplants to potted bulbs. Problems to be aware of:

- Aphids can attack the succulent foliage to suck plant juices. Wash them off with a forceful spray of water or use a homemade soap spray.

- Flying gnats can also be a problem, but are easily controlled if you keep the soil surface clean of debris. Allow the soil to dry out between watering, and set up yellow sticky

■ *To catch whiteflies and other flying insects, use sticky traps, small pieces of paper that are coated with a sticky substance.*

traps. Gnats are not harmful to the plants, just more of a nuisance in the house.

- Overwatering potted bulbs can result in rot that destroys the entire bulb, roots and all. If this should occur, discard the rotting bulbs. Monitor your watering practices to avoid keeping the soil too wet.

EDIBLES
Be on the watch for aphids, spider mites, and whiteflies on plants that are spending the winter indoors. You can keep most of these pests at bay by washing them off with a homemade soap spray (see page 220) or rinsing off the foliage under the kitchen faucet. If infestations are severe, use an insecticidal soap. Read and follow label directions.

LAWNS
Check for grass mites by rubbing the palm of your hand over the exposed grass. If your hand turns a brownish or reddish color, mites are invading that portion of the lawn. Mites can also be detected by examining the leaf blades up close and personal to find the tiny moving dots.

The best control is to "winter water" those areas since this will discourage mites from causing extensive damage. A homemade soap spray will also work to eliminate mites in addition to the application of water. See page 220 for homemade soap spray recipe.

PERENNIALS
Be ever vigilant for activity from deer, elk, rabbits, meadow mice, and other critters that may visit your garden. As their food sources may become scarce they will make early morning or evening visits to your garden. Any foliage that remains somewhat green may be vulnerable to nibbling. You can spray the stems and foliage with hot pepper spray. This will help to temporarily repel critters that like to graze.

ROSES
Forced-air heat in our homes decreases humidity and can cause indoor roses to become more susceptible to spider mite invasion. Be on the watch for fine webbing developing among the

stems and leaves. Foliage may become stippled and have a "salt and pepper" look. You can make a homemade spray by mixing 1 tablespoon liquid Castile soap into 1 quart of water. Pour into a spray bottle and apply to the foliage and stems. More severe pest invasions may require the use of insecticidal soap or a systemic pesticide applied to the soil. Read and follow label directions.

If you're growing miniature roses indoors for winter color, keep a close eye on them for signs of fungus gnats, spider mites, and powdery mildew disease. A white powdery coating on the young stems and foliage is often a sign of powdery mildew. Increase air circulation around the plants and remove infected plant portions. If fungus gnats become a problem, place yellow sticky traps around the plants to capture these nuisance pests. Allow the potting mixture to dry out slightly between waterings to discourage larvae in the soil.

SHRUBS
Be on the watch for rabbit, deer, field mice, and other critters nibbling at stems or upper branches. It may be time to apply more homemade repellent (see homemade remedy on page 221).

Construct protective wire cages around plants that are most vulnerable to deer and elk. Cages should be tall enough to deter deer that stand on deep snow cover. If permitted in your area, an electric fence will keep them at bay too.

TREES
Check trees for any signs of past pest damage, especially borers. You should be able to detect tiny entry or exit holes if borers were a problem. Control them later in the year when they become active.

VINES, GROUNDCOVERS & ORNAMENTAL GRASSES
Deer and elk can be damaging to vines, groundcovers, and ornamental grasses when their natural food sources are scarce. They will nibble on the tender shoots, leaves, berries, and stems to sustain themselves during the cold, harsh winter. Spray vulnerable plants with the homemade critter repellent (see page 221) or a commercial product to keep them away. Repellents will need to be reapplied as they break down over a period of time.

February

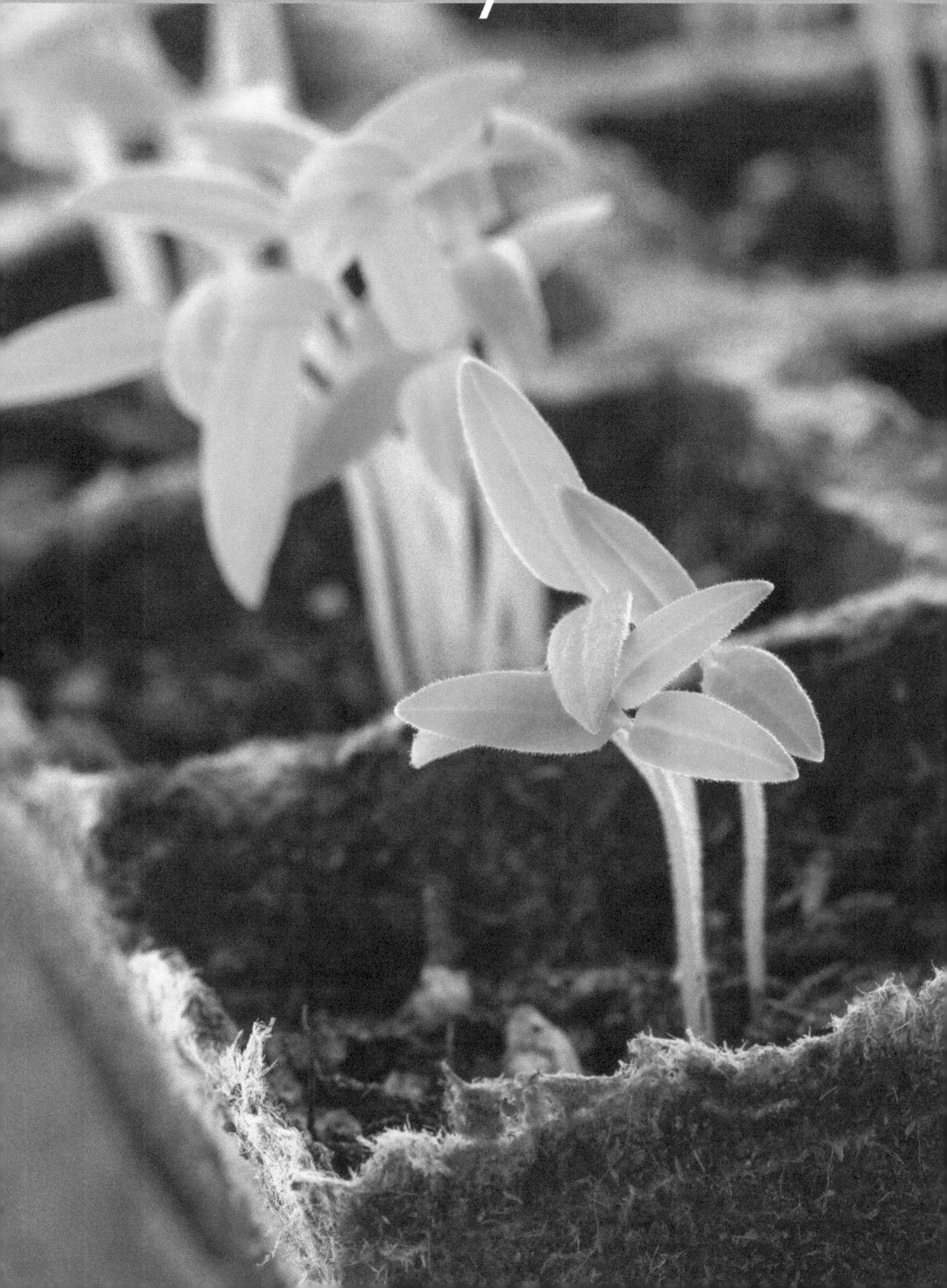

Uncertain weather in the Rockies makes gardening tricky with bright warm sunshine for a week or more followed by cold, frosty conditions that can devastate landscape plants. If you're itching to do some gardening, now is a good time to get a jump on the season by starting seeds of cool-season crops, including broccoli, cauliflower, cabbage, and onions, indoors. Some perennial flowers can be started early. Annual flowers that can tolerate cool weather, such as pansies, violas, and calendulas, can be started indoors six weeks before the last spring frost. For any seed starting, check the back of the seed packet for specific timing for planting indoors.

Visit your local garden stores to check out plastic flats and containers that are specially designed to start seeds successfully. Choose a proper seed-starting mix that has been pasteurized or sterilized to avoid damping-off diseases (fatal to emerging seedlings). Some seeds may germinate more rapidly with heating cables or heating mats.

This is a fun month outdoors as we experience some warm sunny days. Get outside to see early color from snowdrops and winter aconite. These are a welcome sight to the winter garden tucked among rocks and other parts of the landscape. It's a sign that spring is not too far behind.

If you did not mark the location of your bulb beds, do so when they start emerging and blooming. This will prove helpful for locating the spots when it's time to overplant or work the soil this spring. You don't want to dig or rototill areas where hardy bulbs are located.

It's not unusual to have dry periods in February with the lack of snow or persistent snow cover. If it does snow, periods of warm weather will melt it fast. If prolonged periods of dry weather settle in, get outdoors and check the lawn, trees, shrubs, and perennials. Those that are planted on slopes, in southern and western exposures, may need water.

If you haven't already started, make a rough sketch of new flowerbeds or your vegetable garden. Pick locations with good soil drainage or consider gardens in raised beds.

PLAN

ANNUALS

Place your orders of annuals as soon as possible. Garden retailers are beginning to stock their seed racks, so look for special buys locally. Some annuals are started from seed several weeks before the last spring frost in your area, so it's not too early. Some mail-order catalogs offer annuals and biennials that are already young transplants. If you plan to purchase them, get your order in early to be sure the company will have your first choice. The young plants will be delivered at the appropriate planting time for your area.

Annuals that can tolerate cool weather such as pansies, violas, and calendulas can be started indoors six weeks before the last spring frost. Check the back of the seed packet for specific timing for planting indoors.

BULBS

If you want to plant perennial groundcovers in bulb beds, plan on doing so before the bulb foliage is all gone. Groundcovers over bulb beds keep the beds tidy, yet allow the bulbs to grow normally and undergo their natural dormancy. Some of

■ *Seed packages on display*

my favorite groundcovers are sweet woodruff, veronica, and woolly thyme. Consider planting pansies as an undercover for bulbs too. (Undercover, or underplanting, refers to growing shorter plants, such as groundcovers, under taller-growing plants.) They will provide color when the bulbs' foliage is yellowing and ripening.

■ *Planting pansies under flowering bulbs will help disguise the yellowing foliage of the bulbs later.*

Plan to order summer-flowering bulbs from mail-order catalogs early to get the best selection. These will help to fill in some of the empty spots in the flowerbed and provide interest to the garden. Your order will be sent in the mail at the appropriate planting times.

EDIBLES

As the days begin to lengthen, our gardening urges stir. It is time to inventory your supplies and make a shopping list for starting seeds indoors. Include seed-starting mixes, trays, covers, water-soluble fertilizer, seed inoculant, and fluorescent lights. Also, consider investing in new tools if necessary. Check your supplies of garden insecticides and other pest controls. Many products have a shelf life of only a few years and should be discarded once the container begins to shrink, leak, or show signs of degradation. Check with your local EPA office for disposal sites and dates of chemical pickup in your area. Dispose of according to the label.

Plan to visit your local garden stores to check out plastic flats and containers that are specially designed to start seeds successfully. Choose a proper seed-starting mix that has been pasteurized or sterilized to avoid damping-off diseases, which are fatal to emerging seedlings. Some seeds may germinate more rapidly with heating cables or heating mats. See page 40.

Lack of light can be one of the most limiting factors in growing seedlings indoors. Plants tend to become spindly and weak before you can plant them. You can solve this problem by purchasing or building a seedling stand with artificial light. This way, you can control the amount and quality of light the plants receive. To build a light stand, see page 22.

If you're thinking about planting a home orchard, now is the time to make a plan. Locate the orchard in a sunny spot with a gentle slope. This will reduce frost damage in spring. If you haven't already ordered fruit trees, do so soon. Pick varieties that are hardy in your area. Check with local nurseries or gardeners who have experience growing fruit in our region for recommendations.

Fruit trees can be obtained as standard, semidwarf, and dwarf, depending on the growing space you have.

The rootstock on which a tree is grafted will determine whether the tree is a dwarf. Keep in mind that standards take longer to mature and produce fruit.

Grafted trees can sometimes have their own problems, including suckering from the rootstock. You will have to prune the suckers off each summer as they appear. Many heirloom fruit trees are grafted onto hardier rootstock, which allows them to be grown in a wider variety of soils.

Trees growing on their own roots are preferred. They will acclimate and establish much stronger. Determine your needs, and grow fruits that you and your family will enjoy. Oh, by the way, birds will eventually share your crop, too! Plan to have some bird netting around when the cherries start blooming.

If you're thinking about growing a fruit tree from seed, *think again*. These generally will not come "true" from seed. There will be much variability in the resulting progeny, and you may be disappointed when the plant finally produces fruit, if it ever does.

LAWNS

If you didn't have a chance to get your lawn mower tuned up previously, February is a good time to do so. Your local lawn-care equipment service center is

■ *Put sand, crushed gravel, or the actual fertilizer you'll use into the spreader and test it on a driveway or other hard surface. This will help you determine how fast to walk and whether the unit is distributing in a uniform pattern.*

HERE'S HOW

TO FORCE SHRUB BRANCHES TO BLOOM

1. Prune the branches on a warm day when temperatures are above freezing. Be somewhat selective so you don't disfigure the natural growth form of the shrub.

2. Cut the branches at 6 to 12 inches long; longer branches are good to use if you're creating larger floral arrangements.

3. Bring the cut branches indoors, and make a second cut on a slant just above the original cut before placing the branch in water. Then, make several 1-inch-long slits in the end of each cut stem to expose more surface area for water to soak up.

■ *Forsythia can be forced to bloom indoors.*

4. Place the cut ends in a bucket or vase of water into which a flower preservative has been added; see the homemade flower cocktail on page 221. Place the container in a cool, dark spot where temperatures are 45 to 50 degrees Fahrenheit.

5. When the buds start to expand and show color, move them to bright light, but keep them out of the direct sun. Lower temperatures will prolong the life of forced blooms if you plan to use them in floral arrangements.

6. Some, like pussy willow, will root in the water and can be carefully transplanted outdoors later in the spring. Have fun!

likely to have more time now than in early spring when everybody else gets the same idea.

For the handyman: Sharpen the lawn mower blade, clean the undercarriage, and replace the spark plug. Change the oil and replace the old air filter with a new one. Your mower will be in top running condition when the time comes to use it.

Check your lawn fertilizer spreader. Is it still in good shape or is it rusting out? It may be time to purchase a new one. If your spreader is in good condition, it is helpful to calibrate it ahead of time so you know that you are applying the correct amount of fertilizer come spring.

PERENNIALS

One of the primary reasons we like to plant perennials is that they generally return year after year; that is, if the crown and root system survive the winter. Plan to select plants suited for your area. Refer to the *Rocky Mountain Getting Started Garden Guide* for recommended perennials that grow and survive without a lot of fuss.

Most local garden retailers and nurseries routinely stock perennial plants that are best suited to the local climate, soil, and temperature regimes. Talk to fellow gardeners to find out what grows best for them. They can provide invaluable advice on which plants have performed well in their gardens over the years. If you decide to order from catalogs, do your research ahead of time. Be sure the plants you want are cold hardy for your part of the region. Otherwise, plan to protect the "marginally hardy" perennials by mulching or planting them in a microclimate.

ROSES

Valentine's Day is this month, and who doesn't like to receive roses during a winter month? A bouquet of long-stemmed roses is a classic gift of love at

Valentine's Day, but a long-lived rose bush will keep on giving.

Catalogs may be arriving in the mail this month. Before ordering, it's always best to sketch out a plan to make sure you have the proper location and space for your desires. Now is a good time to learn about the various roses and how they might fit into your garden style.

Make plans to order bare-root roses so they will arrive at the appropriate planting time for your area. Most mail-order companies are good about sending the plants at the proper planting time for your locality. Many will allow you to make your request for shipment to ensure they do not arrive too late in the spring.

SHRUBS

Shrubs provide framework and background for other plants, including flowers, groundcovers, and lawns. They create a transition from the lawn to the home and other structures. Shrubs can be utilized to create privacy from a nearby neighbor, enclose a patio or deck, or provide a barrier to traffic—but are not as expensive or intimidating as walls and fences. Plan

■ *Protect a tree with wire mesh to guard against rabbit and rodent damage.*

to use them more in your landscape if you don't already. A well-planned and well-designed landscape with a mix of shrubs, trees, vines, flowers, and groundcovers will enhance your property.

The cold days of winter are a good time to evaluate the positioning of shrubs in your landscape. A shrub in the wrong place can hit the sides of the house, grow over a pathway, or obstruct your view from a window. If the plant is healthy, make plans to move it yourself or hire a professional landscaper to do it for you in early spring. Get the new site ready on the warmer days of the month.

How would you like some early spring color indoors during the winter? Though I don't recommend pruning at this time, a little bit can be trimmed in late February to force blossoms indoors. Spring-flowering shrubs whose flower buds were formed on last year's wood can be coaxed into early bloom indoors once their dormancy requirements have been met. While this varies between species, at least eight weeks of temperatures below 40 degrees Fahrenheit is generally sufficient for most blooming shrubs.

TREES

You still have some time to order bare-root trees, but don't delay. Bare-root stock needs to be planted early before it leafs out.

Now is the time to get outdoors on warm sunny days, walk around your trees, and give them a good inspection. You may discover some interesting features and appreciate their winter structure.

Look for any nibbling on the bark of the lower trunk from rabbits or other critters, including meadow mice, voles, or pocket gophers. They are particularly fond of the young tender bark. Many critters will set up residence in heavy mulch, leaves, or persistent snow around the base of young trees. Take time to pull back mulches to check for visible damage.

You may need to place protective collars around the trunk to thwart rabbits, deer, elk, meadow mice, and voles. Even with these protectors, rabbits can still damage the bark if they can stand on the snow and reach above the protective collar, so plan accordingly. Of course, the taller critters can reach beyond the protective collar to nibble branches and tender twigs. Wire fencing may be needed to exclude deer, elk, and roaming livestock.

Ice and snow can damage trees. Following a storm, check whether any damage has occurred, and prune accordingly. Make a list of tasks to improve the shape and form of your trees.

VINES, GROUNDCOVERS & ORNAMENTAL GRASSES

Winter is a good time to read the *Rocky Mountain Getting Started Garden Guide* and make notes about the various vines, groundcovers, and ornamental grasses that are suited to our region. Evaluate your landscape, and determine which areas need more winter plant interest. Ornamental grasses work especially well for vertical lift and texture, and vines will add cover and texture to arbors and fencing. Some are very attractive spilling over large stones or retaining walls. Be creative, and experiment. Sketch some of your ideas. Visit public gardens in winter to see what they use to make the landscape attractive.

If deer are a problem in your area, use this time to plan appropriate fencing. The fence will need to be 10 feet tall or taller.

PLANT

ANNUALS

Growing your own transplants from seed offers you a wide choice of varieties that are usually not available at garden retailers. However, you will need adequate light and time to care for the seedlings.

See January, page 22, to learn how to make a light stand.

There are a couple of ways to grow your own transplants from seed. In the one-step method, sow the seeds directly into individual containers or cell-packs. These can be transplanted directly outdoors when they are ready and frost has passed.

The two-step method involves sowing the seeds in trays or flats and allowing them to grow until the "true leaves" emerge. Then, the seedlings are transplanted into individual pots for further growth before moving them to their permanent homes outdoors.

BULBS

Later in the month when pansies and violas become available locally, plant them where bulbs are growing. They combine well with tulips, daffodils, and hyacinths. Cool-weather annuals will add color and interest when interplanted with bulbs and fill in the gaps.

EDIBLES

It's a bit too early to start many vegetable and herb seeds indoors, but you can start cool-season crops such as onion and cabbage that can be set out in the garden in April. If you have a small garden and don't have enough space or time to tend seedlings, buy young plants at a garden store.

You can plant herb seeds such as chives, cilantro-coriander, dill, fennel, salad burnet, sage, winter savory, French sorrel, and thyme at the end of the month or in early March. Start these seeds in a sterilized seed-starting mixture to prevent damping-off.

Fill individual seed trays with moistened seed-starting medium. If the mix is too dry, it will float to the top with seeds and all when it's watered in. Sow the seeds at the recommended depth on the seed package. Cover them with a tiny bit of the mix, and mist to water them in. Record the name of the herbs on plant labels for each tray or container. Use a pen with moisture-resistant ink or a wax pencil. Then, gently cover the tray with a plastic bag to maintain humidity until the seedlings begin to sprout.

As soon as you see the seedlings, remove the plastic, and set them under the fluorescent lights so that the top leaves are just a few inches below the lights. The light fixtures should be adjustable so they can be raised as the seedlings grow. This will keep the plants growing vigorously and strong.

Water new seedlings carefully to avoid waterlogging them and causing rot. Wait until the surface of the seed-starting mixture begins to dry out, then water either from the bottom or lightly from the top.

LAWNS

Delay planting seed or sod until soil begins to thaw and gradually warm up. Temperatures during the day should stay consistently at 55 to 60 degrees Fahrenheit for the best results with overseeding or installing new sod.

PERENNIALS

You can still plant perennials from seed indoors. If you don't have a space with enough natural light, such as a sun porch or greenhouse, try growing them under artificial lights. Fluorescent lights work well and can be suspended from the ceiling with adjustable cables or chains. This will allow you to keep the light source within inches of the seedlings as they germinate. Lack of light will make plants weak.

Be sure to read the directions on seed packets and follow the guidelines for growing perennials indoors. I like to sow seeds directly into a cold frame and let nature take its course. Pansies, violas, columbines, larkspur, California poppies, and other cool-season perennials prefer cooler temperatures to germinate and develop. The plants will be acclimatized and will transplant with less shock.

As seedlings begin to grow, lower the fluorescent lights to within an inch or two of the sprouts. Provide fourteen to sixteen hours of daily artificial light if you don't have any natural sunlight.

Do not allow the seedlings to dry out, but on the other hand, don't waterlog the growing mixture. Too much moisture can result in diseases that will kill the seedlings.

ROSES

It's still too early to plant roses outside, but if you are growing miniature potted roses indoors, they

■ *A cold frame can be simple or complex but it serves the same purpose. Locating it adjacent to your home provides added warmth.*

HERE'S HOW

TO START SEEDS INDOORS

Steps for starting seeds indoors:

1. Fill the containers or seed flats with moistened soilless potting mixture.

2. Place one or two seeds in each pot and sow a row in the flat. Cover the seeds with the mixture. Plant at the depth recommended on the seed packets.

3. Water each pot or the seed flat. Individual pots or containers should be placed in a tray for easier transport to the windowsill or plant stand.

4. Cover the containers with a sheet of plastic or Plexiglas to prevent the growing medium from drying out.

5. Give the pots or seed flat warmth from a heat mat or heating cables to help germination.

6. Remove the plastic or cover when the seeds have sprouted. Move them to bright light or artificial light that can be adjusted so they are consistently about 2 inches above the seedlings as they grow.

7. Snip off the second or less vigorous seedling in pots so there is just one per container. Thin plants in the seed flat so they are 2 to 3 inches apart. This will make them easier to transplant later.

8. Water the growing medium when it is getting dry to the touch. Do not keep it too wet, as this will cause damping-off disease or seedling rot.

may need to be repotted. Check the root system by carefully slipping the soilball out of the pot. If the roots are growing towards the inside of the container or coming out through the drainage hole, it's time to move the plant to the next larger pot size. Use a quality potting mixture that has good drainage when repotting miniature roses. They are fussy about moisture and don't tolerate being waterlogged.

SHRUBS

Even though the soil may be beginning to thaw, don't jump the gun to plant new shrubs or transplant existing ones quite yet. A good timeline for planting is when the garden stores begin to bring out their nursery stock of shrubs. Transplant shrubs in your yard when their buds are just beginning to swell, but before it's totally leafed out.

Dig out and dispose of problem shrubs that are diseased, dying, or otherwise too old to rejuvenate. Then, later in the month you can transplant existing shrubs that are positioned incorrectly to new locations in the landscape.

If you placed an order via the mail, bare-root shrubs may be arriving in your area. If the ground is still frozen when they arrive, store bare-root stock in a cool place and keep their root system moist until planting time. An unheated garage or cool basement will work for temporary storage.

TREES

This is not the time to plant trees in the Rocky Mountain region.

VINES, GROUNDCOVERS & ORNAMENTAL GRASSES

It's still too early to plant outdoors, but if you have space and time, start annual vines from seeds indoors. This should be done towards the end of the month so the seedlings won't become too leggy before planting time. Read the seed packet to determine how many days to plant ahead of the last killing frost in the spring.

If you start seeds indoors, use sterile containers or seed flats. Plant them in a clean, soilless growing mixture. A plant stand would be handy if you are growing many different kinds of plants indoors. Use fluorescent lights to make the seedlings grow strong and vigorously.

Violets, violas, Johnny-jump ups, and pansies will be available by month's end and can be planted as a winter groundcover as the weather permits. Plant some in outdoor containers for a splash of winter color.

CARE

ANNUALS

When the seeds have sprouted, remove the plastic covering and put them in bright light or under artificial light. A combination of one 40-watt cool white and one 40-watt warm white fluorescent light is very effective and inexpensive. Set the containers or seed-starting tray on your light stand and adjust the lights so they're just a few inches above the leaves. Keep the lights on for sixteen hours each day. An automatic timer will help save time.

Pinch back the leggy growth of annuals as they stretch for more light. You can take cuttings during this process and root more plants. This is a good time to root geranium, impatiens, begonia, and coleus cuttings.

BULBS

The early blooming hardy bulbs will be emerging now, and many will be blooming to add color to the winter garden. Those planted in warmer sites, near buildings or heat-retaining walls, may start pushing out of the ground with green shoots. This is normal, as the bulbs are following their internal clock. A light freeze or snowstorm will not harm them. If the bulbs were mulched, this will keep the soil cooler and help to delay early emergence.

During prolonged dry spells in February, you may need to do some "winter watering" of bulb beds to maintain soil moisture and keep the ground cool. Apply water when the ground is not frozen and early in the day so it can soak down. A light watering is all that is required; use the frog-eye sprinkler to complete this chore.

Check on tender summer-flowering bulbs that are stored in the garage or basement. Dahlias and cannas should be kept cool so they won't sprout. Usually a temperature of 45 to 50 degrees Fahrenheit is ideal. If any of the bulbs are getting mushy or have completely dried out (tubers of dahlias and cannas) discard them.

Gladiolus should be kept dry and cool. I store them in old mesh bags that oranges and grapefruit are sold in. This allows good air circulation and prevents molds from growing on the corms. In a month or so, you can bring some of these out and pot them up in containers to give them a head start.

EDIBLES

Watch newly planted seedlings so you can customize a watering schedule just for your indoor environment. As the seedlings sprout, remove the plastic cover to prevent them from pushing up against it. Condensation in the plastic that constantly covers the leaves can result in rot or other leaf diseases. Did you know that by gently brushing your hand over the tops of growing seedlings daily, you can flex their stems and help them grow stronger? Give it a try. It is good plant and human therapy.

Prune currants, raspberries, and gooseberries starting in mid- to late month. Remove all the weak, spindly canes, and winterkilled wood. Every year, remove all but half a dozen of the older branches to the ground. This will rejuvenate these fruits to produce new vigorous growth. Begin to prune grapes late in the month or wait until March.

Continue to pinch or prune back herbs that are successfully growing indoors as needed. This will keep them compact and in shape. It will also promote denser foliar growth.

LAWNS

Take precautions to avoid walking over the lawn if it is frosted or snow-covered. New grass blades are vulnerable to damage from foot traffic, as the ice crystals on the leaf blades tear away membranes when they are crushed. This will leave noticeable footprints in the lawn. Snow-packed areas result in compaction around the growing crowns and may promote snow mold diseases.

Keep de-icing salts off lawn areas, as they will kill spots in the lawn and nearby flowerbeds and shrub borders. Use non-salt alternatives on sidewalks, driveways, and patios to avoid harmful salt accumulations.

Frosted grass is brittle and breaks easily if walked upon.

PERENNIALS

As the weather permits, take a walk around the landscape to check out your perennials. Where frost has heaved the soil, make sure the crowns and roots have not been exposed to the drying winds. Replant or reset, if needed, any plants that have been disturbed. If the ground is frozen, pile mulch or evergreen boughs over the plants temporarily. Replace mulch that may have blown off the beds exposing crowns and roots to drying winter winds.

To prevent early perennials from emerging prematurely in extended warm, sunny periods, maintain a layer of mulch over the plants. Winter mulch holds in some of the chill and helps to delay early growth until there is less risk of damage from late freezes and extreme temperature fluctuations.

It is always tempting to get outdoors and clean up the perennial garden. Resist the urge, however, as the natural growth and dried stubs help to catch and hold snow cover. This provides needed moisture and a winter mulch.

Pick up dead stems and other debris that may have blown into the perennial bed.

Check for signs of the early emerging bulbs like snow crocus (*Crocus tommasinianus*) and dwarf iris (*Iris reticulata*). Avoid walking on the soil if it is wet, as this will compact the ground and impede the movement of air and water to plant roots.

ROSES

Check the mulch placed around the base of your roses to make sure there are still adequate amounts for good insulation from temperature fluctuations. A 2- to 3-inch layer of mulch to cover the graft union is recommended. Hybrid tea roses are typically more susceptible to winter injury because they are grafted. The graft union is the swollen knob, located at the base of the rose bush. If it is not protected from winter temperature fluctuations, the top portion of the rose will die and growth will come from the rootstock. This wild stock grows vigorously and produces smaller blooms than the grafted variety, or none at all.

My favorite roses for our region are the hardy old-fashioned shrub roses that are typically grown

Crocus tommasinianus, *sometimes called "tommies," emerges very early.*

on their own roots. They are not as susceptible to winterkill as their crowns and roots survive to regrow new shoots the following season.

If you did not apply a horticultural oil in the autumn, pick a warm day and apply to the bare canes of roses that have a history of insect or disease problems. Dormant oils kill pests by smothering overwintering insect eggs and fungal spores. This reduces the incidence of problems during the growing season. Read and follow label directions on the product label when using any pesticides in your rose garden. Heavy horticultural oils should only be applied when the roses are leafless and dormant. Light, or superior oils, can be applied anytime of the year.

Periodically check indoor roses for insect pests and powdery mildew disease. Remove and discard portions of the plant that may harbor these problems. Leaves that have fallen around the base of the plant should be picked up and disposed of. Not doing so will encourage little black fungus gnats that soon become a nuisance in your home.

Prune gangly twig growth from vigorously growing indoor roses to encourage better air circulation, which reduces the incidence of diseases.

SHRUBS

Routinely check any structures or snow fence you set up to protect your shrubs to makes sure they are still functional. Until the chances of snow and severe weather are over, they can still be useful.

For weak-wooded shrubs, including dogwood, willow, forsythia, and lilac, carefully remove snow from the branches, particularly if it is a heavy, wet snow. Use upward strokes from *beneath*, not from the top. Start knocking snow from the lower branches first so that snow from the top ones will not overburden, and possibly break, the lower branches. Use an old broom, and gently bump it upward from underneath to dislodge and scatter the snow. To finish up, redo the lower branches to clear the snow that had fallen from above.

Do not disturb stems or branches that are iced over because they are likely to break. When the ice melts, they will resume their former posture. Check the shrubs after every storm, and take action to prop up those that need it, and prune out severely damaged branches.

You can commence late-winter pruning of shrubs to remove broken or damaged branches, but remember that pruning spring-flowering shrubs, such as lilac and forsythia will remove their flower buds and reduce flowering. Wait to prune spring bloomers until after they have finished blooming. Minor renewal pruning can preserve most of this year's flowers though, so prune gently.

It's time to renew shrubs that produce colorful winter bark such as the red-twig and yellow-twig dogwoods. Cut out at least one-third to one-half of the oldest canes to the ground with a pruning lopper. Older stems tend to lose color after a few years and can become infested with scale and canker diseases. Any overly long or scraggly branches can be headed back to shorter branches that are growing in the same direction.

To get an early spring feeling indoors, selectively prune some budded branches from spring-flowering shrubs. See details on forcing branches in the Plan section. The closer to their natural blooming time you cut the stems, the more quickly they will bloom indoors.

TREES

■ *Winter is a great time to study the structure of bare trees to see if there are any crossing branches. If there are, prune them out.*

Heavy, wet snow and ice accumulation can damage evergreens that have multiple leaders or trunks. Remove the weight of snow carefully. Snow-laden branches can snap if you move them too vigorously, so gently lift the snow off with an upward sweep of a broom or rake (never downward).

When removing snow from walks and driveways, avoid piling it up around the base of tree trunks. It can create a haven for critters to set up residence. Meadow mice or voles can girdle trees by chewing the bark all the way around the trunk. Instead, shovel the snow around the trees' drip lines (the area where the outermost branches extend) to provide moisture to the root zone.

The limbs of ornamental trees can be protected from snow and ice breakage with flexible supports. You can use old bicycle tire inner tubes; loop the rubber tubes around weak branches and the trunk to provide extra support, yet allow some flexibility. You can also create horizontal supports by securing bungee cords throughout the framework of the tree and attaching their ends to posts oriented on the outside of the tree. At the end of winter, examine your trees and prune out any broken or dead limbs.

You can continue to prune when the coldest days are past and before new growth begins. February is a good time to study the structure and form of your trees to determine which branches need removal. To safely remove large, heavy branches or limbs, follow the three-cut method to prevent the branch from tearing or stripping the bark farther down the trunk as it falls.

Wait to prune evergreens until new growth begins to emerge. This will allow for better shaping and a stronger branch structure to develop. With pines, the best time to prune is when the new growth is just beginning to expand or "candle."

VINES, GROUNDCOVERS & ORNAMENTAL GRASSES

Some hardy bulbs may soon be emerging from the soil and poking through groundcovers like vinca, veronica, and thyme. They add welcome color to the landscape, and later the groundcover will mask their ripening foliage. Remove any accumulation of leaves, as these can smother groundcover growth.

Cut back ornamental grasses as their stems and seedheads collapse to the ground. Choose a warm, sunny day and shear the clump to allow the new

shoots room to grow. Cutting now will prevent you from cutting the tips of new shoots later when they start to emerge in spring. Chop or shred the clippings, and add them to the compost pile.

WATER

ANNUALS

Keep young seedlings growing indoors moist, but not waterlogged. Water the young plants by spraying the growing mix with a fine mist or water from below. Water young potted plants when the growing mixture feels dry about an inch down. Do not overwater, as this can encourage fungus gnats.

BULBS

■ *One way to check moisture of overwintering potted plants is to stick your finger down 2 to 3 inches to test the soil; another is to use a moisture meter.*

Hardy bulbs in the outdoor landscape may need attention to watering if the winter has been dry. Water early in the day when the ground is unfrozen. Mulched bulb beds will require less attention, as the winter mulch will help to retain moisture and keep the soil cool.

EDIBLES

Learning to water vegetable and herb seedlings indoors in an art. It is better to keep the plants a little too dry than too wet. If there is excess water in the drainage saucer, discard it after a half-hour to discourage fungus gnats and soilborne diseases.

Watering too often from the bottom will increase the incidence of soluble salts. These will be noticed as a white crust on the rim of the trays or containers. Flush the soil with clean water from the top to leach salts out the growing medium.

LAWNS

Even though the majority of the lawn remains dormant, there may be some areas that are beginning to awaken. The lawn will still need some moisture if rainfall and snow are in short supply. If there has been no rain or snow for more than a month and the ground is not frozen, winter watering is necessary. See January's recommendations.

PERENNIALS

If your perennial beds have been properly mulched, they are less likely to dry out, but prolonged periods of dry weather can damage crowns and roots. Though dormant, perennials do need moisture.

Dig down to a depth of 4 to 6 inches when the ground is not frozen, and check subsoil moisture. If it is beginning to dry out, get out the garden hose and frog-eye sprinkler for winter watering. Do not overwater native plants and rock garden perennials as this can rot their crowns.

For seedlings growing indoors on the cold frame, remove the plastic covering and let them gradually acclimate to less moisture. When the soil is dry to the touch, either water from the bottom or sprinkle lightly with a mister to avoid damaging the tender seedlings.

Do not overwater as this will often result in damping-off diseases.

ROSES

Water the rose garden if you're experiencing clear, dry weather conditions for extended periods. Giving the rose garden a good drink on a warm, sunny day when temperatures are above freezing will ensure their survival. This only needs to be done every five to six weeks during dry spells and as long as the ground remains unfrozen.

Indoors, miniature roses should be watered regularly to compensate for the lack of humidity and the drying conditions of forced-air heat. Poke you finger into the potting soil to the depth of your second knuckle; when the soil begins to feel dry to the touch, give the plant a thorough watering such that water runs out the drainage hole. Discard excess water from the drainage saucer after an hour or so.

SHRUBS

Water shrubs whose soil is not frozen solid if there has been little or no appreciable snow or rainfall for a month or more. Water early in the day to allow the water to soak down to the roots.

Well-mulched shrubs usually survive better than those left unmulched since the mulch helps to retain moisture and prevent the soil from heaving.

HERE'S HOW

TO WATER FOR LATE FALL AND WINTER

Use a twin-eye or frog-eye sprinkler to give plants a good, deep drink. Set the sprinklers over the root zone early in the day when temperatures are above 40 degrees Fahrenheit. Let the water run for fifteen to twenty minutes (or until it starts to run off) in each area, then move to achieve good overlap. Lawns facing south or west will benefit from a drink of water too; this can also prevent damage from mites.

TREES

Be sure to get outdoors on those sunny warm days, and check whether your trees need winter watering. This goes for both evergreens and deciduous trees. Just because they are dormant on top doesn't mean they don't need water in the root zone.

When temperatures are above freezing and the ground is not frozen solid, set out a frog-eye sprinkler, and water around the root zone. Place the sprinkler at the drip line, and water for ten to fifteen minutes. Then move as needed to cover the entire root area. Water early in the day so the water can percolate into the soil. The roots are not able to take up moisture when the soil is frozen.

Afterward, disconnect the garden hose and store it back in the garage or garden shed.

VINES, GROUNDCOVERS & ORNAMENTAL GRASSES

During periods of warm, windy, dry weather, it may be necessary to water vines, groundcovers, and hardy ornamental grasses. Take advantage of the winter thaw and water when the ground is not frozen. Water early in the day to allow the water to percolate into the root zone. Winter watering may need to be done every four to five weeks, depending upon local weather conditions.

FERTILIZE

ANNUALS

Young sprouts will not need fertilizer for a few weeks. It is easiest to add a granular, slow-release fertilizer to the growing mixture prior to transplanting. Follow the label directions on the package. Otherwise, use a water-soluble fertilizer diluted to half strength.

BULBS

It is too early to apply granular fertilizer to bulb beds now. If you will be potting up tender summer-flowering bulbs later in the month, add a slow-acting granular fertilizer to the potting mixture. Follow label directions.

EDIBLES

You don't need to fertilize young seedlings immediately after they sprout. This can do more damage than good. Wait until the stem growth begins and a second set of leaves emerges on the seedlings. Then, use a water-soluble plant fertilizer such as 10-10-10 or an equivalent at half the recommended strength.

LAWNS

It's still too early to apply lawn fertilizer.

PERENNIALS

It is too early to fertilize outside perennials, but you can stock up on slow-release, organic-based fertilizer and other supplies if you find them on sale.

As the perennial seedlings develop their first set of true leaves (not just the initial small leaves), you can lightly fertilize them. Soilless growing mixtures do not contain much in the way of nutrients, so use a water-soluble plant fertilizer such as 10-15-10. I prefer to apply it at half the strength recommended on the label to avoid burning the tender seedlings.

ROSES

Outdoor roses do not need any fertilizer now, but this is a good time to apply a layer compost over the root zone of your roses to improve the soil conditions and fill in low spots. It doesn't matter if the ground is frozen, as snow and rain will moisten the compost and allow it to work into the soil as the spring thaws start up.

Miniatures indoors will benefit from a light fertilization of liquid plant food with an analysis of 10-20-10. Follow label directions.

SHRUBS & TREES

It's still too early to fertilize shrubs and trees in our region.

VINES, GROUNDCOVERS & ORNAMENTAL GRASSES

Delay fertilizing until new growth emerges later in the spring.

PROBLEM-SOLVE

ANNUALS

Continue to monitor plants for attacks by aphids, whiteflies, and mites. Spray persistent pests with a soap spray or commercial insecticidal soap, following label directions. Whiteflies can be trapped with yellow sticky boards.

Watch out for damping-off disease (see January Problem-Solve, page 30). Always use a sterile, soilless growing medium to reduce this problem. Maintain good light exposure and air circulation to avoid making the plants more susceptible.

BULBS

As the bulbs begin to emerge from the soil and some early crocus are blooming, critters may arrive too. Sparrows and finches seem to like to feed on crocus by tearing away at the blossoms. You can prevent this by covering vulnerable areas with bird netting.

Moles are active even in winter, often pushing up softened earth.

Snow mold on grass

Squirrels, however, are bolder creatures. They may dig up tulip and crocus bulbs and find them as tasty morsels early in the season. Bird netting is not strong enough for them. Construct a screen using hardware cloth to lay over threatened bulb beds.

Deer may also arrive to nibble on the foliage and buds of tulips and crocus. They won't bother daffodils, however. Spray the plants with a homemade critter repellent to keep them at bay (see page 221). Repeat after a rain or snowstorm.

EDIBLES

Be on the watch for damping-off fungus disease, which will kill seedlings rapidly. The stems will turn black, flop over, and die. This is the reason to water sparingly. Always use a sterilized growing or seed-starting mixture, or sterilize regular outdoor garden soil by baking it in the oven to an internal temperature of 160 degrees Fahrenheit. Garden soil will need to be amended with sphagnum peat moss and perlite.

LAWNS

A disease known as snow mold is common in higher elevations where snow cover is prolonged and accumulative. As the snow becomes compacted, this disease may attack bent grass or Kentucky bluegrass. After the spring thaw, patches of dead grass may be evident. Symptoms appear as a white or gray fungus or matting, dead grass that is slightly pink in color.

PERENNIALS

Weeds are always opportunistic and will pop up unexpectedly in perennial beds. Be on the watch for the first signs of downy brome or cheat grass. If it appears, handpull or dig it out when the soil is moist. You can also suppress the growth of winter annual weeds by applying a shallow layer of mulch over open areas.

Damping-off diseases can be a problem on seedlings you've started indoors. Cutting back the frequency of watering can control it. Increase the amount of light and provide better air circulation around crowded seedlings. Sometimes it helps to thin seedlings and transplant those you wish to save.

ROSES

Be on the watch for critters that nibble at the rose canes during the winter. Deer, elk, and rabbits are notorious for chewing on landscape plants when there is a lack of natural winter feed. To protect valued roses, surround them with wire cages tall enough so the deer cannot reach down inside. You can also spray the exposed canes with my homemade critter-repellent. See page 221 for the recipe. Remember, if the snow is unusually deep, critters will be able to reach higher on the plant than usual.

If you live in an area where mice, voles, and pocket gophers are a concern, periodically check the mulch around the base of the roses. They can be nesting in the mulch and will feed on the bark and damage or kill the stems. If you find the nesting site, pull away the mulch and destroy the nest. Reapply the mulch as needed to continue winter protection. Surround the mulch with a wire cage to discourage pests from nesting. To prevent critter damage in the future, delay winter mulching until after the ground freezes so that such rodents will seek other places to build a home. If necessary, spray the homemade critter-repellent on the canes, repeating applications after heavy snowfalls.

SHRUBS

Continue to be on the watch for damage by deer, elk, rabbits, and other critters. They will nibble on tender branch tips and the succulent stems of young shrubs. The only dependable deer and elk deterrent is a deer-proof fence. Check with your local Division of Wildlife for more information on deer-proofing your landscape.

If you are relying on spray repellents, it's a good idea to repeat applications every few weeks as they breakdown in sunlight and are washed away after snow begins to melt or rainfall splashes it off the stems.

TREES

Check for signs of insect damage or possible overwintering eggs on the branches or limbs. If necessary, you can apply a horticultural oil spray when temperatures are above freezing. Read and follow label directions.

Signs of rabbits include distinct round droppings around plants, gnawing on stems of older woody plants, clean-cut clipping of young stems and leaves, and—in winter—tracks.

VINES, GROUNDCOVERS & ORNAMENTAL GRASSES

Be on the watch for rabbits and deer. They will show up to nibble tender stems and new buds. Prevent damage by wrapping exposed stems with chicken or rabbit wire; protecting with a hardware cloth ring is a good idea, especially for plants in open areas where critters are common. You can also spray vulnerable plants with a repellent as directed on the product label. Try the homemade critter repellent described on page 221.

If mice or voles are a problem, you may have to set traps to eliminate them. Bait them with peanut butter. Also, keep mulches away from the base of the stems and crowns of plants to discourage critters from nesting there.

March

The signs of spring are all around and March can be a busy month. The soil outdoors is becoming more workable. If you didn't add organic matter to flowerbeds last fall, do so this month, at least several weeks before planting outdoors. Get a head start on the growing season by using cold frames and row covers. They warm the soil to help speed seed germination and establishment while protecting plant leaves and stems from freezing temperatures.

Many kinds of cold frames are available through mail-order catalogs, or you can make your own. Several types of annual seeds can be started in a cold frame, so if you don't have room for starting seeds indoors, you can start them outdoors. Add a heating cable or heating mat for seeds that require bottom heat for germination.

An easy-to-construct cold frame can be made by using straw bales to make three sides of a square, with the open side facing south. Put an old storm door or window on top and "close" the open edge with another piece of glass or Plexiglas set at an angle. Remove the front glass on sunny, warm days so the plants don't cook.

During warm, dry, and windy weather in March, it's not unusual to see daffodil, tulip, and hyacinth shoots prematurely emerge from the ground. Often, early emergence is seen on the southern or western exposures or next to buildings. Bulb plantings can be mulched with 2 to 3 inches of compost or shredded wood chips, bark, or pine needles to keep the soil cooler and suppress early emergence.

March can be tricky in the Rockies. It can be snowy, cold, dry, windy, or a mixture of all! If it's too muddy to plant, wait until the soil begins to dry out. Never work wet soil, as this destroys soil's structure and leaves you with lots of hard clay clods.

The time you put into an early start this month will pay off in big dividends. Enjoy the warm days, colorful early blooming bulbs, and wild birds returning to your garden.

PLAN

ANNUALS

Figure out the number of plants you'll need to plant in your annual flowerbeds. Calculate the square footage of existing or new beds by multiplying the length times the width to get the square footage of the planting beds. This information will help determine the number of plants and amount of fertilizer you will need. See the plant spacing chart below.

BULBS

Plan on replacing those bulbs that are waning. Consider adding more early blooming minor bulbs. These little wonders will add a welcome touch of color when you're awaiting springtime. Snow crocus, grape hyacinth, winter aconite, snowdrops, and Siberian squill are a few little gems to plant.

EDIBLES

If your plant stand is filling up, cool-weather seedlings can be moved outdoors to a cold frame until they

PLANT SPACING CHART

Follow this chart to calculate the number of plants you'll need. Divide the square footage of the garden by the spacing factor. The result is the number of plants you'll need.

Spacing (In.)	Spacing Factor	Plants Needed (Sq. Ft.)			
		25	50	75	100
4	0.11	227	454	682	909
6	0.25	100	200	300	400
8	0.44	57	114	170	227
10	0.70	36	72	107	143
12	1.00	12	50	75	100
15	1.56	16	32	48	64
18	2.25	11	22	33	44
24	4.00	6	13	19	25
30	6.25	4	8	12	16
36	9.00	3	6	8	11
48	16.00	2	3	5	6
60	26.00	1	2	3	4

are ready to plant. Make plans for getting the garden plot ready. Prepare your garden rakes, shovels, trowels, and cultivators, and tune up the mechanical garden tools' small engines. Rake or till the garden when the weather is nice and the soil is not too wet.

Planting dates for specific crops vary throughout our region. Check with your local weather reporting station or state university, or chat with experienced gardeners for the average last frost-free date to guide your planting schedule.

For early crops, it is important to warm up the soil prior to setting out transplants. Plan on covering the prepared garden bed with clear or black plastic several weeks in advance. You can start this now to get the soil ready. This will absorb the sun's heat. Later, when planting time arrives, cut holes in the plastic, and plant through it so the plastic continues to warm up the soil for the young transplants.

Plant protectors to keep on hand include cardboard boxes, fiber pots, 5-gallon plastic buckets, and frost blankets to cover plants if extreme cold is predicted.

Now is the time to make plans to buy bare-root fruit trees. These are available through mail-order catalogs and local nurseries. They are harvested from the growing fields, bundled, and stored in cool storage. The majority of my fruit trees can be planted bare-root in early spring with great success. The root system adapts to the soil conditions very favorably and has strong growth early in the cool season. If you haven't tried bare-root trees, give them a try, but be sure to plant them before they leaf out. Dormant stock suffers less transplant shock and will get off to a quick start.

LAWNS

Your lawn is still dormant in the shady areas, so plan to get it in shape as the soil thaws. In sunny exposures it can suffer drought stress, so plan on some early watering to thwart lawn mites and their damage. But as weather conditions begin to warm up and spring showers arrive, the lawn will awaken and begin to turn green.

If your lawn needs repair and reseeding, select the right grass for your needs and the sun exposure of your lawn site.

PERENNIALS

The "winter roses," also known as hellebore or Lenten rose (*Helleborus*), are beginning to bloom. Plan to get outdoors and take in the beauty of your perennial beds. Clean up and oil garden trowels that were not taken care of last fall. Sharpen pruners yourself or have this done professionally. It is *much* easier to prune perennials with sharp tools.

Take advantage of early garden sales for stakes, wire cages, and other supports for taller perennials like delphiniums or floppy ones like peonies. Stock up on compost, slow-acting fertilizer, and horticultural oil for tackling chores as the weather permits.

Plan to expand or reduce the size of a perennial bed, depending upon your wants and maintenance routine. Consider a raised island bed to reduce the size of the lawn area. Sketch a plan of your proposed garden in a notebook to determine how many plants you will need.

ROSES

Spring is approaching, and the snow is beginning to melt. As the days get longer and temperatures rise, rose bushes begin to awaken in the garden. You'll see signs of buds swelling and little sprouts starting to develop at the base of the plants. Don't get in a hurry to prune too early. Pruning will stimulate new growth more rapidly, but there is still a chance of late spring frosts that will damage tender new growth.

Pull back the mulch a bit to check the condition of the canes. If they are still green and firm, they have survived the rigors of winter. Rose bushes that have no signs of green or those that have turned brown or black all the way down to the graft union are most likely damaged. Plan to order or buy replacements as needed.

SHRUBS

Now is the time to get serious about purchasing new shrubs for your landscape. Make a sketch or a detailed plan so you choose the proper shrub for the proper site. If the location receives full sun, partial shade, or shade, select plants accordingly so they will perform in that area. Check soil conditions to make sure the area is well drained, or make plans to improve that area prior to planting. Once

you have an accurate list of shrubs that will fit into your landscape, you are ready to place an order with the nursery or garden store.

By now, some of the mail-order stock may be arriving at your door. If the soil is ready, it's time to plant. If your area is not ready to plant, store bare-root plants in a cool spot and keep their roots moist up to planting time.

TREES

Begin shopping for the more unusual trees. Check with garden centers and specialty nurseries to locate your desired species. Shop early to find the best selection. Diversity in the landscape will make it interesting.

VINES, GROUNDCOVERS & ORNAMENTAL GRASSES

Can you feel and smell the arrival of spring? As the days get longer, our garden urges stir. Consider eliminating large expanses of lawn. Are there slopes that are difficult to mow and are just "a pain in the grass?" Consider one of my favorite evergreen groundcovers, *Juniperus horizontalis* or 'Blue Rug' juniper, as an alternative to turfgrass. Once established, it is a very hardy and reliable groundcover for difficult slopes, with year-round visual appeal.

For shady areas, consider *Vinca minor* or periwinkle, one of the most adaptable covers for areas under tree canopy. Study the *Rocky Mountain Getting Started Garden Guide* for more plant selections. Identify where you'll plant ornamental grasses as accents in your yard. They are virtually foolproof, and once established, can be very drought enduring. Leave them standing in the autumn and winter for added texture in the winter landscape.

PLANT

ANNUALS

Some annuals can be directly sown in the garden even though the soil temperatures are still cold. If the soil has been worked previously, snapdragon, sweet peas, pansy, and viola are a few that can be directly sown outdoors. Their seeds need cool conditions for proper germination. Check their seed packets for more specific information

Creeping juniper can solve many landscape "problems" and even replace turf for some areas (pictured is Juniperus chinensis procumbens nana*).*

and timing. See "Here's How to Read a Seed Packet" on page 55.

By midmonth, it's time to sow indoors seeds of warm-season annuals that need six to eight weeks lead time before transplanting outdoors. Determine the last frost date for your area in spring and count back the number of weeks indicated on the seed packet. (You will be planting *after* the last frost.)

If you did not transplant seedlings into larger pots last month, now is a good time to do so. If there is no granular, slow-release fertilizer incorporated into the potting mixture, add some prior to transplanting. This will save time for fertilizing later.

Otherwise, use a water-soluble fertilizer at half the recommended strength. Apply to a moistened potting mixture every other watering.

Transplant overwintering geraniums, begonias, impatiens, coleus, and other annuals that were in the basement or porch. Use a good-quality sterile potting mixture. Cut tall leggy plants back to balance them in their containers. Water in well.

BULBS

If you want a headstart for the tender, summer-flowering bulbs, it's time to pot up begonias, dahlias, cannas, and caladiums indoors. I use 1-gallon plastic containers with a well-drained potting mixture. Start them in an attached garage where the emerging sprouts will not freeze. Once the sprouts appear, provide light with a light stand to make them grow strong, sturdy stems.

Outdoors, snowdrops have completed blooming and the foliage persists. During the next few weeks, you can divide crowded clumps of snowdrops if the ground is workable. Having the leaves intact makes it easy to separate the clumps for new transplants.

Pansies, forget-me-nots, violas, and primroses are good companion plants for spring-flowering bulbs, and can be planted now. Many cool-tolerant annuals will be available at local garden retailers.

HERE'S HOW

TO DIVIDE SMALL BULBS

1. Gently dig masses of minor bulbs, and shake away the excess soil.

2. Tease apart the individual bulbs, being careful not to tear the roots or break off the foliage.

3. Discard any bulbs that are damaged or appear diseased.

4. Replant some of the bulbs in their original spot; bury about 3 inches deep and space 3 inches apart.

Tulips, daffodils, hyacinths, and lilies are often given as gifts during the Easter season. These have been forced to bloom in their pots, but can be planted in your garden once they finish blooming and the soil outdoors is workable. Before planting, snip off the flowers; leave the foliage so it can grow to produce food energy for the bulb. Grow indoors until the danger of frost has passed and then plant outside in an area where the soil has been enriched with compost. Work a little slow-release fertilizer into the planting holes. These bulbs will readjust to the outdoor schedule and bloom next year in your yard.

EDIBLES

If the soil is workable and not too wet, set out bare-root asparagus plants, rhubarb, horseradish,

TO READ A SEED PACKET

1. **Common name**

2. **Scientific name**

3. **Plant type**
   Annual flowers complete their entire life cycle during one growing season. They sprout, bloom, and die in one year. They do not come back from year to year from their roots, as perennials do.

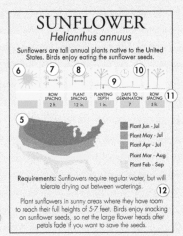

SUNFLOWER ①
Helianthus annuus ②
annual ③
15 grams ~OR~ Enough to cover 20 ft. ④

SUNFLOWER
Helianthus annuus
Sunflowers are tall annual plants native to the United States. Birds enjoy eating the sunflower seeds.
⑥ ⑦ ⑧ ⑨ ⑩
ROW SPACING 2 ft. | PLANT SPACING 12 in. | PLANTING DEPTH 1 in. | DAYS TO GERMINATION 7 | ROW SPACING 5 ft. ⑪
⑤
Plant Jun - Jul
Plant May - Jul
Plant Apr - Jul
Plant Mar - Aug
Plant Feb - Sep
Requirements: Sunflowers require regular water, but will tolerate drying out between waterings. ⑫
Plant sunflowers in sunny areas where they have room to reach their full heights of 5-7 feet. Birds enjoy snacking on sunflower seeds, so net the large flower heads after petals fade if you want to save the seeds.

4. **Weight of seeds in packet**
   Seeds are packed by weight, not volume. Often, the weight is accompanied by information about how much space you can plant with the seeds contained in the packet.

5. **When to plant**
   Most seed packets have information about when to plant. Some packets will tell you how warm the soil needs to be for seeds to sprout, but most packets have zone maps that allow you to locate your approximate zone to see when's the best time to plant outside. (Zone maps tell you when to plant outside—not when to start seeds inside.)

6. **Light requirements**
   Most annual flowers grow best in the sun, though there are a few shade-lovers. Always match the light requirement on the seed packet with the conditions in the location where you plan to plant the seeds.

7. **Row spacing**
   The amount of space you need to leave between rows of seeds.

8. **Plant spacing**
   How far apart to plant the seeds.

9. **Planting depth**
   How deep to plant the seeds.

10. **Days to germination**
    How many days it will take for the seed to sprout after planting. In general, plants germinate faster when temperatures are higher and slower when temperatures are lower.

11. **Plant height**
    The height of the fully grown plant. You don't necessarily need to plant tall plants in the back of the bed and short plants in the front, but you will want to look for plants that have different heights so that every plant in the flowerbed isn't the same height. Staggering the heights makes it easier to actually see your flowers and plants.

12. **Water requirements and suggestions**
    Every plant has different water requirements. Always plant things with similar water needs next to one another.

and onion sets. Asparagus is one of my favorites, and it's hardy throughout the region. Considering the cost at the supermarket, why not grow your own?

Test the soil before digging in by squeezing a handful. If it crumbles in your hand, it's workable. If water drips when you squeeze or it remains in a sodden ball, wait a week or so before digging.

Although Saint Patrick's Day is the traditional time to plant garden peas, the soil in our region may be too moist and cold. The soil temperature should be 45 degrees Fahrenheit or more. Use your best judgment; I usually wait until early April.

Herbs that were started indoors should be hardened off (acclimated to the outdoors) for a few weeks before they are completely set outdoors later in the month. When nighttime temperatures are above freezing, let them spend the night outside.

Around the middle of the month, start warm-season vegetables including tomatoes, peppers, eggplant, and okra. Spinach, Swiss chard, endive, and leaf lettuces can be planted directly outdoors in late March.

LAWNS

As the weather warms up and sod growers begin their harvest, you can install new sod. Just be sure to have the soil prepared at the site of new sod installation. A minimum of 3 cubic yards of organic matter per 1,000 square feet should be added to "fill dirt" to build a good soil for deep and healthy root growth. You can add up to 5 cubic yards of organic matter per 1,000 square feet if your budget allows.

Once the soil is amended with organic matter, scatter and scratch in some granular starter fertilizer such as 18-46-0. Follow label directions. Smooth the planting area, then seed or sod. Lightly press the seed with the back end of the rake to make sure the seed is in contact with the soil.

Water seeded and sodded lawns daily if spring rains are scarce and infrequent, supplying ¾ to 1-inch of water weekly. This is where an automatic sprinkler system is time saving and worth the money. The seedbed must be kept moist to ensure uniform germination.

■ *Keep turfgrass seedbeds moist until the grass germinates.*

PERENNIALS

Put together a planting plan before getting new perennials. Complete a plant list and try to include the number of plants species you will need. See the Plant Spacing Chart on page 52 for help.

Perennial seedlings started indoors may need transplanting. If their roots are growing through the drainage holes or the mixture dries out rapidly, it's time to move them. Gently remove the seedlings by tugging on the top set of leaves, not the tender stems. Transplant into a container half full of soilless growing medium, with slow-release fertilizer added. Set each seedling into the new growing mixture at the same level it was growing. Fill in around the seedling with more medium and lightly press down the growing mixture. *Remember: do not plant too deep.* Water and return the transplants to good light.

You can divide and replant many perennials, including chrysanthemums, asters, coneflowers, sedum, phlox, ornamental grasses, and many others. Lift clumps out of the soil with a spading fork and separate clumps into healthy, vigorous sections.

ROSES

Now is a good time to transplant roses that need relocation in your landscape if they are not growing in full sun. Prepare the new site in advance to make the job easier. You can begin transplanting established plants as soon as you see the new rose buds swelling. Don't wait until the rose bush leafs out; there will be more transplant shock if you do.

This is an excellent time to plant bare-root roses. Be careful about working the soil; don't work it if it is too wet, as this can destroy the soil structure and

HERE'S HOW

TO DIVIDE PERENNIALS

1. Cut back the foliage on an overgrown perennial by about one-half to reduce water loss in the transplanting process.

2. Use a sharp spade to cut around the plant and gently lift as much of the rootball out of the ground as possible.

3. Smaller rootballs can usually be cut into pieces using a sharp knife. Larger clumps can be sliced with a sharp spade or pried apart using two back-to-back garden forks.

4. Remove excess soil from the rootball so you can see what you are working with and remove any rotted or damaged roots.

5. Replant the new plants as soon as possible at the same depth the plant was growing at or slightly higher to allow for settling, and water the soil thoroughly. If you can't replant the same day, pot up the divisions and keep well-watered until they are established.

leave it lumpy. Allow the soil to dry out slightly so that it is crumbly when you grab a handful.

SHRUBS

As the soil begins to dry out enough to work, you can begin planting. Plant bare-root stock while it is still dormant; it will suffer less transplant shock than if you wait until the buds leaf out. Keep bare-root nursery stock in a cool location and the wrapping moist until you plant them outdoors.

TREES

Bare-root deciduous trees are best planted while they are still dormant, about a month before the last freeze in your area. Plant them as soon as possible after they arrive in the mail or after buying bare-root stock locally. Unwrap the root system and soak in a bucket of water at least six hours before planting. If there are any broken or damaged roots, prune them back cleanly to behind the break.

If you need to move small trees and shrubs in your landscape, now is the time to get started. Transplant before they leaf out to avoid transplant shock. Dig the new planting hole two to three times wider than the rootball. Prepare the new site by adding one-third by volume of compost or sphagnum peat moss.

VINES, GROUNDCOVERS & ORNAMENTAL GRASSES

As the pansies and violas arrive at local garden stores, plant them in spring-flowering bulb beds to provide early spring color and serve as a groundcover around the bulb foliage. They love the cool weather and will grow and bloom with gusto.

Bare-root vines and groundcovers that arrive via mail-order can be planted anytime the soil can be worked. I like bare-root plants since they are economical and acclimate so well to our native soil conditions.

Divide ornamental grasses as soon as the soil can be worked.

CARE

ANNUALS

Annuals that you started from cuttings last fall should be thriving with the increased daylight

TO DIVIDE ORNAMENTAL GRASSES

1. Begin by cutting back last year's old stems if you haven't already done so.

2. Dig down around the outside of the clump until you begin to feel the clump dislodge from the ground.

3. Lift the entire rootball out of the ground to expose the massive amount of roots and crown.

4. Cut the clump into manageable rooted divisions by slicing down with a sharp spade or machete.

5. Replant each division as needed to other parts of the landscape, or share extra clumps with friends and neighbors.

6. An alternative way to divide grasses is to split them right where they grow. Use a sharp spade to slice down through the grass clump while it is still planted.

7. Pry apart chunks or wedges of the grass as if cutting a piece of pie.

8. Remove the divisions by digging under and around them, leaving the main rootball in place.

9. Fill in the empty holes with garden soil.

10. Replant the grass divisions to new areas or give them away.

hours as spring approaches. They may need to be repotted into larger containers before you actually set them outside. This is a good time to refresh the soil and cut back some of the leggy growth. Top with fresh potting soil as needed.

Continue to adjust the light over young annual seedlings as they grow to provide optimal growing conditions. Keep the lights a few inches above the plants to encourage strong, sturdy growth. If seedlings are being grown in a windowsill, rotate the containers every few days so that light falls on every side. This will keep the plants from leaning too much and encourage sturdy stem growth.

Gently brushing your fingertips or an open hand over the tops of seedlings a couple of times daily will also encourage the development of sturdier stems.

You can keep annuals from getting too leggy and tall by regularly pinching back the tips of their stems. This will stimulate the plant to grow more lateral stems and compact foliage. You can do some pinching of annuals purchased at the garden store as well. This will get rid of the lanky growth if the light conditions have been poor.

BULBS

To naturalize bulbs in your warm-season lawn or other parts of the landscape with low to moderate moisture, delay mowing the lawn to allow the bulb foliage to ripen and store energy. *Iris reticulata*, crocuses, and snow crocuses are wonderful bulbs for naturalizing an area, whether a lawn or open space.

To tidy up the bulb garden, pinch off the faded or spent flowers to keep them from spreading. This is particularly true of grape hyacinths since they can spread throughout the garden bed. If you are naturalizing an area, this is not necessary.

EDIBLES

If you have overwintered carrots and parsnips and other root crops in the garden, dig them out before they start to grow. Once they start to regrow, they loose their sweet flavor and will go to seed.

To grow herbs in limited space, plant them in large containers such as strawberry pots or terracotta

planters. Use a fresh, soilless potting mixture that has good drainage, and be sure the containers have drainage holes.

Pinch herbs growing indoors that are growing leggy to keep them growing more compact. These include basil, rosemary, thyme, and mint. Thin out seedlings planted directly in the garden or raised beds to allow proper spacing for vigorous growth.

Finish pruning your small fruits including raspberries, blackberries, and elderberries before the buds swell. Remove the weakest canes, and oldest wood, leaving six to eight canes per plant. You can head back the remaining canes of red raspberries to 3 to 4 feet tall. On black raspberries and blackberries, cut back lateral branches on remaining stems to 10 to 15 inches long. If desired, after pruning bramble fruits, tie them to supports for easier maintenance.

If you grow everbearing raspberries for a late summer or fall crop, you can get out the lawn mower or pruning loppers, and cut the canes to the ground. The new canes produced this spring will bear an abundance of fruit without any further pruning. Remove damaged canes and dead wood from currants and gooseberries.

LAWNS

When the soil underfoot is no longer frozen and you can poke a screwdriver down 6 inches or more, you can begin to core-aerate the lawn. This will breathe new life into the lawn by allowing water, air, and nutrients to become more available to the grass plants. A good aeration will also break through thatch layers and help microorganisms begin the process of breaking down heavy thatch layers. See "Here's How to Use a Power Core-Aerator" on page 60. Do not use a power rake on lawns that are beginning to green up.

If annual weeds such as crabgrass, goosegrass, or downy bromegrass chronically invade your lawn, it will soon be time to apply a pre-emergent herbicide. Wait until the forsythia shrubs begin to bud and bloom as a guide for applying the pre-emergent.

Pre-emergent herbicides kill weed seeds as they begin to germinate. An environmentally friendly pre-emergent is made from corn gluten. I highly

TO USE A POWER CORE-AERATOR

1. Water the entire yard lightly a few hours before you aerate to ensure that the soil is moist—but don't overwater or you will bog down the machine in mud.

2. Flag all sprinkler heads, shallow sprinkler lines, and shallow buried cables, wires, and utility lines. Clear the lawn of other debris such as small tree branches.

3. Set the depth gauge on the coring machine to maximum. Run the machine across the lawn, back and forth in one direction. Then run it again, perpendicular to the original direction.

4. Allow the cores pulled up by the aerator to dry for a day, then gently rake across them to break them up so that they decompose more quickly.

Pre-emergent herbicides do *not* distinguish between "good" and "bad" seeds. Do *not* apply to areas where you intend to overseed with lawn grasses or other groundcover plants. It takes several weeks for the pre-emergent to become ineffective. Read and follow the label directions on the herbicide package prior to application. It is best not to core-aerate a lawn after applying a pre-emergent.

recommend this for the bird- and wildlife-friendly landscape. As the corn gluten breaks down, it also adds fertilizer to the lawn. It is very useful to place beneath bird feeders to prevent the germination of wasted birdseed that falls at the base of the feeder.

PERENNIALS

Perennials that are established in the garden can cope with the vagaries of nature's spring weather. They have a built-in time clock that will let them know when to awaken. Perennials planted on southern or hot exposures may be fooled into growing too soon. Protect them with additional mulch or a light watering to keep the soil cool.

It is inevitable that some perennials will emerge early and start to bloom. If a hard cold snap is predicted, pick some flowers to enjoy indoors.

Late frosts are the norm, but established perennials can usually cope. When a heavy, wet snow is on its way, have 5-gallon buckets or boxes on hand to cover the foliage of plants that have already emerged and those that are subject to damage from the weight of snow.

Some perennials you've ordered may start arriving via the mail. If the soil is workable and not too wet, go ahead and plant them in their designated homes. Bare-root perennials will transplant easily and root in nicely while conditions are cool.

If conditions are too soggy or cold, store bare-root plants in a cool, dark place so they will stay dormant until actual planting time. Keep the roots moist.

This is the time to begin garden cleanup. Cut back dried grasses, stems, and flowerheads to tidy up the garden and make way for the new perennial shoots.

ROSES

As your rose bushes begin to grow, you can start to remove the winter mulch. If you leave the plants covered in extended warm weather, the new shoots will be etiolated (white and weak) and may die back if exposed too late. Nature's signal for removal of mulch is when the forsythia shrubs are flowering.

If you have overwintered tree roses in trenches, carefully dig them out and reset them in their upright position. Climbing roses should be inspected for winterkill, and damaged stems pruned back to healthy, green wood. Tie up climbers to their supports.

Spread a 2-inch layer of mulch over the root zone of roses to keep the soil from baking and to discourage annual weed growth. Mulches also help conserve moisture.

As nature signals the expansion of new growth and winter protection has been removed, it's time to prune. Prune roses to maintain their health and shape the plants to fit their designated areas. How much you prune depends on the type of rose shrub and your method of growing and training.

Make sure pruning loppers, hand pruners, and pruning saws are sharp and ready. Remove all dead and damaged canes on all types of roses. Roses that have signs of winterkill should have stems pruned back to healthy live wood that is solid; cut as low as needed.

Disinfect pruning tools between cuts by spraying the blades with rubbing alcohol or household disinfectant. Pick up and discard fallen debris that may harbor insects, eggs, or fungal disease spores.

Hybrid tea, floribunda, and grandiflora roses do best with a hard pruning. Keep the center of the shrub open to sunlight. Select three or more healthy young canes spaced openly to form a vase shape. Cut them back 7 to 9 inches tall. Cut off all other canes at the base with pruning loppers. Make the cut ends approximately ¼ inch above an outward-facing leaf bud; angle the cut so the water will drain away.

Landscape roses benefit from rejuvenation and renewal pruning. Remove about one-third of the older canes and weaker branches. Reduce the height of the remaining canes by one-third their length.

Polyanthas and miniature roses need basic grooming. Prune back stems to 3 to 6 inches. Cut off twiggy growth and open up the center of the plant to allow more light to the plant and promote more flowering.

Groundcover and hedge roses can be sheared. Prune the canes to about 6 inches.

SHRUBS

You can gradually begin to rake out old leaves and other debris that has collected in your shrub beds during the winter. Collect fallen leaves and put them in your compost pile or send them through a shredder and work them into the vegetable garden. Take care not to disturb any emerging perennials or spring-flowering bulbs.

Gradually remove winter protection from shrubs by mid- to late month. Keep a watch for any damage to the shrubs from the winter, such as broken branches or critter-feeding injury.

Neglected shrubs can be renovated now. Those showing lots of overgrown, tangled, or dead wood can be pruned back hard. Shrubs that are overgrown or neglected can be renewed by pruning out one-third of the oldest canes to the ground. This will not severely reduce the bloom this season, but will encourage new, healthy, vigorous growth. Head these plants back when flowering is finished. Cut back another third next year. Cut back the final third the year after that. In this way you have renewed an old shrub with new, vigorous, and more flowering stems.

■ Cutting stems back to ground level will renew old shrubs.

Rejuvenation pruning can be done before spring growth expands, either before leaf or bud break. Prune evergreens before the new, soft needles form. On old, tired deciduous shrubs, systematically cut back every stem to 4 to 6 inches from the ground. Use sharp loppers or pruners; in some cases, a chainsaw will be needed to remove thick, large canes.

As young replacement growth begins to appear, you can clip or pinch off some of the weaker canes to encourage the development of fewer, but stronger remaining ones. These will make up the basic structure of the shrub.

Shrubs that are growing in their natural form and are well balanced can be pruned to thin out crowded or crisscrossing stems. As the stems grow 6 inches, pinch out the terminal bud to promote more branching, if desired. New branches will emerge just below the pinch.

Prune early spring-flowering shrubs like forsythia and quince when they finish blooming. Avoid pruning other shrubs that bloom later, such as potentialla, blue mist spirea, and weigela, as this will remove the flower buds.

TREES

Newly planted bare-root trees that are exposed to high winds may need to be staked to keep them from blowing over. The wire from the stakes should be attached to nylon tree straps to protect the bark of the tree. Make sure that the supports are secured at the lowest point on the trunk to allow movement back and forth. This will encourage a strong, thick trunk. Remove the supports after one growing season.

Remove broken or dead branches. Trees that tend to "bleed" or excrete sap profusely, such as maple, elm, aspen, and birch, should not be pruned now. Although bleeding is unsightly, it is not harmful.

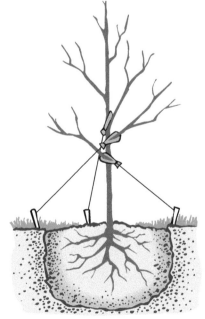

■ If you must stake a newly planted tree, remove stakes and wires after one year.

To minimize bleeding, prune these trees after the leaves have expanded and green up in the summer and the shoot stops growing. Some arborists recommend fall pruning to reduce bleeding, but this practice must be weighed against the possibility of making the trees more susceptible to winter injury. Use your best judgment when making this decision for your particular climate conditions.

Thin out suckers or upright growth on trees. Some trees like the Bradford pear will produce a lot of upright branches that grow closely together on the trunk. Weak branch growth makes a tree more vulnerable to snow, ice, and wind breakage.

To keep evergreens such as pines and spruces from growing out of bounds, you can trim the new growth or "candles" back each year. Timing is critical; do this pruning when the new needles are about a ½ inch long. Pruning the candles at this time will allow the new shoot buds to develop below the cuts. These will sprout next year.

Pines, spruces, firs, and most junipers should not be pruned back to older, bare branches. Any needleless branch will eventually die and this will result in a hole or gap in the evergreen.

VINES, GROUNDCOVERS & ORNAMENTAL GRASSES

Some perennial vines will awaken from winter dormancy this month. Check their supports to be sure they are secure when growth really gets going. There's an old adage about perennial vines: "The first year they sleep, the second year they creep, and the third year they leap!"

Check newly planted groundcovers, and mulch around them to suppress weed growth early in the season. It can be a real challenge to control weeds in groundcovers once the weeds get a stronghold. Spread a 2- to 3-inch layer of pine needles, shredded cedar chips, pole peelings, or chopped leaves over the soil between the groundcover plants.

Later in the month, you can begin to prune back Jackmanii clematis and other clematis that bloom on new wood. Spring-blooming varieties that bloom on the previous year's wood should be pruned after flowering, no later than mid-July.

Finish cutting off the old tops of ornamental grasses, and recycle the clippings to the compost pile. Be careful not to damage any new green shoots if they are emerging.

Gently rake over groundcovers to remove any accumulation of leaves and other debris that may have blown in. Prune out dead tips and broken branches, if needed.

WATERING

ANNUALS
Keep potted annuals watered as the potting mixture dries out. Poke your finger down about an inch; if dry, it's time to water the plant. Don't overwater.

New seedlings and transplants should be kept moist, but not too wet. It is okay to allow the growing mixture to dry out slightly between waterings.

Water plants with tepid water rather than directly from a cold-water faucet.

BULBS
If there has been a prolonged dry spell and the ground is dry, water bulb beds to maintain uniform

THE WHEN AND HOW OF PRUNING CLEMATIS

Pruning methods vary. Spring-blooming clematis that bloom on previous year's growth should be pruned after flowering (no later than mid-July) to allow for the production and ripening of the new growth. Remove dead wood or winterkilled tips. Deadheading can often stimulate new blooms later in summer and early fall. Summer-flowering and early fall-blooming varieties do best if cut back in early spring. Prune stems back to a pair of plump buds, and thin out weak and dead wood. Late-flowering cultivars and species produce flowers on the current season's growth, so prune in early spring and remove the previous season's stems down to a pair of plump, healthy buds, 6 to 12 inches above the ground.

moisture for healthy strong growth, and to keep the soil cool to help delay premature emergence. Water areas where the ground is unfrozen.

EDIBLES

When watering homegrown seedlings, use a spray bottle that will deliver water without knocking the plants over. Don't overwater, as this increases the chances for damping-off diseases and fungus gnats. Before setting transplants directly into the garden, water them a few hours ahead of time to reduce transplant shock.

LAWNS

If the spring is dry for extended periods, you will need to water your lawn so it can start growing. This is the time to encourage deep root growth while the soil is cool. Water deeply, but infrequently. Usually once a week is adequate. Apply 1 inch of water per week when rainfall or snow is lacking.

Keep new sod and seeded areas moist for a period of twenty days to ensure strong and healthy establishment. Check with your local water provider for updates on water restrictions and apply for a watering permit if you need to establish either a new seed or sod lawn.

PERENNIALS

Check the garden soil before watering the perennial bed. March snow and rains can often provide adequate moisture. If, however, we are experiencing a prolonged dry spell over two weeks, get out the garden hose for spot-watering. Use a frog-eye sprinkler to water dry areas for ten to fifteen minutes. Avoid overwatering native plants and rock garden plants that do best with very good drainage and thrive on just the natural precipitation.

Keep new perennial seedlings watered as needed, but allow the soilless mix to dry out slightly to harden up the plants. Move the transplants outdoors during the day into a semi-shady spot to help them acclimate if they were started indoors. Bring back inside at night to prevent freezing.

SHRUBS

Water newly planted shrubs as soon as the soil begins to dry out. Established shrubs need a deep watering every few weeks. To avoid waterlogging

the soil around your shrubs, always check soil moisture with a soil probe, or dig down several inches with a garden trowel.

TREES

During mild spells when there is little or no precipitation, water trees. Pay particular attention to fall-planted trees and evergreens. They are most vulnerable to desiccation during dry, windy weather.

Use a frog-eye sprinkler to spot-water trees that are planted in open exposures.

Apply water early in the day to allow it to soak down to the root system.

Mulch newly planted trees with a 2- to 3-inch layer of compost or other organic material to help retain moisture and prevent excessive weed growth at the root zone.

VINES, GROUNDCOVERS & ORNAMENTAL GRASSES

Hopefully we have a wet spring, but this is not always the case. If we experience a dry, windy spell of weather, water newly planted groundcovers, vines, and ornamental grasses. The soil moisture is essential to sustain the root system.

Pansies and violas used as underplantings around bulbs will need regular watering during their peak blooming season. Mulched plantings will need less frequent watering and will survive the drier conditions more favorably.

FERTILIZE

ANNUALS

In the milder parts of the region, you may be able to get outdoors and work some fertilizer into annual flowerbeds. My preference is to use a slow-release fertilizer as it saves time and lasts longer into the growing season. Follow the label directions for the amount to use.

BULBS

Since bulbs, corms, rhizomes, and tubers are specialized plant structures, they store energy from the previous growing season. They generally do not need fertilizer in the spring until after they have finished blooming. Once the flowers have faded and the leaves continue to grow vigorously, scatter a slow-acting granular fertilizer throughout the bulb bed and lightly cultivate into the soil. Water the fertilizer in thoroughly. This will provide nutrients so the foliage can build up food reserves to store in the underground bulbs. One application of slow-release fertilizer is all that is needed for the spring season.

EDIBLES

Fertilize indoor seedlings weekly with a water-soluble fertilizer diluted to half strength. Apply the fertilizer to a moist soil, never to dry soil. Keep the plants in bright light so they utilize the nutrients.

To fertilize the outdoor garden for transplants, add a slow-acting fertilizer ahead of time, or add a water-soluble fertilizer at half strength as you plant. Do not add fresh manure to the garden prior to planting because its high soluble salts will "burn" the transplants. Add manure to the garden in the autumn, and till it so winter freezes will break it down.

LAWNS

If you applied an autumn fertilizer in October, it is still too early to fertilize the lawn.

PERENNIALS

As the soil begins to dry out and perennials start to show signs of growth, you can apply a slow-acting granular fertilizer throughout the perennial bed. A slow-release formula will provide a more consistent, uniform supply of nutrients than a fast-release formula. Some will last for several months. Read and follow label directions.

Lightly fertilize perennial seedlings (use at half-strength) every few weeks. It won't be long they can be transplanted to the garden directly.

ROSES

With established roses, now is a good time to apply a slow-release fertilizer around their root zone. Lightly cultivate the fertilizer into the ground and water in well. Follow label directions for application rates. Fertilizer can be sprinkled over organic mulches and scratched into the mulch. Rain, snow, or your

own watering will move the nutrients into the soil and to the roots.

TREES

Don't be in a rush to fertilize your trees. Trees growing in lawn areas generally receive adequate nutrients from the application of lawn fertilizers. (Don't use weed-and-feed combinations around the root zone of trees as this will eventually cause damage.)

The best time to fertilize trees is at the start of budbreak, when new growth begins to emerge in the spring. Use a complete fertilizer analysis such as 20-10-10. Follow the label directions for the amount of fertilizer to apply for the type and size of tree you are about to fertilize. Aerate around the root zone and scatter the granules over the area. Water the area to move the fertilizer down to where the roots can assimilate it.

VINES, GROUNDCOVERS & ORNAMENTAL GRASSES

Once groundcovers are established, they require minimal fertilizing, unlike turfgrasses. You can

■ *Amend raised and other beds before planting.*

scatter a slow-release granular fertilizer around the plants and water in well. This will provide nutrients for the entire growing season. Organic matter worked into the soil will also encourage microbial activity and help in the decomposition of other plant debris.

PROBLEM-SOLVE

ANNUALS

Be on the watch for spider mites on indoor annuals. You will notice symptoms of mottled foliage, a "salt and pepper" look to the leaves, or fine webbing on the undersides of the leaves. Wash the plant in tepid water from the faucet or in a bathtub to remove the mites and their eggs. You can also spray a homemade soap solution or spider mite spoiler remedy and rinse off the foliage in the sink or tub. (See page 220 for some homemade remedies.)

If leggy stems are a problem on seedlings, this is an indication of insufficient light. Lower the artificial lights closer to the seedlings.

Damping-off disease can threaten seedlings that are too wet or have poor air circulation.

In the outdoor garden, be on the lookout for weeds starting to pop up. Pull them or cultivate the soil to get them while they're still young. Spread mulch over the soil if needed to discourage weed seeds from germinating.

BULBS

Check shallow-rooted bulbs for frost heaving. Those not mulched or those without snow cover are more prone to freezing and thawing temperatures. These fluctuations cause the soil to shift pushing plants right out of the soil. Gently push heaved plants back in place using your hands and water.

If foliage has emerged early, remember the leaves are pretty cold-hardy, but it can be protected with a layer of mulch if frigid temperatures occur. A well-drained, sandy loam soil can be added to about 1½ to 2 inches in depth to help protect foliage and add soil depth to the bulb plantings.

With added soil depth, bulbs should be later to emerge the following season.

EDIBLES

Unexpected late frosts may threaten new transplants or tender seedlings. You can cover them with polyspun garden frost blankets, also known as floating row covers, or use cardboard boxes, burlap, buckets, or wooden crates. Remove coverings during the day so the plants get sunlight and air circulation.

■ *Floating row covers will protect vegetable beds against frost.*

Be on the watch for rabbits and protect plants with a low fence or garden netting.

Soil-inhabiting insects such as cutworms can clip off the stems at ground level, so place collars around vulnerable plant stems of plants. Use plastic cups with the bottoms cut out; slip over the plant with 2 inches set into the ground.

LAWNS

Be on the watch for the germination of annual weeds that may have been missed by pre-emergent applications. Winter annuals including the mustard family, kochia, and cheatgrass may have already invaded bare spots in your lawn. Deal with them by handpulling or digging when the soil is moist. You can spot-treat weedy areas with an appropriate herbicide; try to avoid routine weed-and-feed combinations or broad applications of weed killers over the entire lawn.

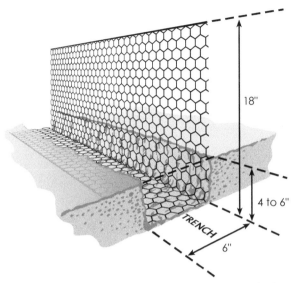

18"

4 to 6"

TRENCH

6"

■ *A rabbit fence should go 4 to 6 inches into the ground to keep the rabbits from digging underneath it.*

Dandelions are beautiful and invite honeybees, and I rather like them. They make a mean and tasty Italian salad or dandelion wine. To you, however, dandelions may be just another weed. Resolve to dig them out before they form their characteristic fuzzy seedheads and proliferate like tiny parachutes.

PERENNIALS

Be on the watch for pests in late March including aphids and flea beetles. Check under organic mulches for slugs and their eggs, which look like mini-fish eggs (caviar anyone?). If you find them, destroy the eggs, handpick overwintering slugs, and get ready to set out slug traps.

Continue to monitor emerging weeds. Pull them by hand or spot-treat with an appropriate herbicide. Read and follow label directions.

ROSES

Now is the time for early prevention measures in your rose garden. Proper pruning assures removal of dead, diseased, and insect-ridden wood. Pruning also creates better air circulation to prevent leaf diseases. Good sanitation techniques of removing debris will eliminate disease spores and overwintering insect pests.

Choose disease-resistant rose varieties (the rose descriptions in catalogs should tell you) to reduce

the use of pesticides in your garden. Prepare the soil to encourage healthy and vigorous growth.

SHRUBS

Be on the watch for overwintering insects, including aphid eggs and scale that can be spotted on the stems and branches. You can control them effectively now by applying a dormant oil spray before bud break. Lighter oils can be applied even during leaf emergence. Read and follow label directions for application rates and timing. Do not use oils on bluish green evergreens as it will remove the waxy coating that produces the evergreens' coloration.

TREES

Inspect trees for signs of insect damage or overwintering eggs that are getting ready to hatch. If you detect a problem, you still have time to apply a horticultural oil to suffocate insect eggs and some of the overwintering adult and nymph stages of pests. Oils will help to reduce the onset of disease spores too. Read and follow label directions when using oil sprays.

Do not apply oil sprays to blue spruce or other evergreens that have the bluish bloom on their needles. Oil will dissolve the bloom and thereby turn the evergreen a sickly green.

VINES, GROUNDCOVERS & ORNAMENTAL GRASSES

Control weeds in groundcover plantings while the weeds are still accessible. Handpull or dig young weeds when the soil is moist. You can also apply pre-emergent weed control products over the soil around groundcovers to stop the germination of annual weed seeds. Read and follow label directions when using herbicides. Once groundcovers grow dense enough, weeds will not be as aggressive.

Grasses growing in groundcovers are the most difficult to control. If you can, dig the offending grass plants when they are young and not yet well rooted. It's easier to pull out clumps following a good rain or watering of the garden. Established weedy grasses may need to be spot-treated with a grass control; protect the ground from spray drift by covering with newspapers.

Frosts are now a thing of the past in all but Zones 4 and 5, and our plants are growing rapidly in the mild temperatures and April showers of mid-spring. Gardeners are busy planting warm-season vegetables and flowers while harvesting the bounty of the garden. Wildflowers paint meadows and roadsides as parents plop their kids down in patches of bluebonnets for the annual photographic ritual.

The weather is mild, making working in the garden such a pleasant activity. Take advantage of the mild temperatures now to reduce work later when things heat up for summer. Mulch your flowers, vegetables, and woody ornamentals to eliminate most of your weeding chores for later and to get longer-lasting benefits from the water you apply during the upcoming months.

If you haven't begun a garden journal and notebook, this is a great time to start one. Your journal tracks your activities while your gardening notebook is a collection of pages on various topics for later reference. It could include newspaper and magazine articles about a new plant or gardening practice, notes and handouts from a lecture at the botanical garden, free publications from your County Extension office, and even photos of plants, pests, and designs taken in your landscape or others that you visited. A well-organized notebook is a wealth of inspiration and gardening knowledge that will grow into a prized gardening resource.

Out in the landscape, hedges need to be sheared to maintain density while individual shrubs can use a snipping here and there to keep their natural shape. It's time to thin the crop on fruit trees. The flower garden is bursting with color and with some deadheading and fertilizing will continue to look great. Our southern lawns have been awakened from their cool-season slumber and are asking for a little extra nutrition.

April is indeed a busy time in our gardens and landscapes.

PLAN

ANNUALS

As soil temperatures warm up, get ready to plant some of the early-blooming flowers including pansies, violas, primroses, and sweet peas to grow up on a trellis. They grow and thrive best with cooler spring weather. Visit your local garden centers and nurseries for the early arrivals of plants and other supplies you will need for the annual garden.

Plan to clean up containers, box gardens, window boxes, and hanging pots prior to planting. Top off with new, sterile potting mix, if needed.

GARDEN STORAGE IN A MAILBOX

If you're tired of making trips between your garden and tool shed, here's a nifty short cut. Install a large mailbox close to the garden. A mailbox is a great place to store gloves, pruners, scissors, and various other small garden tools. Your equipment will be close at hand and still protected from the elements.

Visit your local hardware store, and purchase a wooden fencepost (4 inches x 4 inches or 6 inches x 6 inches). Set the post with about one-third of the total length buried in the ground. In clay soils, dig the posthole twice the diameter of the post. If you prefer, anchor the post with a concrete collar (a layer of concrete placed in the posthole around the post and extended slightly above ground to shed water). Once the post is set, secure a mailbox to the top for tool storage. You can be creative and decorate it to match your gardening style.

BULBS

As spring bulb beds sprout, take time to update your garden journal regarding what's doing well and mark locations for future planting and transplanting. Use weatherproof labels or make your own out of old vinyl window blinds. Cut 6- to 8-inch pieces of the old blind and use them for labeling rows and plants.

Look for spots in your garden beds where summer-flowering bulbs such as dahlias, glads, and begonias can be planted to fill in the gaps left when spring bulbs die back. Garden retailers are stocking up on packaged summer-flowering bulbs, and the sooner you can purchase them, the better. Left in their bags unattended, bulbs may dry out or rot. You can store them in a cool garage or basement until it is time to plant.

Photograph the beds and take a few close-ups. Also, record notes in your garden journal to indicate times of blooming and when the bulbs are at their peak.

Plan to leave the healthy green foliage growing as the bulbs finish up their blooming cycle. Even though you may be tempted to cut it back, the foliage is necessary to store food reserves for next season.

EDIBLES

To maximize the production from your garden, have young warm-weather transplants ready to go into empty spots after harvesting the cool-season crops. Successive planting with snap beans, beets, carrots, more radishes, Swiss chard, and spinach will fill in the voids. If your homegrown transplants didn't fare so well, buy young, healthy transplants from a reputable garden store.

You still have time to start more warm-season seedlings such as tomatoes, tomatillas, squash, and cucumbers to fill in the blank spots that will come. Read and follow the timing sequences on seed packets for planting indoors and transplanting outdoors.

LAWNS

Check the lawn for thin spots that may need overseeding or can be laid with new sod. Have compost ready to add to bare soil and build a healthy soil foundation for good germination. If you prefer, check with sod growers to see if they have sod available to patch bare spots.

Take time to check your lawn for problems that may arise with the arrival of spring weather. Rub the palm of your hand over the lawn and see if a red streaking appears. If so, that means grass mites are active. Plan to get the hose out and water south and west exposures where mites frequent.

Plan to control weeds in warm-season grasses such as buffalo grass and blue grama before they start to green up.

Make sure you lawn mower is tuned up, blade sharp, and ready to go.

ROSES

Although we can expect more cold and spring snows, make changes in your rose garden early in the season. Replace roses that are not doing well or tend to be more susceptible to disease problems. Select hardy rose varieties that are more disease resistant.

Have you ever tried integrating roses into other parts of your landscape? Their colors and forms blend well with many perennials and can be used as a backdrop. Many hybrid tea, miniature, floribunda, and tree roses are adapted to grow in large containers on the patio or deck. Plant fragrant roses where you entertain or sit to relax so the fragrance can be enjoyed. Some of my favorites include 'Double Delight', '4th of July', 'Mr. Lincoln', and 'Scentimental'.

SHRUBS

Now is the time to have a camera ready to shoot pictures of spring-blooming shrubs. Take photos at the different stages of blooming to keep track of the succession of bloom and foliage over the season. Pictures are helpful when evaluating plants in your landscape.

It is planting time, but before you purchase, be sure of your shrub choices. Will they suit the location and not outgrow the area? Consider the exposure; is it full sun, partial sun, or shady? Check soil drainage and amend as needed prior to planting.

Watch for the flowering cycle of conifers including pines, spruces, and junipers. On a windy day you can see the air fill with yellow pollen as it blows from the male flowers that look like tiny cones. Later in the season, you may see the true cones on pines and spruces that develop from the female flowers.

TREES

This is the month when many states celebrate Arbor Day. You can take part in this celebration by planting a new tree in your landscape. If you don't have space, think about donating a tree to a park or other community center where many can benefit from a tree's beauty and function.

Learn more about trees for the Rockies in the *Rocky Mountain Getting Started Garden Guide*. This will help you become more familiar with various tree selections that are best suited to our unique climate and soil conditions. Visit parks and preserves to see native trees in their natural environments. Take notes on what grows well in your particular area. Take photographs of the trees and show them to knowledgeable plant experts to help you identify them, or use a good field guide with color photos and line drawings.

When choosing a tree for your landscape, consider its ultimate size. A small spruce may be cute planted near the house when it is only 3 feet tall, but this tree will grow and spread to encroach on the house and surrounding sidewalks or driveway.

VINES, GROUNDCOVERS & ORNAMENTAL GRASSES

If you have arbors, pergolas, or latticework in your landscape, grow some vines on well-constructed and anchored structures. They add interest throughout the year. You can even hang a nesting house for songbirds from an arbor, and the vine will provide extra protection as it leafs out. Use vines to break the monotony of a wood fence or to screen a chain-link fence.

Consider ornamental grasses to provide accent in the center of a flowerbed, or use them as a living screen to block the sounds from the street. Use your imagination to create something original and enticing.

PLANT

ANNUALS

Let the weather and soil temperature be your guide for planting. Keep frost protection such as row covers, cardboard boxes, and blankets handy to protect new transplants from unexpected drops in temperature.

HERE'S HOW

TO HARDEN OFF INDOOR-GROWN TRANSPLANTS

1. Move them to a cold frame or protected location two weeks prior to planting.

2. Water thoroughly, but allow the potting mix to go slightly dry between waterings.

3. Stop fertilizing.

4. At the same time, gradually introduce plants to full sun conditions. Start by placing them in a partially shaded location. Give them direct sun for a few hours. Increase the amount of sun the plants receive each day.

5. Cover the transplants or move them indoors when there is danger of frost.

6. By the end of two weeks, the transplants are ready to plant into the garden.

As weather permits, plant hardened-off cool-season annuals, such as violas, pansies, snapdragons, and dusty miller in mid- to late April.

If you have window boxes and other empty planters, grow some pansies now to brighten the scene.

Sow seeds of hardy annuals including cleome, four o'clocks, cosmos, nigella (love-in-a-mist), portulaca, and sweet alyssum. They can be sown directly in a prepared flowerbed where you want them to grow.

Do not disturb the areas where self-sowing annuals such as columbines, larkspur, California poppies, and cosmos went to seed last fall. There will be new sprouts appearing soon.

BULBS

When the snowdrops, glory-of-the-snow, and Siberian squill have finished blooming and only their green leaves remain, it is a good time to thin them out and transplant them to new areas, if you desire. Lightly lift the clumps and separate the bulbs, then poke them into workable soil, an inch or so deep, leaving the foliage intact—that's all there is to it. These are great little gems to use for naturalizing areas in the landscape.

Soon it will be time (mid-month) to plant summer-flowering bulbs directly outdoors. The soil needs to warm up to 55 to 60 degrees Fahrenheit and should not be too wet. Be sure the soil has been amended with compost, sphagnum peat moss, or a combination of both. This will improve drainage, retain nutrients, and allow better root growth.

If you haven't already started stored begonia, dahlia, canna, and caladium bulbs indoors, you still have time. Nudge them out of dormancy by potting them up in fresh potting soil and watering them. It is still a bit too early to set them outdoors. Wait until the danger of frost has passed in your specific area.

If the soil is workable, this is a good time to set out forced bulbs you've been growing in the house. Keep any remaining foliage intact and plant them at least 6 inches deep so they will survive in winter.

Later in the month you can direct-plant gladiolus corms, cannas, and dahlia tubers outdoors. Be sure the soil is ready where they are to be planted. Plant at the depth recommended on the label or package. If the soil is still too wet or cold, wait a few more weeks before planting.

EDIBLES

Plant cool-weather crops early in the month as weather permits. Radishes, spinach, leaf lettuce, and green onions thrive in cooler weather. In very high elevations, you may need to wait until late May or early June.

Transplant strong, vigorous transplants that you've hardened off, and make room for more seedlings indoors. Direct seed cucumbers, melons, summer squash, pumpkins, and watermelons when the soil is warm (55 degrees Fahrenheit). They are fussy about being transplanted.

Continue to plant asparagus, parsnips, rhubarb, salsify, and onion plants. As mid-April approaches and the weather is milder, sow seeds of cabbage, beets, lettuce, parsley, and garden peas. When they're available in the garden centers, transplant young cole crop seedlings such as broccoli and cabbage. Plant horseradish roots and early cabbage at the same time.

Many herbs and vegetables can be combined with flowers in containers or raised beds for a handsome effect. Use a well-draining potting mixture, and be sure the containers have drainage holes. Shallow-rooted vegetables and herbs grow well in containers. Lettuce, radishes, onions, short carrot varieties, beets, and herbs need a container that is at least 8 inches deep and 6 to 12 inches in diameter. When grouping plants together, use larger pots such as half-whiskey or wine barrels, 5-gallon buckets, or even an antique bathtub. Let your imagination guide you.

HERE'S HOW

TO MOVE ESTABLISHED BULBS

If you must move established bulbs, now is as good a time as any.

1. Carefully dig the clumps out of the ground with a heavy-duty spading fork. Take care not to damage or break the foliage.

2. Gently tap or brush excess soil from the bulbs and carefully separate them, teasing apart the tangled roots at the base of each bulb.

3. If a larger bulb has developed several good-sized baby bulbs with roots, you can divide these from the mother bulb by carefully breaking them apart, or you can plant the entire clump intact. Remember, keep the leaves intact so they can capture sunlight and produce energy for the transplanted bulbs.

4. Check the bulbs for injury from insects or diseases. Discard those that have become soft, show signs of mold, or have started to rot. Discard any that are suspect.

5. Replant some of the bulbs in their former location if there is still adequate sun; space them 4 to 6 inches apart and about 6 inches deep. Water in thoroughly.

6. Plant the remaining divisions elsewhere, or give them away. The smaller bulb divisions generally will not bloom for a year or two, so be patient. This transplanting technique is ideal for naturalizing areas with an overflow of bulbs.

■ *Spread mulch around the vegetable transplants. If you live in a warmer area, this will help keep water in the soil during those hot, Indian summer fall days. In cooler areas, the mulch acts to insulate the vegetables, helping them stay warmer longer into the fall. Straw is good for vegetable gardens because it is lightweight. Most garden centers and home-improvement stores sell bales of wheat straw. Just ask for it if you don't see it.*

Indoor tomato seedlings should be hardened off outside before transplanting directly to the garden. You can transplant them into larger pots if it is still too cold to set them out permanently. They will continue to grow and develop and may even begin to set flowers.

As the soil warms up to 50 degrees Fahrenheit (late April), plant beans, cucumbers, melons, squash, and pumpkins in the garden. If you live in a cold area, wait to plant these towards mid-May.

Plant sunflowers in late April, or as soon as the soil temperature warms up. They add height to the garden and can provide support for pole beans. Later the seeds are a welcome food source for birds and squirrels.

LAWNS

Sow new grass seed or install sod as it is becoming more available. Cooler weather is ideal for establishing new lawns. If there is weed competition, spray or pull, or hoe out the weeds prior to seeding or sodding.

Allow one to two weeks for effective weed control prior to seeding or sodding, so plan accordingly. Don't procrastinate.

HERE'S HOW

TO PLANT CONTAINER-GROWN ROSES

- Plant container-grown roses anytime the ground is not frozen. If you purchase them ahead of time and the weather doesn't cooperate for planting right away, keep the soil in the container uniformly moist until planting time. Dig the planting hole as deep and twice as wide as the container in which the rose is growing. Add compost or sphagnum peat moss to the soil removed from the hole at the rate of one-third by volume and mix it in. This helps to improve drainage and adds porosity to the soil for healthy root development. Reserve this prepared soil to fill the hole.

- Carefully slide the rootball out of the container, taking care not to break the rootball or damage healthy roots. Prune or slowly untangle any roots that are matted together or circling the inside of the container. Set the rootball into the planting hole. The top of the rootball should be level with the ground.

- If this is a grafted rose, set the plant 1 to 2 inches *deeper* to allow added winter protection. (The plant tags may not state whether the rose is grafted; look for the graft union to make sure.) Look for a knob at the base of the plant; plant the rose a bit deeper so this knob will be covered with an inch of soil when you fill the hole with prepared soil you dug out. Mix in a handful of granular, slow-release fertilizer formulated for blooming shrubs or roses.

- Water the entire root zone thoroughly. To help maintain moisture and reduce weed invasion, spread a layer of organic mulch around the base of each rose bush. This will aid the establishment of the plant.

PERENNIALS

If you haven't already hardened-off your indoor perennial seedlings, get to it. Here's what to do: gradually expose them to outdoor conditions by moving them to a cold frame or unheated porch for at least a week before planting in the garden.

Plant bare-root perennials as soon as they arrive in the mail or when you purchase them locally. It is best to get them in the ground before major growth resumes. This encourages a strong, healthy root system to support the plant.

ROSES

Container-grown roses are readily available this month and are easy to transplant. Just be careful not to break the rootball during transplanting. Many garden retailers force roses into early bloom so you can experience the fragrance and see the colors of the various types. See "Here's How to Plant Container-Grown Roses" on page 74.

SHRUBS

This is the best time to finish up planting bare-root shrubs before they fully expand their buds into leaves. Shrubs are available as container-grown and balled-and-burlapped. Getting them in the ground early will allow them to develop a strong root system before the onset of hot weather. They will have become well-established before winter arrives and better equipped to survive.

TREES

It's a good time to plant container-grown trees and also larger trees that are balled-and-burlapped. Pay careful attention to the watering during their establishment phase. Most of us are likely to overwater a newly planted tree, and this will often lead to its demise. See "Here's How to Plant a Balled-and-Burlapped Tree" on page 76.

VINES, GROUNDCOVERS & ORNAMENTAL GRASSES

April is the prime time to plant ornamental grasses, vines, and groundcovers. These plants need sufficient time to get established before the heat of summer. Bare-root plants are more economical, but many can be purchased already growing in containers. To reduce transplant stress, plant the bare-root plants as early as possible before they fully leaf out.

When planting ornamental grasses, here's a simple rule for spacing: Place plants as far apart as their eventual height. For example, grasses that can grow to a height of 3 feet can be planted 3 feet apart from center to center. See "Here's How to Plant Vines, Groundcovers, and Ornamental Grasses" on page 78.

CARE

ANNUALS

Young transplants that are thriving in a cold frame should gradually be exposed to outside temperatures, both day and night. This will harden them off before they are set outside permanently. Prop open the glass cover on hot days so that the plants don't cook in the heat. If temperatures are predicted to go below freezing, close the cover at night.

As the end of the month approaches, many of the transplants growing indoors should be readied to be set outdoors. Set them outside in a semi-sunny spot daily for increasingly longer times to adjust to the outside weather. Bring them in at night until it is mild enough for planting. This is called the "hardening-off" process that acclimatizes plants to the outside so they experience less transplant shock when they are finally planted in the garden.

Pinch back leggy stems of seedlings as they mature. Plants growing in pots or those retained from last year will benefit from a light pruning as well. This will make them grow out more lateral stems thereby creating a more sturdy and compact plant.

Pick bouquets of pansies and violas and put in a decorative drinking glass or bowl to add color indoors. Picking them will encourage these plants to form more blossoms.

BULBS

Check lily bulbs, gladiolus, begonias, caladiums, cannas, and other frost-tender bulbs before you purchase them. Avoid those that have bruises or show signs of rot. You can divide dahlia tubers where they are attached to the main stem. It is critical to keep an "eye" or growing tip with each tuber division. Some dahlia growers will even take stem cuttings from plants started indoors earlier, and plant these up to increase their collection.

HERE'S HOW

TO PLANT A BALLED-AND-BURLAPPED TREE

1. Dig a hole no deeper than the depth of the rootball but at least twice as wide, preferably three or four times wider.

2. Amend the soil, if needed, to create a well-drained soil in the correct pH range. To do this, mix the planting soil with organic matter such as well-rotted compost or manure.

3. If the wrapping is real burlap, you simply have to cut and remove the fabric on top of the ball and peel the burlap down the sides so it stays below the soil line. It will eventually decompose. Synthetic burlap must be removed completely. Remove the wire basket that surrounds the rootball and burlap, if present.

4. Place the plant in the hole and adjust the hole depth so that the plant is about 1 inch higher than it was planted in the nursery (to allow for settling of soil). Use a shovel handle laid across the hole to help determine the proper depth.

5. Shovel in the amended soil around the rootball, stopping to tamp down the soil when the hole is half full.

6. Fill the rest of the hole with loose soil and tamp down again to ensure good contact between the soil and the roots.

7. Soak the planting area with water. Once the soil has settled, build up a 2- to 3-inch basin around the plant to catch rainfall and irrigation water. However, do not build a basin if your soil is very heavy and doesn't drain well.

8. Apply 2 to 3 inches of organic mulch such as shredded bark or wood chips, keeping the mulch a few inches away from the trunk.

Begonias and gladiolus that have developed smaller bulbs can be increased by carefully breaking off the bulblets or corms from the original bulb. Since they are small, they will not bloom this year but will increase in size for next season.

Continue to cut off, or deadhead, faded tulip, daffodil, and hyacinth flowers as soon as they finish their bloom cycle. Cut back the stems to where the leaves begin, but never remove the foliage. Remember, the leaves are the food factories that build up energy for next year's blooming cycle.

EDIBLES

As the seeds you've sown in garden rows or raised beds begin to sprout, be sure to thin out plants. Refer to the spacing on the seed packets. Plants that are planted too thickly will not perform to your

expectations. Instead of pulling out plants, snip off the excess seedlings to avoid removing too many.

Discourage weeds, and help retain soil moisture by applying an organic mulch around plants that are 4 to 6 inches tall. If you prefer, lay down landscape fabric and transplant seedlings through the fabric, which in turn will warm the soil. This is especially good for warm-season crops. Top the fabric with

wood chips, dried grass clippings, or organic materials if weeds are a concern and this will keep the fabric anchored down too.

To get an early crop of tomatoes and peppers, provide additional protection to warm the soil and air temperature at night. Set up clear plastic tunnels over raised beds, or surround plants with plant protectors like Wall O'Water™ season

HERE'S HOW

TO PLANT VINES, GROUNDCOVERS, AND ORNAMENTAL GRASSES

1. To prepare the planting area, dig out the weeds and turn the soil with a shovel or rototiller. Add a generous supply of compost to improve drainage and hold nutrients.

2. Rake the area smooth, and stake the spots where the grasses are to be planted. With groundcover plants, make sure they are spaced equidistant from each other to allow them to spread to their mature width as indicated on the plant tag.

3. Dig a hole for each plant as deep as its pot is tall. If you are planting on a slope, dig the hole straight up and down so the plant will be sitting vertically.

4. Remove the plant from the nursery pot. Tease any tangled roots and set the plant in the hole. Fill in with the backfill soil you set aside.

5. Water the plants in thoroughly for good root-to-soil contact.

6. Mulch new plantings to maintain uniform moisture and suppress weed growth.

extenders to hold in the heat at night. There are many ingenious plant protectors on the market, so give some of them a try.

Pinch or prune back woody herbs including sage, rosemary, and lavender that grew back from last year. This will help them regenerate compact growth. Pinch the tips of basil grown indoors and other herbs monthly to encourage compact branching.

LAWNS

You still have time to core-aerate your lawn, both cool- and warm-season grasses. Make sure there is moisture in the soil so the aerator will remove deep plugs. You don't need to remove the plugs. If you do, recycle them to the compost pile.

■ *It's fine to leave the plugs of soil and grass on the lawn. They will disintegrate quickly.*

■ *Set the mower height so that you're mowing at the tallest recommended height for your grass type. Most mower adjustment brackets are next to the front wheels, but consult your mower manual for specific instructions for setting the mower height.*

It's lawn-mowing season this month to keep the lawn looking in top shape. Set the mower blade at about 2 inches for the first cut, then raise it to cut at 3 or 3½ inches as the weather warms. The length of the grass blades correlates to deeper root growth, and shades the soil to keep weed seeds from germinating.

Mow the lawn when it is dry to obtain a more uniform cut. Dry clippings will fall into the turf rather than mat together in clumps. This also reduces the chances of disease organisms infecting the grass.

Mow with a sharp mower blade. Dull or nicked blades bruise the grass foliage, allowing a larger surface area for fungal diseases to enter the plant. Frayed leaf tips dry out faster, giving the lawn a yellowish brown cast.

Don't allow the grass to get so tall that you're mowing a hayfield. I recommend that you mow one-third of the leaf blades at each mowing to maintain a clean, healthy cut. Cutting more than this will often stress the grass plants and leave a yellowish cast. Spring lawn growth is fast, so expect to mow more frequently than you would in summer. Growth will slow down later in the season as temperatures warm.

PERENNIALS
Mulch newly planted perennials, and renew mulch around established plants as needed.

Pinch or prune back perennials you desire to keep at a specific height. You can pinch back the new growth until the later part of June for fall-blooming perennials to make them grow more compact.

Pinching is a technique that removes ½ to 1 inch of each growing shoot, up to 2 inches of shoot tips if desired. When you pinch perennials, they will produce more, but smaller flowers than plants that are left untouched.

Pinching is also used to stagger the blooming times of plants, particularly hardy garden chrysanthemums. It prevents them from growing too tall and straggly. Experiment pinching different perennials. I like to pinch back asters, Joe-pye weed, turtlehead, spike speedwell, 'Autumn Joy' sedum, and others. You may like the results you can create.

If the young perennials you started indoors are growing too tall, pinch them back, too. Snip or pinch to a node above the second set of leaves. This will stimulate them to develop into more compact plants.

ROSES
By the middle of the month, it is probably safe to remove mulch surrounding rose bushes, but if a hard frost is predicted, throw garden blankets or burlap sacks over tender plants for the night hours.

■ *Climbing roses are often grown as vines but they are not true vines. These plants have long canes, or stems, that must be tied and trained into place to encourage them to grow upward. Use twine or twist ties if stems are light; insulated wire or rubber strips if they are heavy and woody.*

Replace old mulch with fresh mulching material. Add just enough to provide a 2- to 3-inch layer around the root zone. Do not allow the mulch to touch the rose crowns or stems as this can promote rodent damage and reduces air circulation.

Begin to train climbing roses as their canes start to expand and branch out. Climbers produce the most blooms on canes that grow horizontally within a 45-degree angle of the ground. Train along fences and retaining walls to create a spectacular display.

If you have not done your final pruning yet, now is the time to prune climbers and ramblers to remove any winter-damaged, dead, or broken canes. A pruning rule of thumb from a horticultural colleague: "Prune when the daffodils are in bloom." Start just as the leaf buds are beginning to enlarge, but it is better to prune later than too early.

SHRUBS

Prune early-flowering shrubs, such as lilac and spring-flowering spirea, and forsythia after they finish blooming if you need to shape them or gradually renew an older shrub that is losing vigor. Remove dead or damaged stems and branches. Use sharp pruning tools.

Renew older shrubs by cutting out one-third of the oldest stems to the ground each spring. This will help them grow new, vigorous shoots. Cut the taller remaining branches to shorten them if desired. Prune to an outside bud that is growing in the same direction as the longer stem to maintain the natural growth pattern.

Prune hedges to shape them to your liking. The best way to reduce storm damage to hedges is to prune the shrubs to a narrower top and wider bottom. This will allow better shedding of snow and will reduce stem breakage. It is better to thin out weak stems and older wood than to just shear away the tops.

If you did not prune the stems of butterfly bush in late fall, now is the time to remove any winterkill or cut the shrub back to within 4 to 6 inches of ground level. This allows healthy, vigorous growth that will bloom this summer.

Mulch shrubs to maintain uniform moisture and conserve water. A 2- to 3-inch layer of mulch over bare soil under and around shrubs will hold in soil moisture, eventually enrich the soil, and discourage weeds. Do not put the mulch in direct contact with the stems at ground level. It can create a problem if rodents nest and nibble on the tender bark. Keep the mulch 4 to 6 inches away from the crown to promote better air circulation and reduce disease problems.

TREES

Now that it's mowing time for cool-season grasses, take precautions to avoid bumping into tree trunks with the lawn mower or weed trimmer. A manmade disease called "lawnmoweritis," caused by skinning the bark with lawn machines, will give diseases and insects entry into the tree. Any wound on a trunk can be quickly colonized by fungus diseases or infested by borers. A ring of mulch or a living groundcover such as vinca minor or ajuga around the root zone will protect the trunk.

Stake tall, newly planted trees only if they are vulnerable to windstorms or other harsh weather conditions. Remove any staking from trees planted last spring. Check others to see if the supports and ties are getting too tight for the growing tree. Left unchecked, nylon and rubber straps can girdle the bark.

■ *Shrubs that have numerous stems coming out of the ground can be thinned by cutting some stems all the way to the ground.*

Staking should only be done if newly planted trees are located on very windy, exposed sites. This artificial support system encourages tall growth, often at the expense of a supportive trunk and root system. The end result can be a weak tree.

Small trees generally don't need to be staked after transplanting. It is better to allow them some movement to encourage stronger trunk development and healthy root systems. However, in very windy and exposed areas, trees will benefit from staking the first season or two, especially if they are top-heavy. You can string wire through a section of garden hose to protect the bark from injury or use nylon tree ties. The staked tree should still be able to sway somewhat in the wind.

Remove vertical suckers that grow within the framework of fruit trees and various ornamental trees including Callery pear, hawthorn, aspen, and crabapple. When pruning out diseased branches from crabapples, disinfect your pruning tools after each cut by spraying them with a disinfectant, or wipe them off with 70 percent rubbing alcohol. Do not use bleach, as it will rust metal parts.

VINES, GROUNDCOVERS & ORNAMENTAL GRASSES

Well-established groundcovers need very little maintenance other than cleaning out debris in the spring. For a fresher look, lightly prune plant tips that have been dessicated by winter winds.

If you haven't finished cutting back ornamental grasses, get this task done before new growth starts to expand. Cut back to within a few inches of the ground.

Prune out dead and damaged stems from established vines.

WATER

ANNUALS

If it's a good year, Nature should provide adequate moisture with rain and spring snows to keep the soil moist. If there is a prolonged dry spell of two weeks or more, you will need to water newly planted annuals as the soil begins to dry out. Plants that have been mulched will need less frequent watering.

In areas where seed has been sown, lightly moisten the soil down an inch or so to help germination. You don't need to water deeply yet.

If you have biennials growing in the flower garden from last season, water them deeply, as they do have a more extensive and deep root system. This includes foxglove, money plant, and forget-me-not.

BULBS

Water bulb beds as the soil dries out. If there is a lack of rain or spring snow, water these flowerbeds every three to four weeks. Spot watering may be necessary to ensure the bulbs will have good root growth and produce full blooms. If it gets too dry, bulbs may become stunted and bloom poorly.

HERE'S HOW

TO PRUNE VINES AND GROUNDCOVERS

Buds will begin to expand and leaves emerge on clematis, honeysuckle, Virginia creeper, trumpet vine, and others as the temperatures warm up. You can tell how healthy a vine is by its annual growth. To stimulate more vigorous growth and flowering buds, cut back the vines by 30 to 50 percent. This process will rejuvenate the vine and make it grow more prolifically. Thin out dead and damaged stems and branches that may have suffered "winterkill." If you have a hardy wisteria, cut back the excess growth along the main stem; prune back to the already formed flower buds on the spurs of last year's wood.

If you have potted bulbs in containers, allow the potting mixture to dry out between waterings. As soon as it feels dry to the touch an inch deep, it's time to water the potting mixture. Don't keep the mix too wet, as this will cause rot.

EDIBLES

Before setting out transplants, moisten their root systems. This reduces transplant shock. Watering also helps settle transplants and seeds into the soil.

Vegetables and herbs may need daily watering if rainfall is scarce. The roots of transplants and germinating seeds are shallow and tend to dry out quickly until they develop. Once the plants are established, you can wean them off an every day schedule.

Water container gardens regularly to ensure germination of seeds and establishment of transplants. Soilless mixtures dry out rapidly and need more attention. Use a watering can or a gentle sprinkling from the garden hose.

LAWNS

If spring rainfall is infrequent or scarce, it is critical to keep newly seeded and sodded lawns watered. Frequent light sprinklings on newly seeded lawns

■ *Check sod strips for separation gaps or any areas that you have cut short. Fill these with a combination of sterile soil and grass seed that matches the species in the sod.*

■ *After you've planted everything, water each plant by placing the water breaker on the hose at the base of each plant and counting to ten. To make quick work of watering, put a soaker hose around your plants to water them. You can snake the hose in and out of rows and use wire pins called sod staples to hold down the hose. If the hose is in the middle of two rows, the water from it will reach plants on each side of the hose.*

will help them germinate. Sodded lawns needed to be soaked good daily for the first two weeks. Following these guidelines will make your lawn develop a vigorous, deep root system that will endure even during short drought periods.

Inspect automatic sprinkler systems to make sure they are operational and there are no broken heads or leaks. Adjust watering pattern if needed.

Water the edges of newly installed sod since it tends to dry out quickly. I like to spread a topdressing of compost along the edges of new sod to help reduce the drying out and wicking effect of the freshly cut sod. In a few weeks the sod should be anchoring and knitting together before the onset of hot weather.

PERENNIALS

April showers may be sufficient to keep emerging perennials in good shape, but as this may not be the norm, it's often necessary to water the plants as the soil becomes dry. Test the soil with a garden trowel around a perennial's root system. When needed, water deeply and infrequently to encourage more drought-enduring plants. Newly transplanted perennials will require a bit more attention for the first few weeks to become well established.

ROSES

Keep newly planted roses watered deeply once a week or as the soil begins to dry out. Check the soil every few days to determine a schedule that works best for your soil conditions and the rose's exposure to sun and wind. Roses that are mulched will require less frequent watering.

Unmulched soil will need to be checked by digging down with a small garden trowel for dryness every three to five days. When watering roses avoid watering the foliage, particularly at night.

SHRUBS

Newly planted shrubs will need to be watered weekly if there is insufficient rain. Set a slowly running hose or frog-eye sprinkler beneath the shrub at the root zone and let it run until the ground is saturated or the water-holding reservoir is filled. In soils that are clay, water ten to fifteen minutes, let it soak in; then resume watering for another fifteen minutes and let that soak in.

If your budget and time allow, install a soaker hose or drip irrigation to save time and ensure a good, deep watering. Be careful not to overwater shrubs during their establishment. More shrubs are killed by too much water than by not enough. Established shrubs need, on average, about an inch of water a week either from rainfall or from you. More watering is needed in hot weather, less when it is cool. Check the soil with a soil probe or dig down with a garden trowel.

Mulched shrubs may go longer between waterings. Dig underneath the mulch to check soil moisture. This will help you in determining a schedule for watering in your soil conditions.

TREES

April showers are usually not adequate to keep your trees deeply watered. Dig down around the root zone and check the subsoil moisture. If it is beginning to dry out to a depth of 4 inches, it's time to bring out the frog-eye sprinkler and give the roots a good soaking. With cooler weather, I recommend that you deep-water every two to three weeks during the spring to maintain subsoil moisture for spring growing conditions. Let the weather guide you, and check the soil moisture before watering.

VINES, GROUNDCOVERS & ORNAMENTAL GRASSES

April showers are usually adequate for most groundcovers, vines, and ornamental grasses to survive, but if has been dry, it's time to bring out the hose and water.

Use a frog-eye or similar sprinkler set at the drip line of the plants, and water for ten to fifteen minutes. This will allow uniform coverage of the root zone and sustain the plants during dry spells. If you have installed a drip irrigation system, use it to give the plants a deep soaking. Inspect it for leaks and replace cracked or broken emitters.

Remember, mulched plantings will need less frequent watering than those that are growing on bare ground. As groundcover plants begin to mature, they naturally shade the soil and this attribute makes them more drought tolerant.

FERTILIZE

ANNUALS

When the soil is dry enough to be easily worked, this is the time to prepare the annual beds for new plants. Rototill or dig and turn over shovelfuls of soil to loosen the bed. Mix in slow-release granular fertilizer as you prepare the soil. Follow label directions on the fertilizer package.

If you did not incorporate organic matter such as compost, aged manure, or sphagnum peat moss into the soil last autumn, do so now. Organic amendments will help to improve drainage, retain nutrients, and aid in moisture retention.

HERE'S HOW

TO FERTILIZE PLANTS BY SIDEDRESSING

Sidedressing is the process of applying granular fertilizer to an established plant. Sprinkle the granules around the plant being, careful not to get granules on plants leaves; it can burn them. Then gently scratch them into the soil, being careful not to damage roots, and water well.

BULBS

Fertilize hardy spring-flowering bulbs to help them grow healthy foliage, but wait until after they finish blooming. Do not overdo the application of fertilizer. I recommend a slow-release granular applied at the base of the bulbs, lightly cultivated into the soil and watered in.

EDIBLES

Add a slow-release granular fertilizer as the garden beds are prepared. This saves time later and will provide nutrients for a more extended period. Some slow-acting fertilizers will last up to twelve weeks.

Fertilize container gardens more often because frequent watering leaches nutrients out of the soilless mixes. You can mix in a granular, complete slow-release vegetable fertilizer such as 10-10-10 into the potting soil or purchase a soilless mix that already contains one.

If you use a water-soluble plant fertilizer, apply according to the manufacturer's recommendations. Do not overdo, because a soluble salt accumulation may damage plant roots.

Fertilize fruit trees at the rate of a ½ pound of slow-release granular 12-12-12 or something similar per tree. Water thoroughly after applying fertilizer to help it percolate down to the root zone.

LAWNS

You can apply pre-emergent weed controls if warranted for problem annual weeds such as creeping spurge and crabgrass. Read and follow label directions. Crabgrass controls can be timed around the time the forsythia shrubs bloom.

If you want to encourage a more lush and greener lawn earlier in the spring, you can apply fertilizer around Easter. Just remember, you will have to start watering and mowing earlier when growth kicks in.

Iron chlorosis (yellowing of the grass blades) is a common problem in our region. Alkaline soils are the reason for this chlorosis because iron, while present in the soil, is not in a form available to lawn grasses. To keep your lawn uniformly green, you may need to apply a lawn fertilizer containing iron or apply a separate chelated iron supplement.

PERENNIALS

If your garden soil is not very fertile with humus or other organic matter, sprinkle slow-acting granular fertilizer around newly emerging and established plants. Avoid the use of quick-release nitrogen, as this will make the plants grow spindly and topple over.

ROSES

Wait to fertilize roses until after the new growth has started to develop. Apply a slow-release rose fertilizer at the rate of 2 pounds per 100 square feet or 2 heaping tablespoons per rose bush.

Lightly cultivate the fertilizer around the bush and water in thoroughly.

SHRUBS

Newly planted shrubs need one growing season to promote strong roots outward into the planting hole and beyond. They do not need to be fertilized the first year. For a boost, however, you can apply a slow-release 5-10-5 granular fertilizer over the root zone. Do not use a high-nitrogen product. Lightly

HERE'S HOW

TO KNOW WHEN AND HOW MUCH TO FERTILIZE YOUR LAWN

- An easy way to remember when to fertilize your lawn is to schedule applications around the holidays. Begin with the first application around Easter, the second on Memorial Day, the third on July 4, and the fourth on Halloween. The recommend rate is 1 pound of nitrogen per 1,000 square feet per application.

- The amount of lawn fertilizer to use can be determined by dividing 100 by the nitrogen number (the first number on the fertilizer bag). For example, if you choose a fertilizer with a formula of 20-10-5, you will need 5 pounds of fertilizer to equal 1 pound of actual nitrogen.

scratch it into the soil and water in well. Reapply mulch as needed. Established shrubs can be fertilized with a complete 10-10-10 or similar fertilizer; use 1 pound per 100 square feet of shrub bed. For individual shrubs in the landscape, apply a cup spread evenly over the root zone and lightly scratch in. Water in thoroughly.

Don't forget to fertilize small fruits at this time, too. Use a slow-release, complete fertilizer such as 10-10-10. Read and follow label directions on the product package.

TREES

Established trees will have begun to bud out and it's time to apply a slow-release granular fertilizer. In lawn areas, core-aerate around the root zone to create channels for the fertilizer to work its way down to the roots. Otherwise, lightly cultivate the fertilizer in the top few inches of soil around the root zone. Select a complete fertilizer such as 10-10-10 with iron and sulfur. An amount to provide 1 to 2 pounds of actual nitrogen per 1,000 square feet once a year meets the nutrient needs for most trees. Regular lawn fertilizing will provide adequate nutrients for trees growing in lawns.

Fertilizer applications are not to be used as a rescue effort for stressed, injured, or declining trees. Do not use combination weed-and-feed products over the root zone of trees.

VINES, GROUNDCOVERS & ORNAMENTAL GRASSES

Newly planted areas that have not yet filled in can be topdressed with compost to improve the soil. Lightly lift the groundcover plants and scatter the compost over the soil around the plants. At the same time, you can add slow-release granular fertilizer around the plants. Water thoroughly to settle in the organic matter and fertilizer. This feeding will last for the growing season.

As established plants begin to show signs of active growth, you can incorporate slow-release granular fertilizer over the root zone. Lightly scratch it in with a cultivator, and then water the fertilizer in thoroughly. One application in spring is all that is needed. It will provide consistent, uniform nutrition for several weeks to months. Check the label of the fertilizer package to determine how often it can safely be applied.

PROBLEM-SOLVE

ANNUALS

It's time for weeds to pop up throughout the annual flower garden too. Lightly cultivating the soil will bring their roots to the surface and make them meet their demise. Winter annual weeds such as downy brome grass, dandelions, and mallow will need to be dug or pulled out, as they have already developed a deeper and stronger root system.

As you set out new transplants, the deer, elk, birds, rabbits, chipmunks, squirrels, and other critters may find it enticing to nibble on the young plants. Protect the new plants by temporarily placing netting over them to discourage wildlife, or construct a fence around plantings. If you prefer, spray a homemade critter repellent on the foliage.

BULBS

Be ever vigilant for sneak attacks from rabbits, deer, elk, chipmunks, and meadow mice, as they find many bulbs gourmet morsels to feed upon. You can spray the foliage with animal repellent or put up a temporary screen or wire cages to protect the flowers and foliage.

Watch for the invasion of insect pests, including aphids that prefer to get into the leaf folds of iris. You may need to use a systemic insecticide or wash them off with a forceful spray of water. When using any pesticide, read and follow label directions.

EDIBLES

Watch for cutworms and armyworms. These soil-inhabiting pests will chew through the stems of young seedlings overnight. Protect the stems with collars made from plastic or cardboard cups. Cut the bottoms out of the cups, and gently lower the collar over the plant, top down, twisting the rim into the soil around the plants' stems.

Protect young seedlings with a cover of netting to thwart hungry birds. Also, set out a bird feeder to divert the birds' attention.

Floating row covers provide a barrier against insect pests such as flea beetles, radish maggots, cucumber beetles, and more.

To avoid killing our beneficial and pollinating bee population, delay spraying fruit trees until after blooming has ended. Then choose something that is environmentally friendly, or use insect traps to keep pests at a minimum. The apple worm trap is very effective for the codling moth. If you detect tent caterpillar nests at the tips of the branches, cut them off, place in a plastic bag, and dispose of these pests in the trash.

LAWNS

Check for an accumulation of thatch in your lawn. Thatch is the layer of dead grass and roots between the actively growing grass blades and the soil surface. Lawns that are three to five years old may develop a thatch layer due to certain management practices (overfertilizing, high nitrogen, poor drainage, compacted soils, poor microorganism activity, sloughing off of old leaf blades, and so forth).

A thin layer of thatch is normal, but as it builds up it will eventually threaten the lawn by reducing water percolation through the soil. Thatch harbors certain fungal diseases and prevents oxygen from getting to the root system.

Core-aeration is the best remedy to break through thatch layers and improve the health of your lawn.

Continue to monitor weeds that pop up here and there. Handpick or handpull weeds when they are young before their roots anchor down deeply. It's easiest after a rain or lawn watering when the soil is moist.

If you've had problems with crabgrass, you still have time to apply a pre-emergent, but get it done by mid-April. Use a natural product like corn gluten which also adds nutrients as it breaks down.

PERENNIALS

Be on the watch for the hatching of insects. As the weather warms up, overwintering adults emerge to feed on the new, tender growth of perennials. Insect eggs will hatch as daytime temperatures remain consistently warm. Check for aphids and slugs.

Leaf miners may show up on the foliage of columbines. They will leave a serpentine tunnel between the upper and lower leaf surfaces. There can be several generations of larvae and adults. Control of leaf miner is simple: crush the tiny caterpillars inside the leaf before the foliage becomes too disfigured or by cutting off the infested leaf.

Diseases, including botrytis blight, may attack peonies, causing the buds to mummify, turn black, and not open up. This disease can also attack the crown, stalks, leaves, and leaf petioles. Remove and dispose of infected plant parts as soon as you spot symptoms. Early in the season when temperatures are still low, you can apply sulfur dust as a fungicide treatment. Read and follow label directions.

Continue to pull or dig weeds before they go to seed.

ROSES

Be on the watch for early aphid infestations on the new, tender growth or succulent rose buds. Masses of pear-shaped, soft-bodied insects will be visible. If there are just a few aphids, carefully rub them off, being careful not to damage the rose's tender shoots. If aphids heavily infest a single shoot, pinch off the shoot and discard in the trash. You can also try to hose them off with a forceful stream of water; do this every few days in the morning hours. More serious aphid infestations can be controlled with insecticidal soap. Spray the aphids on both the tops and undersides of the leaves.

Weed your rose garden diligently. Keep the garden clean by removing yellow or fallen foliage. Monitor the garden regularly for insect pests and encourage beneficial bugs including ladybugs and lacewings.

SHRUBS

Be on the watch for aphids on the new tender growth. Some caterpillars may be showing up now too. If you observe ants running up and down the stems, it usually is a sign of an aphid infestation, as ants like to "farm" aphids for the sweet substance they produce called *honeydew*.

If pest problems are severe, you may have to use an insecticide labeled for that shrub. Read and follow label directions.

TREES

Aphids will soon appear at the tips of the branches where the growth is succulent. You can eliminate severe infestations by spraying them off with a forceful stream of water from the garden hose every few days. If there are major infestations, you may decide to use a homemade soap spray or a commercial insecticidal soap. Read and follow label directions.

■ *Aphids on a rosebud.*

VINES, GROUNDCOVERS & ORNAMENTAL GRASSES

As landscapes mature, shade can pose a problem for some vines, especially if they are not blooming as well as they did in past seasons. You may need to prune deciduous shade trees to increase available light to the vine or groundcover. Thinning out lower branches and raising the skirt on a tree can be helpful in some cases.

If groundcovers develop brown or yellow dead patches, especially at the edges and corners, this could be a sign of salt damage or that "Rover went all over." It is not unusual for dogs and even cats to visit groundcovers to relieve themselves. Their urine will burn the foliage. Clip off dead and brittle portions, and water the area well to leach out the soluble salts. To repel stray dogs and cats, spray with a repellent or exclude them from the area by constructing a fence.

Keep weeds from invading groundcovers and areas around vines and ornamental grasses. Pull weeds while they are young after a rainstorm or watering. Perennial weeds that are tough to pull can be spot-treated with an herbicide that contains glyphosate. Read and follow label directions and precautions.

May

May is the month when spring really arrives! Some of the most spectacular shrubs are in bloom, including lilac, spireas, viburnums, daphnes, and mockorange. Their fragrances permeate the air, especially in the evening. Open the windows and let it in!

The days begin to get warmer, and soon cool ones will be outnumbered. Shrubs are growing vigorously, sending out new foliage, and extending their stem length. Late spring-flowering shrubs are developing their flower buds. Evergreens are extending their soft, paler needles or scales at the tips of the branches that signal they are growing vigorously too.

You'll be getting outdoors more often to get gardening chores underway. Be sure to apply sunscreen and wear a hat, sunglasses, and gloves to protect your skin and eyes from harmful UV rays and your hands from cuts and callusing. Take frequent breaks and be sure to drink plenty of water.

Keep your garden tools handy with the help of a tool caddy, 5-gallon bucket, or a wheeled trash can. Consider converting an old mailbox into a storage unit for your hand tools. Install this handy storage box near the distant garden bed. You'll have hand pruners and nozzles handy when you need them.

Check your garden plan before you start plant shopping and planting. If you're like me, visiting the garden center is like going to the supermarket when you're hungry. A list will help curb your plant-buying appetite and save money. Check out some of the new plants and creative container combinations and hanging baskets. Maybe you have some space to include some of these to fill in the gaps.

Take photographs of garden beds and plants that are coming into their glory. If you see empty spaces, make plans to make new additions to keep garden interest and color year-round.

If you're not around to enjoy your flower garden during the day, create an "evening garden" with annuals that display best in the evening hours. Petunias open by day and release their scent at night. Four o'clocks and datura brighten in the waning sun and provide a last stop for hummingbirds and hawk moths.

PLAN

ANNUALS

Annual bedding plants are available at garden retailers. Some are already in bloom so you can pick and choose your favorite colors and combinations. Plan where you will put all the plants you purchase. A garden plan drawn up before shopping will save you time and money.

If you've grown annuals indoors, make plans to harden them off before planting them directly into the garden. Place plants outdoors in a semi-sunny exposure during the day and leave outdoors at night when temperatures remain above freezing. If frost is predicted, bring plants indoors. Do this for two weeks to acclimatize the plants.

BULBS

The danger of frost is past in many areas of the region, but the last frost date is later in the High Country. As the soil dries out, it is time to set out those frost-tender summer bulbs. If you have grown some indoors in pots, harden them off

■ *Place several stakes in and around the plant clump to serve as a framework and as individual supports. If one branch is particularly large and floppy, put one of the stakes next to it, about an inch away from the plant stem, and loosely tie the stake to the plant.*

before placing directly outdoors by leaving them out in a semi-sunny spot during the day, and bringing them indoors at night. Within a few weeks (late May or early June) they will be ready to plant.

Remember that many of the summer-blooming bulbs including dahlias, cannas, and gladiolus grow tall and need to be spaced appropriately. Set them towards the back or use as an accent in the center of flowerbeds.

Consider planting hardy lilies this spring. They are wonderful plants, not only for background but also for filling in gaps when hardy spring-blooming bulbs are finished.

Take notes on which bulbs did best and when the foliage started to ripen in mid- to late May. Consider planting groundcovers or other companion plants that will help mask the ripening foliage of bulbs.

If you want to stagger gladiolus blooms, make a note to plant some every two weeks. This will ensure that they will continue to provide color and cut flowers every few weeks. Gladiolus are generally inexpensive, and the corms are easy to plant.

EDIBLES

May is the month for planting, growing, and harvesting cool-season vegetables. As the soil dries out and becomes more workable, plan to prepare garden soil by tilling or cultivating the clods and uneven ground. Even though you may have added organic amendments last fall, it is a good idea to loosen the soil in spring. Add more compost now.

Keep a supply of big cardboard boxes, bushel baskets, buckets, large pots, or frost blankets on hand so they can be used to protect your garden plants from a sudden, heavy frost or damaging wet snow. Springtime in the Rockies can bring weather conditions that are more like winter. Be prepared to protect new plants from late spring frost or a sudden hailstorm.

Plan to add trellises or other supports for crops that like to climb including peas, pole beans, and cucumbers. This is also a good time to consider preparing a raised bed. Remember to keep notes in your garden journal.

HERE'S HOW

TO BUILD YOUR OWN TOMATO CAGES

Tomato cages can be used to support a variety of vegetables, and they're easy to make. Here's how:

1. Purchase concrete reinforcing wire, which usually comes in 5-foot widths.

2. Cut pieces 5 feet wide and 3½ feet tall.

3. Carefully roll this stiff wire into cylinders.

4. Leave the wires sticking out at the bottom so they can be used to insert the cage about 6 inches into the ground to anchor the cage.

5. Place cage at time of planting.

LAWNS

If you've just moved into a new home without a lawn, sodding will provide an instant living carpet in the shortest time compared to seeding or planting grass sprigs. Spring is an excellent time to install sod, so make plans before ordering sod. Sodding, like any other lawn planting, requires planning. Take time to prepare the soil in advance since this is your one chance to have it done properly. Most sod companies require a few days to cut fresh sod too, so keep that in mind.

Research to find out what kind of grass will fit your gardening style. You can obtain an updated list of turfgrass varieties from your local sod grower. When planting Kentucky bluegrass, select a blend of several varieties to take advantage of the varying degrees of disease- and drought-resistance in each one.

Plan to take a soil sample in advance to test for pH and fertility levels. The soil test will indicate how much fertilizer, if any, needs to be applied before planting. It will also indicate the level of organic matter and make recommendations on adding soil amendments. Preparing the soil in advance will ensure a healthy and deep-rooted lawn.

PERENNIALS

May is the major planting month throughout most of our region. Plan to visit local garden retailers to see the newest varieties and to get the freshest crop. Start with smaller young plants rather than the bigger gallon-sized plants. Smaller plants are not only more economical, but they transplant better.

Be patient: Unlike annual flowers, perennials are slower to establish and bloom. It may not be until their second year that they really show off their color and display. If you are impatient, plant a few of the larger potted plants to get more immediate results. Choose healthy, vigorous-growing perennial plants, and pass up those that are stunted or yellow.

ROSES

Buds are just waiting to burst into bloom. Some rose varieties are already blooming, including *Rosa foetida bicolor* with its brilliant orange-red flowers. Plan more new additions to your garden. Many garden retailers stock both old and new varieties of roses including the Canadian Explorer series and David Austin English roses. Search out disease-resistant varieties. I am particularly fond of old-fashioned shrub roses that grow on their own rootstock, don't require special pampering, and

■ *'Graham Thomas'*

This is a good month to visit public and private gardens to see shrubs that may have potential in your landscape. Keep a record of those you want to try. Note the height and spread of the shrub so you can determine if it will work in your space. Check with local nurseries for the availability of shrubs you'd like. Some may need to be ordered via mail or the Internet. Note the hardiness of the shrubs you wish to grow. You may have to create microclimates to successfully grow certain species.

TREES

Record your observations in your garden journal. Note trees that are blooming, display interesting characteristics, or have pest problems. You will be able to use this information when you add new trees to your own landscape. For example, if aspen trees are plagued by diseases and insects, you might find it helpful to replace it with a hawthorn or serviceberry.

Keep a list of the trees in your landscape, with Latin names. By knowing their scientific names, you can ask for the same species or cultivar next season if you like—or avoid it if it didn't perform to your specifications.

It's a good idea to photograph your trees to note their progress over the years and note any special care they required. This may include pruning frequency, bracing, cabling, or spraying. This documentation will prove helpful for insurance purposes if trees are damaged by storms or vandalism.

have fragrance. Among my favorites are 'Gertrude Jekyll', a pink; 'Graham Thomas', a fragrant yellow rose; 'L.D. Braithwaite', a good crimson red; and 'William Baffin', a deep pink.

While you're shopping for new roses, consider rose-gardening accessories such as durable pruning tools or a handsome, sturdy trellis to show off your favorite climbing roses. Miniature roses in terracotta or lightweight planters are especially attractive on a patio or deck.

Container-grown roses in full bloom make wonderful Mother's Day gifts. One of my mother's favorites was floribunda 'Europeana'. It has mildly fragrant, deep red blossoms borne in five to seven flowers per cluster. Floribundas are durable and repeat flowering all summer long.

SHRUBS

As shrubs bloom in your landscape, make notes in your garden notebook or journal. Date the observations, too, for future reference. Note botanical names whenever possible, so if you need to replace a shrub in the middle of a hedge, you can match the variety. Monitoring how shrubs grow and develop will guide you in the correct timing for treating insect pests and diseases.

VINES, GROUNDCOVERS & ORNAMENTAL GRASSES

Garden stores are well-stocked with potted plants by now, and you can find a great variety of groundcovers, vines, and ornamental grasses. Grasses and vines are available in various pot sizes so let your budget guide you on what you want to spend. I recommend the smaller plants since they are fast to start up and will often outgrow the bigger rootbound specimens. Groundcovers are available in packs or in smaller 2- to 4-inch pots. Walk around your landscape and make a shopping list (roughly measure the beds first, and know how many you need to buy).

PLANT

ANNUALS

Sow hardy and half-hardy annuals directly in the ground whenever the soil can be worked. Some good choices include larkspur, sweet alyssum, California poppy, spider flower, morning glory, and sweet peas. Wait to sow tender annuals such as marigolds, zinnias, and moss rose until later in the month when the soil has warmed up and the danger of hard frost has passed.

Plant cool-season transplants such as pansies, violas, and primroses in the early part of the month since they will tolerate cool nights. Wait to plant warm-season annuals such as marigolds, zinnias, and begonias until around mid- to late May, allowing the soil time to warm up.

Transplants that have been hardened off can be planted directly to the garden.

Interplant annuals among spring-flowering bulbs to camouflage the bulbs' foliage and fill in empty gaps. Be careful not to dig too deep so you won't injure the bulbs when planting.

BULBS

After the frost-free date in your area, it is safe to set out the first of the tender bulbs you've been growing indoors and those that have been in storage. Check the bulbs in storage to make sure they are not mushy or too dried out. Divide the tubers of dahlias and separate cannas as needed. Remember to make sure a "growing eye" is on each section of a dahlia division.

Be sure that the soil has been prepared where you plant tender bulbs. Set them at the proper depths, and place a stake in the planting hole. Insert the support stake into the ground near the bulb. The stake height should be slightly shorter than the projected height of the plant so the bulb's foliage camouflages it later. Inserting the stake at planting time will prevent you from stabbing the bulb when it has already started to grow. Dahlias, gladiolus, some lilies, and crocosmia will appreciate these supports as they grow, as the supports will help protect them from wind damage.

Follow the package instructions for planting suggestions. To enjoy a continual bloom of gladiolus, plant corms every two weeks until mid-July.

Finish planting out in the garden those gift bulbs (from Chrismas, St. Patrick's Day, and Easter, usually) such as tulips, hyacinths, and daffodils that were forced into bloom. Even the Easter lily can be planted in a protected location (morning sun with afternoon shade) and may bloom again in mid- to late summer.

Amaryllis can be moved outdoors after the danger of frost has past. Sink pot and all in the ground in a semi-sunny location or underneath the canopy of a tree. It will continue to grow foliage and send more energy to the bulb.

EDIBLES

May is an ideal time to direct seed many vegetable crops. Sow vegetable seeds according to directions on the seed packets regarding sun exposure, planting depth, spacing, and days to harvest. Label each row to identify specific crops including date planted and variety. Some root crops such as carrots and radishes can be sown in the same row. By the time the carrots are ready to be thinned, the radishes are ready for harvesting.

Mid-May is a traditional time to sow sweet corn. Planting corn in blocks of nine to twelve plants rather than rows ensures better pollination and requires less space.

Transplant dill, sweet marjoram, basil, sage, and other herbs into the garden now. If you like to grow mint, remember that is spreads by underground roots. Confine it by planting it in a 5-gallon bucket with the bottom cut out. Bury the bucket into the ground with the rim a few inches *above* ground level. This technique usually restricts mint's roots from wandering over the rim to invade other areas of the garden.

Harden-off transplants of cucumbers, melons, squash, pumpkins, and watermelons that were started indoors in mid- to late April so they will be ready to plant in the garden. Be careful not to disturb the roots when transplanting.

HERE'S HOW

TO PLANT OR INSTALL SOD

■ (Left) *Place the first strip of sod along a straight edge such as a front sidewalk. Butt it to the edge as tightly as possible without overlapping the surface. Mist the soil lightly before setting the sod.* (Right) *Continue the row of sod by butting the next strip up tight against the end of the first. Be sure there is no gap and that the strips do not overlap.*

■ (Left) *Cut the first strip in the second row as necessary to create a staggered "brick" pattern. Use a large, sharp knife or sharpened trowel.* (Right) *As you work, stop about every twenty to thirty minutes and spray the strips you've laid—as well as the stack of sod—with enough water to keep them moist.*

1. Spread a 2- to 3-inch layer of compost or rotted manure; use a minimum of 3 cubic yards per 1,000 square feet. You can add up to 5 cubic yards if your budget allows and it will form a deeper foundation when mixed with your native soil. This promotes a deeper and more drought-tolerant lawn with fewer disease problems.

2. Rototill or disc the soil to a depth of 4 to 8 inches and mix the organic amendments into the native or existing "fill dirt." You generally don't have to bring in topsoil, but use what you already have.

3. Right before laying the sod, broadcast a starter fertilize such as 18-46-0, and lightly rake in.

4. Lay sod in a brickwork pattern, staggering the sod sections to make a nice tight fit. I like to spread a layer of compost around the edges of new sod to prevent it from drying out. Check with your local sod supplier for information leaflets that provide complete instructions on sod installation and care tips. Water daily for the first week to ensure root development. As roots anchor in, reduce the frequency.

5. You still have a window of opportunity to overseed thin or bare spots before the weather turns hot. Keep the seeded areas moist by frequent sprinkling. Light waterings two to three times a day should get the new seed to germinate.

At the end of May, it's usually safe to plant peppers, eggplants, tomatoes, and okra. Some garden stores offer transplants of squash, beans, cucumbers, and melons that can also be transplanted. I prefer to direct seed these when the soil is warm (55 degrees Fahrenheit) as they are often fussy about being transplanted. These vegetables will germinate quickly and suffer less transplant shock when direct seeded in a prepared soil.

LAWNS
See "Here's How to Plant or Install Sod" on page 94.

PERENNIALS
No matter how healthy a new plant is, unless it is sited properly and planted in soil with good drainage, it will not thrive or perform to expectations. Check plant labels for the proper sun or shade exposure, cold-hardiness rating, and cultural requirements. See the *Rocky Mountain Getting Started Garden Guide* for more complete information on many plant selections.

Keep newly purchased plants moist—not soggy—until planting time. Then dig the planting hole two times wider than, and as deep as, the plant's container. Slip the plant from its pot and set it in the planting hole. Make sure it is at the same depth or slightly higher than ground level. Fill in with prepared backfill soil, firm around the rootball, and water in thoroughly.

Some perennials can be planted in containers and combined with annuals to provide color during the summer. Use a good, soilless growing mixture and add a slow-release granular fertilizer at planting. However, there are no guarantees that perennials will survive the winter in containers unless special precautions are taken.

ROSES
May is an excellent time to continue planting container-grown rose bushes. Follow planting guidelines in March and April (see pages 56 and 74) for planting.

Bare-root roses may need special attention since it is getting a bit late. If your receive mail-order bushes late, take precautions to "sweat" the canes that are stubborn about sending out new growth.

You can do this by placing a large, 5-gallon bucket over the entire rose plant. Place a large stone or several bricks on the top of the inverted bucket to keep it in place. Within a week or so, buds should start to emerge; this indicates the roots have taken hold and you've saved your investment.

Roses are very compatible with flowering perennials and add special interest in the garden. Climbing roses should be sited at least 1 foot from the side of the house or a retaining wall to allow for proper air circulation and maintenance.

SHRUBS
Container-grown shrubs can be planted from now until early fall. Local garden stores are aware of the impact of shrubs in bloom and will usually have excellent displays to choose from. If you see varieties of shrubs you particularly like, now is the time to add them to your landscape. Planting container-grown shrubs differs from planting bare-root or balled-and-burlapped shrubs. See "Here's How to Plant a Container-Grown Shrub" on page 96.

TREES
Most trees are grown and sold in containers. Container-grown trees are easy to handle and can be planted at almost any time of the year, except when the ground is frozen solid. Exercise caution if planting during extreme heat or drought. Be sure to have the planting site ready prior to planting. See tree planting in April, page 76.

Evergreens, including pine, spruce, and fir, transplant best in spring and early summer when they are actively growing. This allows them to establish a healthy and vigorous root system before the onset of autumn. Plant in well-drained, humus-enriched soil that is slightly acidic to neutral. Add sphagnum peat moss to help acidify the soil. Mulch with compost or pine needles after transplanting.

VINES, GROUNDCOVERS & ORNAMENTAL GRASSES
Since most potted plants are grown in an artificial soilless mixture, the roots are "pampered" to grow faster, so they become rootbound faster. If the plants are set into our unmodified native soils, the roots remain within the artificial soil and are slow to grow outward from the original rootball.

HERE'S HOW

TO PLANT A CONTAINER-GROWN SHRUB

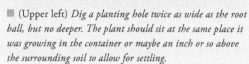

■ (Upper left) *Dig a planting hole twice as wide as the root ball, but no deeper. The plant should sit at the same place it was growing in the container or maybe an inch or so above the surrounding soil to allow for settling.*

■ (Upper right) *Place the container on its side and roll it on the ground while tapping it to loosen the roots. Upend the container and gently pull it off of the plant roots. Do not pull plant by stem.*

■ (Middle left) *Use your fingers to loosen any roots that may be matted, gently untangling them. Roots that are tightly coiled should be cut apart and loosened. Gently spread the roots wide so they are pointing outward as much as possible.*

■ (Middle right) *Set the shrub into the hole.*

■ (Bottom) *Backfill the hole with the original soil. Mound the soil to create a ridge around the plant to hold water. Water well and cover the soil with organic mulch, keeping it a few inches from the shrub.*

I refer to this as the "bathtub effect." To minimize this problem, modify your native soil by adding compost, sphagnum peat moss, or a combination (a 50/50 mix is my preference). Add one-third by volume to the native backfill soil.

CARE

ANNUALS

Get mums to bloom in the fall by pinching off the flower buds during the summer. Chrysanthemums, Joe-pye weed, beebalm, New England asters, phlox, heliopsis, balloon flower, and helenium can all be cut back by one-third in the spring to promote bushier growth and later flowering.

As cool-season annuals begin to decline with the onset of heat, remove them and replace with warm-season annuals including geraniums, petunias, marigolds, and dahlias. Thin out direct-seeded annuals to avoid crowding and to allow for good air circulation, which reduces powdery mildew disease. Provide support for taller-growing annuals for protection from winds. Use bamboo stakes, peony cages, or tomato cages. As the foliage grows and fills in it will hide the supports.

Pinch young transplants after planting, even if it means removing some of the flowers. This helps the plants to become stockier and bushier. Annuals

■ *Pinch off flower buds to encourage continuous blooming.*

such as coleus, petunia, cosmos, marigold, salvia, and sweet pea benefit from pinching. Use your thumb and forefinger to nip out the growing tip of the main stem just above a leaf or pair of leaves.

Deadhead or remove spent flowers from annuals that bloom in flushes. This includes petunias, geraniums, marigolds, and California poppies. This promotes healthier growth and more blooms.

BULBS

Be sure to maintain uniform moisture in newly planted bulb beds, but do not waterlog the ground. Too much moisture can rot the bulbs before they have a chance to develop roots. Covering the bulb beds with a layer of mulch up to 2 inches deep will help retain moisture and keep the soil from compacting.

If you didn't stake tall bulbs when planting, do so as they begin to emerge. Insert a stake gently into moist soil so it does not damage the bulb.

Finish cleaning up the garden. Spent foliage is easily detached from a plant by gently tugging the ripened leaves at the base. Compost this plant debris. Add more compost or mulch in bare spots of the bed to suppress weeds and maintain uniform moisture.

EDIBLES

Even though the weather has mellowed, you can still expect a late spring frost, so be prepared with plant protectors if the forecast calls for a freeze at night. Remove the covers during the day so the plants receive sunlight and air circulation. Floating row covers work well, but 5-gallon buckets, fiber nursery pots, cardboard boxes, and other materials can be used to protect plants overnight.

Thin out crowded rows of carrots, beets, endive, and leaf lettuce. Be careful when pulling out seedlings to avoid removing large clumps. Use small scissors to snip unwanted plants or gently pull when the soil is moist, and space the plants accordingly.

Some vegetables can be grown vertically in the garden, especially those that grow as vines. Cucumbers, squash, pole beans, and garden peas will grow up fences and trellises. This will take up

■ *To save space, grow cucumbers up a string trellis.*

less space, helpful if your garden area is limited, and the vegetables will grow more uniformly.

Keep herbs pinched or pruned to encourage branching and make the plants grow more compact. This will also delay premature flowering so you can enjoy harvesting the foliage for culinary purposes.

Pinch off excessive branch suckers on indeterminate tomato plants to develop stronger central stems that will support the plants throughout the season.

Successful pollination of fruit trees in the home orchard may allow the branches to become laden with excess fruits. Over the next six weeks, thin out the small crowded apples, pears, peaches, and plums so the fruits are approximately 4 to 6 inches apart. This allows better air circulation, reduces insect pests, and promotes larger fruit.

LAWNS

As the days advance toward summer, it is still okay to aerate your lawn if you didn't get it done earlier. Water the lawn the day before you run the aerator over it. The goal is to remove deep cores to break through soil compaction and create channels for

water to soak in and for nutrients to become more available to the roots.

If you inherited a bad lawn, topdress it with compost after aeration. This will allow the organic amendments to filter down into the soil and increase microbial activity and stimulate root growth, which will make the lawn grow thicker. A thick, dense turf will discourage weed invasion.

Mow your lawn regularly and frequently during the spring, as growth is more rapid. Cool-season grasses should be mowed to a height of 2 to 3 inches, while warm-season grasses can be cut shorter. Be sure that the mower blade is sharp for a clean cut that reduces fraying of the leaf blades.

PERENNIALS

As established perennials grow and spread, many will send out stem or root runners to form new plants nearby. Some develop into larger clumps as their crowns enlarge and send up more stems. Either way, perennials reach a point when they become too large or woody for their space in a garden bed.

When they begin to crowd out other plants or to die out in the center, it's time to divide and conquer. Divide perennials before or shortly after they bloom; just avoid digging and dividing in the heat of midsummer. Asters, bellflower, chrysanthemum, daylily, cranesbill, phlox, coneflower, and sedum are a few that can be lifted and divided.

Monitor growth of perennials that may benefit from support, particularly if you live in a windy area. Delphiniums and foxgloves in my garden are in constant need of support from bamboo stakes or tomato cages. Insert the supports 12 to 14 inches into the soil and place them slightly shorter than the plant's maximum height. The stakes will soon be camouflaged by the foliage, but they will protect the plants from wind damage.

Young perennials you started indoors should now be acclimated to the outdoors and can be situated in the garden.

As some of your early spring-flowering perennials have finished blooming, deadhead or remove the faded flowers. This will not only improve their appearance, but many perennials will develop new flowering buds. I like to use a hedge trimmer to clip off the faded small flowers from low-growing perennials such as candytuft, pinks, and creeping phlox. Use a regular hand pruner for larger flowers and woody stems.

ROSES

If you haven't mulched your roses, now is a good time to augment existing mulch that may have settled or blown away before summer's heat.

Support climbing and rambling roses with a trellis, arbor, or stakes, tying the canes loosely with jute twine or plant ties.

If you've acclimated your indoor miniature roses to the outdoors, late in the month is a good time to site them outdoors for the season. Do not place them in the sun immediately, as it will scorch their foliage.

Continue to remove and dispose of fallen leaves and plant debris, as this material often will harbor insect pests and diseases. If necessary, trim back

■ Candles should be removed in spring to control growth on pines and spruce.

rose canes that are encroaching on the sidewalk or pathway. Use your good judgment and common sense to trim back growth.

Pick a bouquet of roses to enjoy indoors. After all, they are to be appreciated inside as well as in the garden. Make rose potpourri for your dresser drawers and for gifts.

SHRUBS

Routinely check the condition of your shrubs. Gently bend stems or branches that appear dead. If they are still flexible, rather than dry and brittle, the stem may still be alive. Do the fingernail test by scraping a bit of the bark off the stem; if there is still green tissue beneath the bark, the stem is still alive. Lightly prune back the stem about halfway, and see if it regenerates new growth.

If you didn't get around to pruning spring-flowering shrubs by now, do so before the end of the month. They will soon start to develop next year's flower buds, and pruning too late will remove next season's blooms. Add fresh mulch as needed around and over the root zone as the mulch layer thins to less than a few inches.

Deadhead or remove the spent flowers from blooming shrubs *unless* you want them to produce fruit for the birds; examples include cotoneaster, ninebark, and honeysuckle. Avoid shearing off the tops or tips of shrubs. This destroys their natural growth habit and causes denser interior growth that is subject to spider mites.

Continue to prune spring-flowering shrubs as they finish blooming. Shrubs perform best when annual pruning removes one-third of the oldest canes to the ground. This makes a shrub produce fresh, new stems for future blooms. Prune back overly long or straggly stems to side shoots growing in the same direction.

TREES

As the new growth expands on pines and spruces, it's a good time to prune the new growth or "candles" to control height and spread. The amount you pinch off depends on how much you want to reduce the tree or shrub's size. It is best to remove no more than half of the candle each year.

As mulch begins to decompose and diminish, weeds may start growing. Renew the mulch layer to 2 to 3 inches to prevent weed invasions and to help retain uniform moisture. Spread the mulch up to, but not over, the root flare at the base of the trunk. Surrounding the root zone with a ring of weed-suppressing mulch will also prevent lawn mower and weed trimmer damage to the trunk.

Remove dead or diseased wood anytime as you discover it in your trees. If you are coping with a disease called fireblight, be sure to disinfect your pruning tools with alcohol or a spray disinfectant. These materials are less corrosive than the traditional mixture of water and household bleach. This can help prevent the spread of the disease to other branches. Dispose of diseased branches so they won't remain to carry the bacteria.

■ *Fireblight*

Cut off suckers that originate at the base of the trunk or those that are appearing in the yard. These will often harbor woolly aphids and other insects that will later spread to the upper portions of the tree.

VINES, GROUNDCOVERS & ORNAMENTAL GRASSES

Newly set-out plants should be mulched to reduce weeds and water loss. Use a 2- to 3-inch layer of compost, shredded bark or cedar, pine needles, or chopped leaves over the soil around the groundcover, vine, or ornamental grass.

Check trellises and other vine supports to make sure they are securely fastened to a wall or post. This will prevent them from falling over when the vines start growing vigorously. Ensure adequate air circulation behind trellises and other supports so vines will not bake in the heat of the sun. Air circulation will also reduce the incidence of foliar diseases later in the season. Construct trellises, arbors, and other supports so they sit about 12 to 18 inches away from a solid wall.

Check on some of the more established groundcover plants that are becoming crowded. It may be time to lift and divide them. This will renew the bed and stimulate healthier, more vigorous growth. Periwinkle, bugleweed (*Ajuga*), and lily-of-the-valley can be lifted and divided every three to five years.

As perennial vines are growing vigorously, prune off straggly stems and shoots to encourage more fullness. Help direct the stems to the supports as needed.

Prune out dead and damaged twigs injured by winter desiccation or windstorms.

Trailing vines such as vinca and ivies should be growing vigorously. Cut back any unruly stems that creep out into the lawn or perennial garden. This will direct their growth where it should be. Boston ivy, English ivy, Virginia creeper, and trumpet vine can encroach on gutters, windows, and chimneys. Don't be afraid to cut them back when they grow so aggressively.

WATER

ANNUALS

Keep new transplants watered regularly to avoid stress. Check the soil to a depth of 2 to 3 inches and water as it begins to dry out. Keep the foliage dry, especially at night, to avoid the spread of foliar diseases.

Black-eyed Susan vine trained to a trellis

During periods of dry weather, water the garden every few days to maintain subsoil moisture so the root systems develop deeply. Use mulches when the plants are 6 inches tall to conserve water and help suppress weed growth.

Container gardens and raised beds drain more rapidly and may require more attention to watering. To determine if the soil needs watering, dig down to a depth of 2 to 3 inches with a garden trowel to check whether the soil is beginning to dry out. If it is, give the garden a good soaking.

If time and your budget permits, consider installing a drip irrigation system to water the vegetable garden. Not only is this a time- and water-saver, but also it puts water at the root zone of the crops and will soak deeply. It reduces the chances of moisture staying on the foliage at night and thereby reduces the incidence of powdery mildew and other leaf diseases.

Placing a soaker hose around your plants to water them is very efficient too. Use landscape pins or sod stapes to hold down the hose.

BULBS
Keep the soil of newly planted bulb beds uniformly moist. Check the soil moisture by probing into it with your finger or a garden trowel. If it is beginning to dry out to a depth of 2 to 3 inches, it is time to water.

Mulched beds need less frequent watering than those that are not mulched.

Container-grown bulbs need closer attention to watering because the potting mixture will dry out faster than garden soil. If the weather is particularly hot, dry, and windy, water accordingly to ensure good root growth and healthy foliage.

EDIBLES
Proper watering is essential to get new vegetable transplants started. Water young transplants before they are taken out of their containers. They tend to dry out quickly when set directly into the garden. Watering will prepare them for the transition.

To make quick work of watering, put a soaker hose around your plants to water them. You can snake the hose in and out of rows and use wire pins called sod staples to hold down the hose. If the hose is in the middle of two rows, the water from it will reach plants on each side of the hose.

LAWNS

Continue to water sod daily for the first few weeks after installation to ensure healthy rooting. After two weeks, start weaning the turf off water by watering it every three to four days. It is best to check for soil moisture by probing the turf with a long screwdriver or garden trowel. This will help you gauge your particular watering schedule.

We can't always depend on natural rainfall, so set your automatic sprinkler for cyclic or interval watering.

Established lawns that were planted on a good soil foundation can go five to seven days without rain or watering if the soil underfoot was well prepared. Compacted soils will not readily accept water and roots are slow to develop.

PERENNIALS

Check perennials weekly for their moisture situation. If the weather has been dry and windy, more frequent watering will be necessary for newly planted perennials.

Use mulch to help conserve water, plus suppress weed growth. Since everyone's soil is different, check the subsoil around your perennials every four to five days. If it is beginning to dry out at that level, give the plants a deep drink of water. Mulched plantings will not have to be watered as frequently.

Some perennials go dormant after blooming later this month. This is normal for bleeding heart, Oriental poppies, bluebells, and other early-season bloomers. These are truly the water-thrifty plants to include in your garden where water is of concern. As these plants go dormant for the summer, they surely will return next year. Just don't overwater areas where they are planted.

ROSES

Keep an eye on the watering of newly planted roses; do not overwater. Allow the soil to dry out slightly between waterings. This will allow the healthiest and strongest root development. Roses need *lots* of water, especially as the weather warms.

Water roses weekly, and if we experience prolonged drought periods, water the rose garden deeply every five to seven days, depending upon water restrictions in your area. Water the soil and root zone, not the leaves. Apply early in the morning to reduce the incidence of leaf diseases. If you must water in the evening, do it early so that any damp leaves will dry before night.

SHRUBS

Continue to water shrubs when rainfall is scarce or during prolonged dry periods. If shrubs are mulched properly, they can go longer between waterings. Dig down through the mulch to check subsoil moisture to determine your watering schedule.

Newly planted shrubs and those in containers need more frequent watering to ensure healthy growth. An inch of water per week will usually suffice. Don't forget to use mulches, even with shrubs planted in large containers. This helps maintain uniform moisture while conserving water.

TREES

Maintain a regular watering schedule for newly planted trees. Research has shown that the establishment time for trees takes up to twelve months per inch of trunk caliper (the trunk diameter measured 6 to 8 inches above the ground). Check the soil moisture to a depth of 6 inches with a garden trowel to determine if it's time to give them a good drink. Avoid overwatering, as this will starve the new roots of oxygen and waterlog the soil. That scenario usually results in the death of the tree.

VINES, GROUNDCOVERS & ORNAMENTAL GRASSES

Keep newly planted groundcovers, vines, and ornamental grasses watered deeply if the weather is dry and windy. Dig down and check soil moisture with a garden trowel. If it is beginning to dry out 3 to 4 inches down, it is time to water the plants thoroughly. Their first growing season is critical so the plants can become well-established and drought tolerant.

FERTILIZE

ANNUALS

If you've already added a slow-release fertilizer to the flowerbed when preparing the soil, you don't need to fertilize again. If you didn't add nutrients, add a granular 5-10-5 at the time of planting. A light scattering around the root zone will help transplants get an extra boost to become established.

If you prefer to use liquid-soluble plant food, it's best to be conservative and dilute to one-half the recommended rate. Too much nitrogen promotes excessive foliage growth, which can make plants floppy and often attracts aphids and other pests.

BULBS

Bulbs, corms, tubers, and rhizomes come equipped with stored food energy to get started. But as the tender summer-blooming bulbs start growing, it is beneficial to provide some supplemental slow-release granular fertilizer for the growing season. I recommend a slow-release granular applied around the base of the plants and lightly cultivated in; then water the fertilizer in. This will last through the summer and early autumn. Read and follow label directions.

Container-grown bulbs may need more frequent fertilizing because you are watering more often and nutrients are leached away. Use a water-soluble flower fertilizer diluted to half-strength and apply at every other watering.

EDIBLES

If you did not add a slow-release fertilizer to the garden soil in the spring, you can supplement with a water-soluble plant fertilizer to give the plants a boost while they are establishing. I prefer to dilute soluble plant fertilizers to half-strength to avoid the accumulation of soluble salts around the root zone. Read and follow label directions.

Too much nitrogen (the first number in the fertilizer analysis) will promote excessive vegetative growth and will often attract aphids and other insect pests. It will also delay flowering and fruiting of many vegetable crops.

LAWNS

If you have not fertilized since last September (around Labor Day), choose a fertilizer with iron and sulfur, and one that has fast-acting (water-soluble) nitrogen for a more rapid green-up to jump-start the grass. The other components of the

fertilizer should have a larger portion of slow-acting nitrogen to maintain uniform, consistent nutrients over many weeks. This allows the lawn to grow the way nature intended. Read and follow label directions for application rates. Use a good spreader or check your own and calibrate it if needed. Follow spreader instructions for details.

PERENNIALS

If you fertilized your perennial garden earlier with a slow-release granular product last month, they do not need any additional fertilizer at this time. Check the fertilizer label for the number of weeks or months the fertilizer will last. Do not overfertilize perennials since this will make them grow lanky and produce fewer blooms.

ROSES

Check your garden journal or notebook to see if it's time to apply more slow-release fertilizer over your roses' root zone. I prefer to use one that will last six months. Some don't last as long as others, and will need reapplication. Refer to the manufacturer's recommendations and follow label instructions.

Roses bloom best with a consistent source of readily available nutrients. It is common in our region for

■ *A walk-behind drop-spreader is the most popular way to fertilize a lawn.*

soils to experience iron chlorosis—a lack of iron because of our calcareous soil conditions. If you have this problem, use a granular fertilizer that contains both iron and sulfur.

Some roses, such as hybrid teas, grandifloras, floribundas, and climbers, are heavy feeders if you want more prolific flowering. If you have time, apply a foliar fertilizer spray or my homemade rose tonic (see page 222) once a month through mid-August as a supplement to the slow-release granular incorporated earlier in the season.

SHRUBS

Any fertilizer should have been applied by now, but if you forgot, you still have time to apply a complete fertilizer such as 5-10-5 or 10-10-10 around the root zone. Lightly cultivate into the soil around the root zones, and water in thoroughly.

Shrubs in containers are watered more often and may need more fertilizer. If using a liquid plant food, dilute to half-strength to prevent excess salt. Apply every two to three weeks during the growing season when the potting soil is moist.

TREES

Look for signs in the foliage and growing tips to determine if your trees are "hungry" for nutrients. Trees grown in lawn areas generally receive adequate nutrients for lawn fertilizer applications. Visual symptoms that trees need additional nutrients include stunted growth, smaller-than-normal leaves, poor leaf color, early leaf drop, and thinning foliage. These symptoms may also be caused by other factors, including poor soil drainage, insects, diseases, or environmental conditions. If you are uncertain, consult with a reputable arborist or horticulturist in your area.

If fertilizer is recommended and you want to encourage more growth, apply it this month. Fertilize with a slow-release, complete fertilizer such as 20-10-10. Read and follow label directions. Water in thoroughly after application.

VINES, GROUNDCOVERS & ORNAMENTAL GRASSES

My preference is to add a granular slow-release fertilizer at planting time so it can be done once

in the spring, then you can "forget about it" for the rest of the year. If you prefer to use a soluble plant fertilizer, use it sparingly, according to the manufacturer's recommendations. It is better to fertilize less often than is recommended on the label. Once a month is adequate. Groundcovers, vines, and ornamental grasses are not big feeders.

PROBLEM-SOLVE

ANNUALS

Aphids, flea beetles, and slugs can become a problem on newly planted annuals.

Cutworms that live in the soil will sever plants at the base of the stem. You can protect transplants with a stiff collar made out of a plastic yogurt cup with the bottom cut out. Push the container 2 inches into the soil with about 2 inches remaining above the ground.

■ *An easy and chemical-free way to protect plants against cutworm damage is to place cardboard collars around plants when transplanting them to the garden*

B.t. (*Bacillus thuringiensis*) is a biological insecticide that is very effective against the larvae of *all* moths and butterflies (*Lepidoptera* classification of insects).

Weeds are opportunistic and will compete with annuals since the soil was disturbed by planting. Get rid of them "the cowboy way" or by hand-digging or pulling as soon as they start to appear. Mulch the soil when annual transplants are 4 to 6 inches tall. This will smother out tiny weed seedlings.

Keep newly transplanted annuals healthy, stress-free, and disease-free by proper watering. Water every few days or as the soil dries out to avoid plant stress. Water from below to reduce the spread of leaf diseases. Space or thin annuals to allow for good air circulation, which discourages fungus diseases.

Tender plants will need some quick protection from late spring frost. Monitor the weather report for predictions of freezing temperatures, and keep a few old blankets, cardboard boxes, or large plastic pots handy. When frost is predicted, cover vulnerable plants.

Record the dates you planted various annuals, including when you direct-seeded them into the garden, so you can track how well they germinated and developed. This can prove helpful in future years for timing your planting and achieving the best results.

BULBS

Aphids are now in full force on iris buds. They will cause the flowers to become distorted or to not open at all. Until their natural predators arrive (lady beetles), you can control aphids by pinching off infested plant parts and discarding them in the trash. Homemade soap sprays and insecticidal soaps may prove helpful too.

Watch for the signs of powdery mildew on plants that have been watered overhead. A powdery white film will appear on the foliage and stems. Make sure the bulbs have good air circulation and try to water early in the morning or early evening so that the foliage goes into the night dry.

Pinch off diseased leaves and stems and discard in a garbage bag. Do *not* place them in the compost pile.

Hand-dig, pull, or hoe weeds while they are still young and you can expose the roots to sunlight and drying conditions. Wait too long, and weeds seem to get harder to dig or pull.

Mulch bare soil to suppress annual weed seeds from sprouting.

EDIBLES

Watch out for hatches of aphids that attack the tender, succulent growth of vegetable and herbs. At the first sight of them, wash them off or use the homemade soap spray. Ladybugs are nature's best predators to keep these pests at bay.

■ *White cabbage butterfly*

The appearance of white butterflies is a sign that cabbageworms are on the way. They chew holes in the leaves of cole crops. Use floating row covers to prevent the butterflies from depositing eggs on the foliage, or use *Bacillus thuringiensis* (B.t.). This bacterial warfare will stop the larvae in their tracks.

LAWNS

Sod webworms may become a problem in lawns. Watch for blackbirds feeding in your lawn. Large flocks may be doing their job of consuming large quantities of sod webworms or army worms. If this is the case, there is no need to apply insecticides, just let nature take its course.

Thinning lawns may be the result of lawn mites, particularly on the south and west exposures. Pay a little more attention to watering these areas and the grass should recover.

Be on the watch for new ant mounds since it is time for them to swarm and start new colonies. Ants normally nest at the edges of the lawn or around sidewalks, pavement or stones. From there, they venture out into the lawn on pest control, so most are beneficial. If ants become a nuisance, discourage them by digging out their nesting site or pouring boiling water over the nests as they reappear. This will make them move elsewhere.

Weeds will continue to have growth spurts in cooler weather. Stay on top of the situation by pulling them out or spot-treating as needed. Get them before they go to seed.

PERENNIALS

If you see ants crawling all over the buds of peonies, don't be alarmed. This is a normal occurrence since the ants are seeking and feeding on the sweet nectar secreted by the peony buds. They actually farm the sweet substance and bring it back to the nest for young ants.

ROSES

Be on the watch for foliar diseases, including leaf spot and powdery mildew. You can prevent these by removing leaves or stems showing early signs of infection. Early applications of my homemade powdery mildew control made from baking soda and vegetable oil can prevent a severe outbreak, and it is people- and wildlife-friendly. See page 220.

If certain roses in your garden develop droopy and deformed buds, this is often a sign of rose midge infestation. This will dramatically reduce the number of blooms. Deadhead and dispose of infested buds and spent flowers. You may need to spray the buds and tip growth with a systemic insecticide labeled for roses. Read and follow label directions.

■ *Powdery mildew can affect all kinds of plants.*

If rose buds or flowers are pierced with tiny holes, and you see bent necks supporting the buds, this a telltale sign of the rose curculio. This attractive maroon to orange-brown snout beetle wreaks havoc in the rose garden with its piercing snout. Remove infested buds, then handpick these tiny critters and drop them into a pail of soapy water. Insecticides can be used also. Read and follow label directions.

SHRUBS

Be on the watch for insect pests; as the days stay consistently warm, insect eggs will hatch. Control invasions with an insecticidal soap spray or make your own homemade soap spray. See page 220.

Lilac borers and other boring insects will make sneak attacks now. Be ready to prevent them. Place pheromone traps in your landscape to detect their presence. This will allow you to apply control measures at the proper time.

If your junipers have a white frothy substance on their branches that resembles spit, it is being invaded by spittle bugs. Hose them off with a forceful spray of water.

TREES

Insect invasions can start to show up on trees this month. Be on the watch for aphids, soft-bodied pests found clustered at the ends of the new tender growth. They feed by sucking the plant sap with their piercing mouth parts. This causes the foliage and new tips to curl and become malformed. Luckily there are many predators that feed on aphids, including birds, lady beetles, lacewings, and syrphid fly larvae.

The ash sawfly may appear later in the month and wreak havoc on the new foliage. They feed by puncturing tiny shotholes in the leaves. On a quiet day, you may hear the chewing if you're standing underneath the tree. The older larvae feed on the leaves more extensively, leaving only the main leaf veins. Sawflies are wimpy pests and are easily controlled with insecticidal soap sprays or a homemade soap spray.

Evergreens may be attacked by a variety of pests including the Cooley spruce gall adelgid, which causes the tips of spruce to develop conelike galls. This kills an evergreen's terminal growth, but does not harm the tree itself. During June, the full-grown adelgids leave their gall homesteads and migrate to fir trees. On the Douglas fir, spruce adelgids are noticeable as the "woolly aphids" that suck sap from the needles. Symptoms develop into yellowing and twisting needles.

To control spruce adelgids and woolly aphids, allow natural predators such as ladybugs and predacious wasps to keep them in check; if infestations become severe enough to cause considerable damage, use a systemic insecticide labeled for evergreens. Read and follow label directions exactly.

■ *Cedar apple rust*

Juniper-Hawthorn rust galls may ooze unique orange "fingers" (the spores of the fungus). It is more common if it's rainy. Control is to prune them out as it can spread to apples causing the leaves to get yellow spots with black centers. Plant disease-resistant apples or remove nearby junipers or cedars.

The emerald ash borer (EAB) has become a more common problem in some areas of the region where it was introduced from firewood harboring live insects. Timely applications of a systemic insecticide that is transported within the tree can be applied in mid-May to late June. Consult with a professional tree service to schedule insecticide treatments. To check if you're in an area where emerald ash borer is a threat to ash trees, check with your State Forestry Service, Department of Agriculture, or Extension Service.

VINES, GROUNDCOVERS & ORNAMENTAL GRASSES

As the weather warms, it is time for slugs to make their sneak attacks on vines and groundcovers. These creatures are active at night. Since they overwinter in moist, organic debris and under mulch, lightly cultivate the mulch to expose them to sunlight and heat. Commercially prepared slug baits are also available, but these *must be used with caution* as they are a threat to wildlife, pets, and small children. Read and follow label directions and observe safety precautions.

Other insects may find vines and groundcovers attractive. Aphids feed on the new tender growth and flower buds. Until there are beneficial insects to prey on the aphids, wash them off with a forceful stream of water. Insecticidal soap sprays or the homemade soap spray can also control aphids. Read and follow label instructions when using any pesticide.

Weevils may feed on the foliage of vines and groundcovers. They chew pieces of the leaves and buds. If you can spot them early in the morning or late evening, handpick them off the plant and drop them in a can of soapy water and discard later.

A disease known as *Phomopsis* twig blight can often attack groundcover junipers and other upright types. The fungus affects the branch tips in the spring, eventually killing them back. Prune out the dead, grayish brown branches to eliminate the fungus spores before they spread to other branches. Keep the plants healthy by proper watering and pruning.

Keep weeds from invading new plantings of groundcovers, vines, and ornamental grasses. A light cultivation when the weed seedlings are young is a good cultural control. Once weeds become more fully established, they are harder to pull or control. The best control is usually spot-treatment with a herbicide.

Early June is the peak planting time for gardeners throughout the Rockies. Air and soil temperatures have finally warmed and seed germination is more reliable and transplants quickly adjust to these warmer outdoor conditions.

Annuals really show off their beauty as warm weather settles in this month. As cool-weather pansies begin to give out, have a few new transplants ready to replace the waning plants.

Take photographs of your flowering bulb beds before they are all finished. This will help you plan future beds and know which plants may need replacing. Consider experimenting with different colors and forms.

Roses are at their peak this month unless "the white combine" (hail) hits your garden. Many of the one-time bloomers will be finishing up depending upon your elevation. Hybrid tea roses are beginning to peak by mid-month. The first flushes of bloom are the freshest and most abundant. Be sure to provide adequate water and a balanced rose food to keep them in their prime. Try the rose tonic in the homemade remedies section.

Continue to make entries in your garden journal or notebook. This will help you keep track of plants that are doing well and those that are not. Note what kinds of pests and diseases are showing up. Jot down these observations so you can refer to them as needed.

Develop a watering schedule that meets the needs of the plants. Gardens differ in soil types, sun, and wind exposure. To find out the moisture needs of your garden, dig down 2 to 4 inches and check to see if the soil is drying out. Then, give the plants a good soaking with an inch of water. Deep watering encourages a deeper root system and better drought resistance.

This is a month of transitions in the Rockies. Spring-flowering shrubs are finishing up bloom, while summer-flowering types are setting bud. The sweet fragrance of mockorange will soon fill the air. Summer, and its rising temperatures, is just around the corner. Visit public and private gardens to get inspired and gather new ideas to incorporate into your landscape

PLAN

ANNUALS

It's helpful to keep a journal or notebook to record information on how well your plants are performing in the garden. This will help you evaluate which plants look and do best. If you need to redesign your garden, notes will come in handy for reference.

Consider planting annuals to fill in the gaps left from some of the perennials that begin to die back, such as bleeding heart and Oriental poppies.

If you're planning a vacation, make arrangements with a neighbor or friend to take care of your garden while you're away.

■ *Disbud mums now to create fuller-looking plants in a couple of months.*

BULBS

As summer approaches, many of the summer-flowering bulbs are forming flower buds and getting ready to put on their show. Consider disbudding some that produce lots of tiny buds, such as dahlias. This will make the main flower grow larger.

Keep notes on which plants are performing best and note where they are planted. Knowing where the bulbs are planted will prevent you from digging or cultivating too deeply when you set new plants around the ripened foliage. Consider marking the designated areas with plant stakes to list the variety and color. You can safely plant companion perennials

and groundcovers in bulb beds to keep the beds looking good year-round.

Photograph your bulb beds before they are all finished. This will help you plan future beds and know which plants may need replacing. Consider experimenting with different colors and forms.

Catalogs featuring spring-flowering bulbs are already arriving in the mail. Pre-ordering fresh bulbs will save you time, and many mail-order companies offer discounts. The bulbs will not be shipped until later in the fall at the appropriate planting time for your area.

Make sure you have enough mulch and compost for the summer season. Use this formulat to calculate what you need: Multiply the area (length times width measured in feet) by the desired depth (in feet) of mulch or compost. Covert this volume from cubic feet to cubic yards by dividing by 27 (the number of cubic feet in a cubic yard). This is the amount of material you will need to have on hand.

EDIBLES

Plan to harvest crops when they begin to reach their prime.

Plan the late-summer and autumn garden. You can start to decide what to plant in cool-weather conditions after certain crops are finished. Some areas of the garden will be vacated after the harvest of bush beans, leaving room for a fall crop of radishes or spinach. Succession planting will keep the garden productive and prevent weed invasions.

Planning means you can start cool-weather seedlings now so they will be ready to set out later in the season. Stock up on fresh seed-starting mixture and other supplies for new transplants. Purchase seeds of cool-weather crops now while they are still in supply. Look for cabbage, broccoli, cauliflower, and Brussels sprouts.

LAWNS

If you normally collect and bag lawn clippings after each mowing, plan to recycle your grass clippings as you mow. If you mow frequently enough, recycled grass clippings can contribute slow-acting fertilizer to the lawn. Grass clippings

If you usually collect grass clippings with a mower bag, consider mulching them with the mower instead, to add nutrients to the soil.

contain up to 4 percent nitrogen, .5 to 1 percent phosphorus, 2 to 3 percent potassium, and smaller amounts of other essential nutrients. Don't waste this valuable fertilizer source.

PERENNIALS

If you haven't started a garden journal, now is the time. Record dates of perennial bloom, how long the flowers last, special cultural requirements, pest and disease problems, and other features. A perennial garden has a relatively short bloom period, though the plants will display foliage for much of the growing season. This is one reason to choose varieties that have attractive foliage to add interest and texture to the garden. By keeping a record of your plant selections, you can determine if you have the right mix of spring-blooming, summer-blooming, and fall-blooming perennials for an all-season display. Consider chrysanthemums, asters, rudbeckia, 'Autumn Joy' sedum, and blanket flower.

ROSES

It is a good time to keep notes on varieties that you like for fragrance, color, and form. You may want to rogue out those that are not performing to your standards.

Rose bushes that are integrated with perennials and other shrubs will manage pretty well on their own. Plan to spend some time deadheading spent flowers and checking for pest problems on a weekly basis. Growing disease-resistant varieties will save you time and energy.

Hybrid tea roses require more of your time if you want them to produce an abundance of flowers. When several roses are planted in relatively close proximity, the incidence of disease and insect pests increases. Monitor these situations daily to prevent severe problems later.

Enjoy your rose garden during its peak blooming. Pick fresh bouquets to display indoors. And remember to keep notes in your garden journal. List some of the following:

- Blooming times of each variety
- Size and condition of the blooms
- Size of the plant
- Disease problems
- Insect pests
- Bushes that should be removed and replaced

Cut roses early in morning or at dusk. Cut blooms in the late bud stage, just showing colored petals. Use sharp hand pruners to make a clean cut, cutting the selected stem at a 45-degree angle back to where a five-leaflet outward-facing leaf bud joins it. Immerse the stems immediately in a bucket of warm water. Place the cut roses in a cool, shaded place, and allow them a few hours to absorb water. Re-cut the stem ends, and create a bouquet.

Cut a rose just above a leaf bud.

SHRUBS

Plan to be on watch for the pests of summer. Routinely monitoring your garden, at least every few days, will help prevent severe problems.

If you don't have shrubs that will bloom later in the season, you still have plenty of time to plant some. Garden stores have container-grown shrubs that will bloom from mid- to late summer through early fall. One of my favorites is butterfly bush (*Buddleia* spp.), which is a magnet for summer's butterflies and hummingbirds. Don't forget to include shrubs that produce attractive autumn berries such as cotoneaster, honeysuckle, firethorn, and snowberry to feed the wild birds that visit your landscape.

Plan to evaluate how shrubs are performing. Corrective pruning may be needed to improve shape and flowering. Some may need replacement because they're just not working for the area.

TREES

This is the month to enjoy the beauty and shade provided by your valuable trees and to visit private and public gardens to see which trees are blooming. These visits will inspire and educate you about what grows successfully in your area. Take a camera and notebook so you can keep a record of deciduous and evergreen trees that are of particular interest. You may want to add one or more to your landscape next year.

VINES, GROUNDCOVERS & ORNAMENTAL GRASSES

Vines need sturdy supports to hold them in place for a good display. Take time to check the bolts, nails, eyehooks, or other types of fasteners holding a wire matrix or wooden trellis out from a wall. Make sure they are secure. Check the footings of arbors and pergolas that must bear the weight of heavy grape vines, trumpet vines, wisterias, or climbing hydrangeas. It's a good idea to have twist ties or soft twine handy to secure the stems of vines that tend to wander. Proper training early in their growth will save time and prevent damage to the stems.

Think about ordering hardy bulbs for interplanting with existing groundcovers. Pre-season discounts from mail-order catalogs should entice you to act soon. As the spring segues into summer, take photographs of your landscape, and record when plants are in bloom.

PLANT

ANNUALS

If you didn't get your annuals planted last month, there's still time to add them to your garden. Look for bargains as garden retailers start to clear out their stock. Even if the plants have gotten a little leggy, cut them back before or during transplanting. Warm weather and proper care will have them blooming in just a few weeks.

Continue to fill in the void spaces left after spring bulbs complete their blooming cycle. Annuals will serve as a living groundcover, shading the soil and reducing weed invasions.

Plant extra annuals in decorative containers, pots, planters, window boxes, and various flea market finds. Let your imagination run wild and create beauty throughout the landscape.

BULBS

It's last call for planting summer-flowering bulbs; they need adequate time to root in, grow, and flower. If you don't have outdoor garden space for dahlias, cannas, begonias, and caladiums, try growing them in large pots. Use a well-drained

■ *Anything can be a flowerpot.*

potting mixture and containers with drainage holes. Plant out another grouping of gladiolus corms so there will be glads blooming in succession when the first batch finishes.

Mix slow-release granular fertilizer into the potting mixture prior to planting bulbs in containers. This will save you time. Most slow-acting fertilizers last for several months.

EDIBLES

In higher elevations with shorter growing seasons, the soil temperatures are rising, and it's time to plant vegetables and herbs in containers or garden beds. Hardened-off plants of tomatoes, peppers, and eggplants should be put in their permanent summer homes. However, there can still be nights with frost, so be prepared to cover the tender plants or have the containers on rollers so they can be easily moved to the garage or indoors overnight.

Early June is the last call for planting pumpkins and watermelons to allow them sufficient time to grow and mature before fall frost. You can purchase seedlings, but my preference is to direct-seed them in the garden the first week in June. Allow plenty of space for these crops as they vine. Bush varieties produce smaller fruits.

If space permits, plant more sweet corn, beans, and late cucumbers. Replant the pea patch with something else as soon as you have harvested all the pea pods. If you plant the early determinate tomatoes, you still have time to plant midseason varieties now. These will grow and produce a fresh crop of tomatoes when the early ones are finished.

HERE'S HOW

TO PLANT VEGETABLE TRANSPLANTS

1. Set out your plants. It is always tempting to cram a lot of vegetable plants into a small space, especially when they're little transplants. Resist that urge! Follow instructions on the package about spacing. You can always thin seeds, but transplants are too expensive to throw away.

2. Plant tomatoes deep and plant everything else so that the plant's rootball matches the soil level surrounding the planting hole. You don't need to put fertilizer in the planting hole.

3. Spread mulch around the plants. Mulch is just as important in vegetable gardens as it is in flower gardens because it helps keep water in the soil, moderates the soil temperature, and prevents weeds from sprouting. Use wheat straw or grass clippings in vegetable gardens. Warm-season veggies like it hot. If you don't have straw or grass clippings, you can actually use black plastic as a "mulch." It will trap the heat in the soil.

TO PLANT A PERENNIAL GARDEN

1. Measure the area where you're planning to plant the garden. Take length and width measurements and multiply them to get the square footage of the planting bed. You'll use these when calculating the amounts of soil, mulch, and plants to purchase for the garden bed.

2. Add 2 inches of soil or compost to the bed. To determine the total cubic feet needed, multiply the area of the bed (length × width) by 2 and divide by 12. (For 3 inches of mulch, multiply the entire area of the bed by 3 and divide by 12.)

3. Use a 4-tine claw or hard rake to mix the soil into the planting bed. In new housing developments, topsoil is scraped off and sold. Adding compost or garden soil replenishes nutrients and helps plants grow.

4. Set the plants out where you want to plant them. Stagger the plants so they aren't arranged in straight lines. You can also create groupings with one of each type of plant and repeat the groupings in several places throughout the flowerbed. If you know you'll have time to plant on the same day that you set out the plants, take all of the plants out of their containers before you set them in the planting bed—you'll save yourself a lot of time.

5. Dig the planting holes just as deep as the rootballs of the plants. If you're planting larger perennials (plants in gallon-sized containers), use a spade or shovel for quick work. Really pay attention to the depth of your planting hole. Perennials can't handle being planted too deep. The top of the rootball of a plant should be level with, or just slightly higher than, the ground around it.

LAWNS

Patch bare spots in the lawn caused by wear and tear or by weeds that choke out the grass. Cut pieces of sod from the edges of the lawn or that has crept into flower or shrub beds and reinstall to the bare spots of your lawn. Keep the newly planted sod sections moist daily for a week or more to ensure that it roots in. It is helpful to prepare the soil where bare spots appear so that the new sod pieces will be able to root in more quickly during the heat of summer. It is getting too late to seed unless you can water diligently.

PERENNIALS

Before the weather turns hot, continue to plant perennials that were grown in containers. Reduce transplant shock by planting on a cool, cloudy day. Perennials that are left in their pots will languish, dry out, and become rootbound.

ROSES

By this time, the majority of your planting and transplanting should be complete, well before the major blooming period. It's too late for planting bare-root plants.

However, you can still remove and replace roses that are not performing up to your standards.

Garden retailers should still have good selections of container-grown plants available. Rose bushes are already in full foliage and are blooming in their containers. They will transplant fairly well over the next few weeks as long as the weather is not too hot or dry. These can be planted up to early fall following planting guidelines from March and April.

Whenever possible, pick a cloudy day to plant, or shade the new plants with a large cardboard box for a few days to allow them to acclimate in hot weather.

SHRUBS

You can still plant container-grown shrubs, but the earlier in the month, the better. Summer's heat can take its toll on newly transplanted shrubs unless you give them extra attention to help them get established. Daily misting of the foliage, covering the shrub with a large cardboard box

for a few days to allow it to acclimate, mulching, and watching your watering carefully are some things to help ensure late-planted shrubs will make it successfully.

It is too late to move established shrubs from one part of the landscape to another; put this project off till next spring. Some shrubs can be propagated now by layering the flexible stems. If a branch of shrub is wounded and the wound covered with a rooting medium—loose soil or sphagnum peat moss—the branch will usually strike roots while it is still attached to the parent shrub. It can then be severed from the parent plant and transplanted as a new shrub. Layering is best done in late spring or early summer; rooting is most vigorous in cooler temperatures.

TREES

So many trees are available as container-grown stock, but the planting time is limited by extremely hot weather or drought. If you plant in June, take special precautions to ensure success. Newly planted trees need regular watering for the first six to twelve months. Unless you are willing to put in the time and commitment, wait until early fall when the odds of successful transplanting are more favorable.

VINES, GROUNDCOVERS & ORNAMENTAL GRASSES

You still have plenty of time to plant containerized vines, ornamental grasses, and groundcovers. These are available at garden retailers and nurseries throughout the region. Get them into the ground as soon as possible, though, before the heat really turns on.

Ornamental grasses do best if planted sooner rather than later so they have time to establish before they begin to set flower stalks. This will allow them to develop a strong root system and survive the winter.

If you have tender tropical vines indoors and like to bring them outside to a covered patio or deck, now is the time. Acclimate them gradually to the outside conditions and sunshine. Bougainvillea, California ivy, mandevilla, and angel's trumpet are a few that can be summered outdoors in filtered sunlight.

This would be a good time to repot indoor vines that are outgrowing their containers. Use a soilless potting mixture and choose a pot that is an inch or two larger in diameter. Carefully remove the vine and support when doing the transplanting, and replace the stake or support into the new container.

CARE

ANNUALS

Always cut and remove the flower stem at the place where it meets the main plant stem. If you only cut off the flower, you'll have ugly stems hanging around.

New growth only sprouts from buds along the main stem.

Keep annuals looking fresh and promote more blooms by deadheading faded flowers. Pinch off or snip with scissors the faded blooms of annuals such as petunia, marigold, annual phlox, verbena, and others. Also, remove yellowing or dead foliage to reduce the spread of leaf diseases.

Thin seeded annuals if they become overcrowded. Plants should be spaced 4 to 6 inches apart. This will ensure that plants will get sufficient light and air circulation to grow into healthy and floriferous

■ *Use your scissors, snips, or hand pruners to snip off dead flowers.*

annuals. Carefully pull up or clip the less-vigorous, overcrowded plants.

BULBS

If your bulbs are getting too leggy, it may be a sign of poor light. As landscapes mature, shade from trees and large shrubs will change the amount and duration of good light in a specific area. Some of these plants may need more staking or wire support rings around them. Make a note of this so you will know where to plant in following seasons.

Pinch off or cut faded blooms. This will stimulate the plants to produce more buds and blooms. Pick up fallen leaves and flower petals at the base of the plants to discourage slugs and other thugs from invading the garden. Remove yellow leaves and broken stems to keep the flowerbed looking fresh.

Dahlias and gladiolus are in bloom and can be cut for indoor bouquets.

EDIBLES

Apply mulch around vegetable rows to suppress weed growth, conserve water, and keep vegetables clean.

As vegetables finish their season, pull out the · bolted (seed-forming) lettuce, spent broccoli stems, and other cool-season crops to make room for the warm-season crops. Continue to thin root crops if they are growing too closely; refer to the seed packet. Use the tops of beets and turnips as salad greens. If you like to grow tall tomatoes with a strong single stem, now is the time to train the plants onto a fence, trellis, stake, or tomato cage. Tomato fruit that is kept off the ground gets better air circulation, ripens more uniformly, and is less prone to insect and disease problems.

Pinch and prune the tips of herbs to delay premature flowering and encourage more branching and compact growth, as well as sweeten the foliage.

To grow indeterminate tomatoes with less suckering, break off side suckers at the point of origin. This will direct energy to the main stem. A few tomato suckers are acceptable and will eventually develop flowers and fruit. Note: determinate tomato varieties grow multiple stems that are not suckers and that will develop flowers and fruit.

Cover your cherry trees with a protective netting and stake down to prevent birds from getting under the netting.

LAWNS

Continue to keep your lawn growing thick to prevent the invasion of weeds. In compacted areas where there is more foot traffic, you can spot-aerate with a hand aerator to break through the soil compaction. This will permit water to soak in and introduce air to the ailing root system. Once the lawn is aerated, topdress with fine compost, and water the areas thoroughly to prevent them from drying out.

Later in the dog days of summer, cool-season grasses such as Kentucky bluegrass will naturally acclimate to drought conditions by going dormant. The green will diminish, but this does not indicate that your lawn is dead. To help cool-season grasses cope during drought periods, encourage them to grow deep roots with good management practices. Use slow-release fertilizers instead of quick-acting types. Core aerate in the spring and autumn. Water deeply and infrequently. Keep weeds at bay.

As the spring growth spurt begins to stall with the onset of hotter weather, your lawn will generally need less frequent mowing. It will depend on the vigor it developed earlier in the season to sustain hot, dry periods.

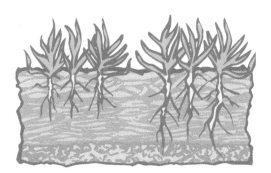

Short, frequent waterings lead to shallow roots, while deep infrequent waterings encourage deep roots.

You will generally be mowing less often this month, unless natural rainfall is abundant. Recycle grass clippings if possible. If you collect clippings, mix them into the compost pile.

Make sure your lawn mower blade is sharp; have a spare in the garage to change periodically. Keep the mowing height for cool-season grasses at 2 to 3 inches so the lawn will not brown out in the summer heat.

Alter mowing patterns to minimize soil compaction and wear on the turf. Mow in horizontal rows one week, in vertical rows the next, and in diagonal rows the third week. It will give your lawn a professional look.

PERENNIALS

If you haven't added mulch around your perennials, do so before the plants get so full that it becomes a difficult chore. A 2-inch layer of compost, shredded wood shavings, or pine needles will work nicely. Do *not* place plastic under the mulch, as this impedes the movement of air and water to the root system. In fact, plastic mulches tend to encourage shallow root growth. If you decide to use artificial mulch, choose a landscape fabric that will allow water, air, and nutrients to get to the roots. However, even landscape fabrics can interfere with the natural propagation process of most perennials.

Support perennials that develop taller stems or large clumps. Waiting too late makes it difficult to set in cages or stakes, and you generally end up breaking stems and flower buds. Train the stems to grow upright early in the season instead of waiting until they begin to flop.

Continue to pinch back the stretching stems of hardy chrysanthemums by half to encourage more branching and a more compact plant. This will result in more flowers in late summer and fall. Pinching will delay the development of buds, so you can follow this technique every few weeks until the end of the month if you want flowers in late August and September. If you decide not to pinch back mums, they will bloom earlier in the season, and this may be your preference.

To train or guide the growth of other perennials, cut back newly growing stems by one-third to half after they have grown a foot tall. This will delay flowering but will control the height and spread of the plants. Try this on beebalm, asters, goldenrod,

■ *Stake tall, floppy plants early or you'll risk breaking their stems.*

and artemisias. Experiment with other perennials too. Plants are resilient and can be trained to fit just about any space.

Prune off the stems of daylilies whose blooms have faded. This will promote development of new flowering stems and buds in reblooming varieties. It also improves the appearance of the plants.

ROSES

Keep the rose garden tidy while the plants are in their prime. Add fresh mulch as needed, and edge the beds if grass is beginning to invade. Pull or dig weeds as soon as you spot them.

Continue to check climbers and ramblers to make sure they are securely fastened to their supports. New growth continues throughout the early season. Flexible rose canes can be carefully woven or tied to supports and will promote more blooming laterals.

Remember that growing hybrid tea roses takes a bit more effort if you want healthy plants and abundant flowering. Deadhead spent flowers daily, remove yellow or diseased leaves, and apply preventative sprays to reduce pest invasions and diseases.

Cut and enjoy your hybrid tea roses for colorful bouquets. Clip off spent flowers to encourage more

blooms. Prune stems back to just above a point where a second five-leaflet faces outward on the stem. This will stimulate the production of new buds and helps control the shape of the bush.

Some landscape roses such as Meidiland®, Carefree, and polyantha do not require frequent deadheading of spent blooms to maintain flower production. However, if you have time, pruning does improve a plant's appearance and helps to keep the bushes more compact and shapely.

SHRUBS

Limit pruning to removing broken, storm-damaged, or diseased branches from now until autumn. Do not shear new growth on shrubs, as this will only induce fast-growing water sprouts or "witches' broom." These succulent shoots are more susceptible to winter injury and desiccation.

Remove spent or dead blooms from flowering shrubs unless they are types that typically produce fruit. This will help to tidy the plant. Don't delay this process, as late pruning will remove flower buds that are developing for next year.

TREES

Use either a ring of mulch or stakes around the bases of tree trunks to protect bark from "lawnmoweritis." Do whatever is necessary to avoid damaging the tender bark.

Remove the support stakes from trees planted last year. The root system has had adequate time to grow and can generally support the tree by now. Trees need to have some natural movement to grow a strong and healthy trunk.

Prune out dead or damaged branches immediately. Summer storms can leave wounds that are vulnerable to insect and disease entry. Consult with an arborist to remove large branches damaged by storms. Be sure the company is licensed and bonded.

If some branches are still bare, don't assume they are entirely dead and prune them off. Be patient. To determine whether a branch is still alive, bend some of the twigs or branches to see if they are flexible. You can also do the "fingernail" test: scrape the bark with your fingernail to see if there

■ *A mulch ring will also protect your tree's trunk from "lawnmoweritis."*

is moist, green cambium beneath the bark. It may take a little extra time for some branches to leaf out if the tree is under stress. Brittle, brown twigs are dead and should be pruned back to where the wood shows signs of life.

VINES, GROUNDCOVERS & ORNAMENTAL GRASSES

Keep newly transplanted groundcover beds, vines, and ornamental grasses mulched with compost, pole peelings, or shredded cedar. This will help conserve moisture and suppress weed growth. Do not pile mulch on the stems of the plants or they can stay too wet and succumb to rot, insect pests, or rodent damage.

Some groundcover plants will do best if they are periodically pinched back to maintain colorful foliage. Routinely pinch off the flowers from lamb's ears, artemisias, and the shade-loving coleus.

Pansies are starting to lose their vigor as the heat arrives. They often become yellow and leggy. You can replace them with other annuals that work as groundcovers such as nasturtiums, portulaca, salvias, marigolds, and creeping zinnias.

Once wisteria has finished blooming, it is known to produce leafy stems with gusto. Prune any excess growth back before the buds for next year start to develop. This should be done no later than mid-July by to ensure you don't inadvertently cut

off the next year's buds. Now is the time to control the spread, size, and direction of the vine.

Pinch back the faded flowers from clematis and honeysuckle unless you want them to produce seedpods. Prune spring-flowering clematis as soon as it finishes blooming. Cut back woody groundcover plants anytime you need to tidy them up. This will allow them to produce fresh, new growth.

WATER

ANNUALS

When rainfall is limited and we experience prolonged dry periods for more than a week, it is important to maintain uniform soil moisture. Water annuals with drip irrigation systems, soaker hoses wound around the plants, or the old-fashioned frog-eye sprinklers. Water early in the day so the foliage is dry by nighttime.

To conserve water, keep the soil cool, and prevent weeds, spread a 1- to 2-inch layer of mulch around transplants. Shredded cedar, pine needles, and pole peelings are some good organic mulches.

To save time and to provide uniform moisture, install a drip irrigation system or wrap leaky, or soaker, hoses around your annuals. They apply water directly to the soil around the plants and reduce overhead watering that may result in leaf diseases.

Check automatic watering systems monthly to make sure they're not clogged. A system that is not working properly will result in stressed or wilted plants.

BULBS

Monitor the watering of bulb beds carefully this month. It is important to let spring-flowering bulbs go into dormancy, so don't overwater to the point where the soil becomes waterlogged. It is amazing how bulbs can survive prolonged periods of drought. Their underground storage organs self-protect the hardy spring-flowering bulbs until their cycle starts again in the fall. Most hardy bulbs prefer and do best with drier conditions. Plant companion perennials and annuals with hardy spring-flowering bulbs that are more drought-tolerant, rather than with those that have greater water needs.

Summer-flowering bulbs will need more attention to watering as they are growing vigorously and setting flower buds. Check the soil moisture by probing into the ground 2 to 3 inches; if it is becoming dry, give them a good watering.

EDIBLES

Deep watering in summer is essential to encourage deeper-rooting, drought-resistant vegetables. Provide at least an inch of water to the garden per week. Use either a drip irrigation system, soaker hoses between rows, or a frog-eye sprinkler that delivers water at a low arc over a larger zone. Set out rain gauges to measure the amount of water applied, and time how long it takes to put on 1 inch of water per garden area.

Tomatoes do best with a uniform supply of moisture, rather than going through a wet-dry cycle. Otherwise, tomatoes (and peppers) will develop a condition known as blossom-end rot (BER).

Keep container-grown vegetables and herbs watered when soilless mixtures feel dry to the touch. Do not allow the plants to dry to the point of wilting because this will make them less productive and more prone to pests.

LAWNS

If we've been experiencing continued drought years, lack of winter and spring moisture, it is critical to begin a deep, infrequent watering regime during the summer. This will maintain a deep, healthy, and more drought-enduring root system.

Water *established* lawns in good soil only when it has not rained for a week to ten days. Then when you do water, water deeply to sustain the roots. Lawns that are growing in poor soil conditions tend to dry out sooner.

Keep *new* sod watered until it is established. Spot-water the edges of the new sod to prevent it from curling up and drying out.

Have your automatic sprinkler system checked to make sure it is delivering water properly and

efficiently. Remember, plants don't waste water, people do.

PERENNIALS

Keep established perennials deeply watered with about an inch of water weekly. Those in sandy soils will need more attention because the soil drains so quickly. Apply organic mulches to help retain moisture and reduce the need for frequent watering. If you mixed a balance of organic matter into the soil at planting time, this will provide better moisture-holding capacity, plus support nutrients that the roots can assimilate.

Since everyone's soil is a bit different, check soil moisture to determine your watering schedule. Use a garden trowel to dig down to a depth of 4 inches or more. If the soil is beginning to dry out, give the

HERE'S HOW

TO MEASURE WATER FROM A SPRINKLER

To determine the rate at which your sprinkler dispenses water to different areas, clean out eight to ten tuna cans (or cat food cans, whichever is available) and place them in a random pattern around the sprinkler. Turn on the sprinkler and let it run for fifteen minutes. Turn off the sprinkler and measure how much water is in the cans. That number times 4 is the hourly rate of your sprinkler, for each different area. If your goal is to spread ½ inch of water in two weekly waterings, determine how long you need to run the sprinkler by dividing .5 by the hourly rate. Supplement the areas that are underwatered as necessary.

perennials a deep soaking. During extended periods of drought, check soil moisture often, and mulch to help reduce evaporation and prevent runoff.

ROSES

Properly mulched roses will get along fine with usual spring weather and can endure much better when summer's heat arrives. Even so, give established roses a deep drink at least once a week to maintain their vigor and promote repeat flowering.

SHRUBS

Check the soil underneath the mulch of newly planted and established shrubs every three to four days. Give them a good, deep drink of water if it is dry. Use a soaker hose or frog-eye sprinkler and irrigate slowly to allow the water to soak in deeply. If you have large planters or containers that are out in the garden, don't forget to water them every few days or as the soil begins to dry out.

Just because a shrub's foliage is wilting does *not* mean the plant needs water. Excessive heat, poor drainage, or root stress may cause wilting. Wait to see what happens later in the day when temperatures fall to check if the leaves remain wilted. If they regain their form and are no longer wilting, it was the ambient heat. Always check the soil before watering.

TREES

During the heat of summer, trees perform best on 2 inches of water per week. This can be critical to their survival during extended drought periods. Water slowly and deeply by using a frog-eye sprinkler, or if feasible, install soaker hoses or drip irrigation underneath the mulch of your smaller, medium, or newly transplanted trees. Use organic mulches under trees to reduce moisture evaporation and prevent runoff of excess water from sprinkling or a hard rain. I find it helpful to core-aerate over tree root zones so water will percolate through compacted soils and reach the roots.

VINES, GROUNDCOVERS & ORNAMENTAL GRASSES

When rainfall is scarce, newly planted groundcovers, vines, and ornamental grasses need supplemental irrigation. Mulched plants will need to be watered less frequently, but check underneath the mulch by digging down 4 inches or so with a garden trowel.

When the soil is getting dry to the touch, it is time to do some deep watering. Most of these plants prefer deep, infrequent watering rather than frequent light sprinklings.

Vines in containers or pots will need checking often to make sure they are not stressed to the point of wilting. Most potting mixtures dry out quickly in the hot sun and wind. Use a water-saving polymer in the soil mix to help retain moisture longer.

FERTILIZE

ANNUALS

If there is no slow-release fertilizer in the soil, you can apply water-soluble fertilizer at intervals recommended on the label. Most annuals are heavy feeders and utilize lots of nutrients from the soil over the growing season.

Organic-based, granular fertilizer can be applied monthly. Sprinkle around the plants and water in thoroughly.

Fertilize annuals in containers to keep them growing vigorously and blooming. Frequent watering of container gardens tends to leach out nutrients more rapidly. Apply fertilizer to a moist soil, never to dry potting soil.

BULBS

If you worked in a slow-release granular fertilizer in the spring for summer-flowering bulbs, there is no need to fertilize at this time.

Bulbs growing in containers may need supplemental fertilizer since you are watering more frequently. Use water-soluble fertilizer diluted to half-strength. Apply every two weeks while the plants are blooming.

When applying liquid fertilizers to container-grown plants, the soil should be moist, not dry. Never apply fertilizer to dry soil or if the plant is wilted and dry.

EDIBLES

If you incorporated a slow-release granular fertilizer into the soil at planting time, you should not need additional fertilizer now. If you prefer a water-soluble plant fertilizer, dilute it to half-strength, and apply at biweekly intervals to a moist soil, never to a dry soil. Plants that may have been slightly damaged by hail or wind early in the season will benefit from a light foliar feeding from a water-soluble plant fertilizer. Apply this early in the morning or later evening so the plants can absorb the nutrients directly through their leaves as well as roots.

LAWNS

If you used a fast-acting, water-soluble fertilizer in the spring, it may be necessary to repeat another application the latter part of the month. I generally wait until the first part of July (July 4) to make the second fertilizer application.

Nitrogen needs to be available to grass plants as it continues to grow with cooler weather. As the temperatures get higher, slow-acting fertilizers are best. These provide nutrients over a more extended period, four to six weeks, depending upon the product. Read the package label.

Never fertilize a lawn that is already stressed by drought or heat. This will only add insult to injury.

PERENNIALS

If you added a slow-release granular at planting time, this fertilizer will continue to provide nutrients as the plants need them. Check the package label to see how long the fertilizer will last.

Perennials growing in containers will benefit from the application of a soluble plant fertilizer since you are watering the soil mix more often and nutrients will leach out. Follow label directions for dilution rates and application frequency. Dilute the fertilizer to half-strength and apply at every other watering to prevent buildup of soluble salts in the soil.

ROSES

Sprinkle a slow-release granular fertilizer over the root zone of container-grown roses planted in June so they get an extra boost after transplanting. Lightly scratch into the soil surface and water in well.

Roses that repeat blooming over the summer will benefit from another application of granular fertilizer as early March applications are becoming depleted by now. Most slow-release products last eight to ten weeks.

Hybrid tea roses and other repeat bloomers appreciate a monthly fertilizer application to give them an extra boost for continued flowering. Use either fast-acting, water-soluble products or the homemade rose tonic on page 222. Read and follow label directions for dilution rates and amounts to apply.

SHRUBS

Once shrubs complete their flowering cycle and produce seasonal growth, there is little need for additional fertilizer. Fast-release fertilizer can stimulate excessive stem growth, which stresses the plant during drought periods, may attract pests such as aphids, and interfere with winter dormancy.

TREES

I recommend that you limit tree fertilizing to spring. Only when you have an expert diagnosis of a nutrient-related problem should you apply a fertilizer this month. For example, if your trees have iron chlorosis (yellowing leaves with green veins), it would be necessary to fertilize. However, do not fertilize when trees are stressed by heat, drought, pests, or disease problems.

Granular slow-release fertilizers release nutrients consistently and gradually over the growing season as soil temperatures and moisture are adequate to help trees utilize the nutrients. Fertilizing in the spring will sustain older trees in your landscape, and the younger ones should do just fine too. Remember that when you apply lawn fertilizer, trees growing in and around lawn areas will benefit.

VINES, GROUNDCOVERS & ORNAMENTAL GRASSES

The application of a slow-release granular fertilizer earlier in the year should suffice for most vines, groundcovers, and ornamental grasses. If you did not apply a slow-release product then, then apply a water-soluble plant fertilizer according to the manufacturer's recommendations. Remember, *it is better to underfertilize* than it is to feed plants too often. Blooming vines do not appreciate high doses of high-nitrogen plant fertilizers and often fail to bloom well.

PROBLEM-SOLVE

ANNUALS

Pests will arrive in the garden as the weather continues to warm up. Aphids are among the first to attach to the soft and succulent growth of annuals, sapping away their energy and vigor. An easy way to combat aphids is by hosing them off the plants as soon as you spot them. Also, make a homemade soap spray to keep them at bay.

Be on the watch for the beginning stages of powdery mildew disease; a light, white powder will form on the foliage and stems. Make sure plants are getting good air circulation and use the homemade mildew control (see page 220) to prevent a severe problem.

If we experience frequent afternoon rain showers, weeds will pop up in the garden just about daily. Hoe, handpull, or dig weeds as soon as you spot them. They are much easier to control when young with a shallow root system.

BULBS

Warmer weather signals the season for slugs (snails without shells) and they are fond of the succulent growth of dahlias, begonias, caladiums, and other tender bulbs. One method of control is to trap slugs with the homemade slug trap. Place shallow, empty tuna cans buried with the rim at ground

■ *Use beer traps or diatomaceous earth to prevent slugs from damaging your plants. To make a beer trap, put a shallow jar or butter lid on the ground next to the afflicted plant. Fill the trap with beer to catch the slugs. Slugs don't like the sharp edges of diatomaceous earth.*

level and fill with a solution of 1 teaspoon sugar and ¼ teaspoon yeast dissolved in a cup of warm water. Slugs crawl in and drown; dispose each morning and reset traps.

You can also discourage them by sprinkling diatomaceous earth (DE) around the base of the plants. The tiny, sharp diatoms will stop slugs in their slithering tracks.

Be on the watch for spider mites making attacks on the foliage of dahlias. Stippled foliage and fine webbing are clues that they are present. Wash down the foliage with water or use a homemade soap spray.

Tiny thrips can attack gladiolus and will rasp at the leaves and flower buds. The leaves will take on a grayish green cast and the buds won't open normally. If they are a major problem, apply a systemic insecticide. Read and follow label directions.

EDIBLES

Insect season is in full swing. Watch for invasions of aphids on herbs and vegetables. At the first signs of invasion, wash them down with a spray of water or use a homemade soap spray (see page 220).

Flea beetles may invade the garden and puncture tiny holes in the foliage of many leafy crops. You can use insecticidal soap sprays or Neem oil to thwart these beasties. Repeat sprays after a rain shower or after overhead watering since this reduces the effectiveness of the control.

Colorado potato beetles can be spotted as oval, yellow-and-black striped beetles that feed on potato foliage. Look for their eggs as masses of soft yellow spots underneath the leaves. Pick them off and discard, or spray with Neem oil on both the upper and lower surfaces of the leaves.

■ *Colorado potato beetle*

Caterpillars of all sorts love the vegetable and herb garden. If you want to encourage the black swallowtail butterfly, be prepared to leave some of the parsley worms (the caterpillars of the black swallowtail) on the dill, parsley, and celery foliage. They will do minimal damage. Otherwise, handpick off excess numbers if they strip the foliage badly.

B.t. is a microbial insecticide that kills caterpillars and should be used with caution if you want to grow host plants for butterfly larvae. The use of B.t. can also reduce the damage from caterpillars that develop into butterflies and moths. Read and follow label directions.

Weeds need to be pulled or dug as soon as they appear in the garden after a good watering or a nice rain.

LAWNS
Be on the watch for white grubs in the lawn. Many will migrate closer to the surface from the deep soil where they spent the winter months as they begin to feed on the grass roots. Symptoms of grub damage can be detected if you can peel the grass back like a carpet. Tiny, C-shaped white grubs will be noticed. A healthy lawn can tolerate a fair number of grubs and the lawn will soon recover because stolons and rhizomes will fill in the damaged areas. However, if grub populations are severe, you may need to treat the lawn with a grub-control insecticide.

■ *White grub*

For the environmentally friendly lawn care provider: try using a biological grub control that consists of predatory nematodes or milky spore (*Bacillus popilliae*), a bacterium that targets soil-dwelling beetle larvae. These biological controls provide relatively long-term control. Follow directions on the label carefully for application techniques and frequency of use.

PERENNIALS
Warmer weather means slugs and other thugs are on the move. Slugs are snails without shells, and they love to invade the garden at dusk and during the night to feed on succulent foliage and stems. Look for the signs of slimy, shiny trails. They are known to hide under mulches or stones, so check these periodically for slugs and their eggs. If you find them, collect them and dispose in the trash or sprinkle them with wood ashes.

Tiny spider mites may be hard to detect. Check for mottling and a salt-and-pepper appearance on the leaves. If fine webbing is noted between the stems or on the underside of the foliage, it is likely that mites are making a run. Hose down the foliage, top and bottom, to discourage them.

If flower buds fail to open, you may have thrips. They feed by rasping the plant tissues and sucking out plant juices. Thrips can be controlled with insecticidal soaps early in the season or systemic insecticides when infestations are severe. Follow label directions for application rates and methods.

Continue to dig or handpull weeds while they are still young, and don't let them go to seed.

ROSES
Continue to monitor roses for infestations of aphids, spider mites, and thrips. Mites favor hot, dry weather and can be discouraged by hosing the undersides of the foliage every other day or two. Insecticidal soap sprays will also help control many rose pests.

Thrips are very small, slender, brownish yellow insects that hide inside the buds and blooms. They cause damage by rasping the flower petals. They can be a problem on white and light-colored varieties. Deadhead and dispose of spent blooms to reduce

■ *Red spider mite*

invasions. Insecticidal soap, Neem oil, pyrethrum-based insecticides, or systemic insecticides can be applied to the buds and blooms. Read and follow label directions.

If caterpillars attack the foliage, apply a product with B.t. (*Bacillus thurengiensis*) to the infested foliage following label directions. Caterpillars will soon become sick and die.

Rose slugs, a type of sawfly larvae, may damage the foliage. They can be controlled by sprinkling wood ashes on them; they soon become crispy critters. Neem oil can also be used for control measures.

SHRUBS
With the heat of summer arriving, it is important to monitor moisture in the soil to prevent stress to the shrubs. A stressed plant is more vulnerable to insect pests and diseases. Spread mulch around shrubs to retain moisture in the soil and prevent weeds.

Insect pest activity may be expected now. As soon as you notice aphids, caterpillars, sawflies, spider mites, and others, handpick or squish those you can reach. Wash off others with a strong stream of water from the hose. But—do not assume that every bug you see is a pest; they are many beneficial insects visiting the garden now. Look for ladybugs, lacewings, and praying mantises that are there to feed on the bad bugs.

Chlorosis may appear on certain shrubs; you will notice the foliage becoming pale or yellowing between darker green veins. This is usually an indication of iron deficiency. Although our region generally has iron in the soil, it is not readily available in a form that plants can utilize. It helps to acidify the soil by adding powdered sulfur over the root zone and watering it in. If the foliage does not green up in a few weeks, it is best to apply a chelated iron to the soil or leaves. Select an iron additive in the form of a wettable powder (WP will be on the label). Read and follow label directions.

TREES
Some trees such as cottonwood, aspen, and crabapples, drop leaves, twigs, bark, and fruit early in the summer, but this doesn't mean that they are in trouble. Some trees are inherently prone

to do this as they mature. Many older trees will routinely slough off strips or patches of bark, and evergreens will shed older needles or scaled leaves (junipers) to make way for fresh growth.

Be on the lookout for more aphids feeding on tender growth. Hose down with a forceful spray of water or use a soap spray. Larger trees may need attention from a professional arborist.

As temperatures begin to rise, spider mites will soon be on the scene. These minute pests will cause the foliage to turn a sickly yellow or brown. Look on the underside of the leaves to detect them. Fine webbing may be noticeable between leaves and twigs. If you have a severe infestation, use an appropriate miticide or consult with an arborist trained in treating for insect and mite problems.

Be on the watch for powdery mildew, a disease that looks like someone sprinkled flour on the leaves. It is usually caused by poor air circulation, and some trees are more susceptible than others. For small ornamental trees, tip-prune the heavily diseased areas, and dispose of the prunings.

Employing bacterial warfare can safely control caterpillars that feed on the foliage. Use B.t. (*Bacillus thuringiensis*) as soon as you see young larvae begin to feed on the leaves.

VINES, GROUNDCOVERS & ORNAMENTAL GRASSES
Aphids may be on the rampage now, so take action to wash them off infested plant parts. Once they fall to the ground in a shower of water, they're done. Pick off heavily infested tips or leaves and dispose in the trash. If you prefer, use a homemade soap spray or appropriate insecticide. Read and follow label directions.

Keep trapping the slugs that make their sneak attacks at night. Slugs and their kin are a nuisance, particularly in the shady areas of the yard.

Black vine weevil can be a serious pest to ground covers such as euonymus and vinca. Applying a soil insecticide may help eliminate these pests. Read and follow label directions and observe precautions when using any pesticide on groundcovers and vines.

July

By now, most planting is done and many get ready for summer vacations. When planning a trip, don't forget to have someone available to check your landscape. Containers will need watering, vegetables must be harvested and tended, and lawns must be mowed. Talk with neighbors and friends who share gardening interests and recruit them to help in your absence.

July is the month of heat and possible drought conditions. It is also a time to enjoy the shrubs in your landscape. Though the spring-flowering shrubs are finished by now, summer-flowering shrubs will continue to put on a show.

Properly placed shade trees make the landscape a wonderful retreat on hot summer days. Birds, butterflies, and squirrels find trees a nice retreat, so look upward to observe the happenings around you. So many things are going on in the landscape now.

Watering will need to be monitored regularly to meet the needs of landscape plants. Good landscaping techniques of choosing water-wise plants, soil preparation, mulching, and deep watering all combine to help conserve water throughout the yard and garden. Observe what grows natively in your area and plan accordingly.

Consider installing soaker hoses or drip irrigation system for ease of watering flowerbeds and vegetable gardens. Add a timer and you can set watering frequency and how long to water specific areas. It frees up your time to do other things and enjoy the summer.

July is one of the hottest months and insects seem to thrive and will attack succulent foliage and flowers. Remember, vigorous and healthy plants will tolerate some insect damage. When populations explode, take action to control pests by handpicking, hosing down with a stream of water, or soap sprays. Encourage beneficial insects such as ladybugs, lacewings, and parasitic wasps to keep bad bugs in check.

Aphids seem to thrive in hot weather and feed on the new tender growth of vines and groundcovers. Wash them off with a stream of water, or use a homemade soap spray (see homemade remedies on page 220).

July is a captivating month with many colorful flowers and you'll be harvesting a bounty of vegetables. Enjoy!

PLAN

ANNUALS

Remember to have someone take care of your plants if you go on vacation. Container-grown annuals can be grouped together near the water spigot and placed out of the direct, afternoon sun. Grouping the plants together will help conserve water, and shade will help reduce the need for frequent watering. If there are some containers that need more attention than others, insert colorful sprinkler-marking flags into those pots to bring attention to those plantings. Before you leave, water everything thoroughly. Weed and deadhead any faded or spent flowers.

If you are growing a cut flower garden and want to dry some of those flowers, plan to begin harvesting later in the month, and then continue into the early fall as the various plants begin to mature and produce near-perfect blooms. Have materials for drying on hand to use the minute you can pick the fresh blossoms that are blemish-free. Silica gel and a combination of borax and sand are good drying agents.

BULBS

Make plans to order your spring-flowering bulbs for fall delivery. The sooner you order, the better the selection.

This is the time to enjoy the many colors and forms of summer-blooming bulbs. Take time to watch the hummingbirds as they visit the blooming spikes of gladiolus.

Be prepared for hailstorms that can quickly damage the foliage and buds. Keep cardboard boxes on hand or large 5-gallon buckets to cover the plants.

Plan to cut some flowers for indoor arrangements, as many summer-flowering bulbs make wonderful cut flowers. Asiatic lilies, Oriental lilies, gladiolus, and dahlias are excellent cut flowers and add dimension to bouquets, plus they last a long time.

EDIBLES

In July, vegetable and herb gardens may be stressed by prolonged periods of heat and drought. Plan on regular watering to maintain healthy growth. If you haven't applied organic mulches around plants, do

■ *Denver Botanical Garden*

so now. Mulches help conserve water and maintain uniform moisture in the root zone. They also suppress weed growth that competes for water and nutrients.

Plan how you'll fill empty garden spots. You may choose a second crop of heat-tolerant vegetables, or you may prefer to mulch empty spots and wait until later to plant cool-weather vegetables. Check the seed packets to determine how many days are required till harvest, and count back to determine seed-planting time.

Plan on doing some insect and disease patrol, and clean up garden debris. If it is insect- and disease-free, add it to the compost pile. Keep the compost layers moist to hasten decomposition.

Make plans to provide supports to fruit-laden branches of peaches, plums, apples, and other tree fruits. The weight of the fruit can result in branches breaking and damaging the tree.

LAWNS

If you are planning a summer getaway, have someone mow you lawn if you'll be away for a week or more. Although the lawn is growing slower now, it will tend to look neglected after seven days and will reveal that no one is home.

It's convenient and time saving if you have an automatic sprinkler system to water your lawn wisely and efficiently. Get bids for installing one later in the season. Modern equipment eliminates the need for trenching, as a sprinkler system can be pulled under the sod and sprinkler heads installed as needed for designated zones.

If you have been plagued by disease and insect problems in your lawn over the years, plan a long-term strategy to combat these problems. Begin to investigate what the underlying causes might be so you can prevent them before they appear. It may be as simple as poor soil conditions, soil compaction, the wrong turf variety for the area, and buried debris underneath the turf. All these cause stress to lawn grasses, making them more susceptible to problems.

Consider having a professional turf expert evaluate your lawn and make suggestions. It will save you

time, money, and effort in the future. Keep a lawn care journal or notebook to help you track your lawn care practices and what kinds of materials you are applying.

PERENNIALS

As the dog days of summer approach, you may find that prolonged heat will cause a pause in perennial flowering. This is nature's way of acclimating the plants for survival. Your perennials continue to thrive through summer with adequate moisture and a bit of maintenance. Plan to add more mulch to conserve moisture where mulch has settled or blown away.

Make notes in your garden journal about which plants are responding best at this time of year. You might want to choose perennials to fill in the gaps for future years. If needed, plan to plant some annuals to add color to the bare spots.

Choose plants that have colorful foliage or variegated leaves to provide interest and texture. This will bridge the gap between peak flowering times of other perennials.

Look for plants with silver, white, yellow, or variegated leaves to add to the color mix even when flowers are insignificant. For recommendations, refer to the *Rocky Mountain Getting Started Garden Guide* for companion plants to use with perennials.

▦ *An automatic sprinkler system head*

ROSES

Monitor your watering schedule to reduce stress and prevent severe spider mite infestations. Plan to check the rose garden daily to assess its needs.

While the garden is in full show, take notes on highlights and disappointments. Note off-color foliage or rose mosaic virus. Rose mosaic causes streaked or mottled leaves and stunted growth. Remove severely infected plants. If certain varieties have been on the decline or plagued by chronic problems, dig them out and throw them away. Then plan to try newer varieties.

SHRUBS

If you are planning a summer vacation, arrange for a friend or neighbor to check your landscape while you're gone. This is especially important if we should experience a prolonged period of heat and drought. An automatic sprinkler system and drip irrigation will help, but is still a good idea to have someone check up on things to make sure everything is working correctly. Leave instructions on what to do if something should go wrong.

TREES

The onset of heat is a good time to evaluate your shade trees and be sure they are healthy and working for you. Check tree locations and their impact on your landscape. Consider adding new trees to the south and west side of your house to reduce cooling costs. For a larger landscape, consider planting a windbreak to reduce energy spending in the winter. Be sure to make notes in your journal or notebook and on your landscape plan.

VINES, GROUNDCOVERS & ORNAMENTAL GRASSES

Plan to have someone take care of your new plantings while you're away. This not only ensures the survival of your plants, but also keeps your property from looking vacated.

It's a time to enjoy the beauty of flowering vines that attract hummingbirds. You can spot them around honeysuckle, trumpet vine, and morning glory. These tiny flying gems love the tubular flowers that provide a source of sweet nectar. Get the camera out and take photos. Record what's blooming and when, identify plants of particular interest, and note which ones are not performing well.

PLANT

ANNUALS

You still have time to plant annuals that are container-grown in market packs, but the sooner the better to prevent them from getting dry. By now these plants are rootbound, so take time to loosen or tease the matted roots. Plant during a cloudy period or in the cool of the evening to minimize transplant shock from the heat, wind, and sun. Water the new transplants in well, then mulch them with compost or shredded cedar.

Early in the month, plant more sunflower seeds that will grow into handsome golden and yellow flowers in the autumn. You will find sunflowers in many kinds of colors and of varying heights these days.

BULBS

You can start digging and dividing irises (four to six weeks after bloom) that have become crowded and those in areas where it has become shady. Dig rhizomes and check for borers. Destroy borers, and remove old rhizomes. Plant the healthy, young rhizomes with the growing points facing out and about 6 inches apart. Set the rhizomes just below the soil surface with the leaves and buds facing upward.

EDIBLES

Sow seeds of bush beans, beets, chard, radishes, kohlrabi, kale, endive, and carrots. When sown directly into prepared garden soil and watered, they will germinate quickly. You can also purchase and transplant seedlings of broccoli, cauliflower, and late cabbage. You'll be rewarded with a late-summer to early-fall harvest.

LAWNS

Buy sod if you need to patch bare spots to prevent weed invasions. Water newly installed sod well and as often as needed to allow the roots to take hold. Spot-watering is usually acceptable, even if you are under water restrictions. If not, consider using gray water to keep the newly sodded areas moist for establishment.

PERENNIALS

See "Here's How to Avoid Transplant Stress" below.

ROSES

If roses must be planted during the heat of summer, take time to cover the re-planted bush with a large cardboard box to provide some protection from heat and wind for three to four days. Mist the plant a couple of times daily to cool the environment. When the foliage is no longer wilting, the covering can be removed.

Consider adding miniature roses in decorative containers. Miniature roses perform well outdoors in the summer and can be transferred indoors for the winter season.

SHRUBS

This is not a good time to plant shrubs, unless there is a period of cool, overcast days. You may find shrubs on sale, but proceed with care. Newly planted shrubs can suffer from heat and drought conditions; you will have to give them extra attention to ensure their survival.

If you must plant shrubs at this time, follow the same guidelines for planting container-grown shrubs.

Periodically mist the foliage on hot days to cool down the plants and help them acclimate as they send out new roots after transplanting. I have often found it helpful to shade new transplants with a large cardboard box or burlap for a few weeks after they are set out in the landscape. This will protect them from intense sun, heat, and wind that may put them under stress.

TREES

Summer planting can be tricky, but follow the proper guidelines for planting trees. Keep the rootball and surrounding soil uniformly moist, not waterlogged, until the trees become established.

VINES, GROUNDCOVERS & ORNAMENTAL GRASSES

You can still plant container-grown plants from the nursery, but special precautions are urged. Choose a cloudy, cool day to plant, as summer heat discourages root growth and wilts top growth. Shade new plants with cardboard boxes or burlap for a few days after transplanting to help them acclimate to the hot weather. Spread an organic mulch around the root zone to keep the soil cool and reduce evaporation.

Be prepared to water as the soil dries out and mist the foliage on hot days to cool the plants and reduce scorch and wilting. A fine mist nozzle that attaches to the garden hose is a handy tool for this purpose.

HERE'S HOW

TO AVOID TRANSPLANT STRESS

As the summer heat advances, it is not advisable to plant or transplant perennials unless absolutely necessary. Although you can buy and transplant perennials in July, follow these guidelines to avoid transplant stress:

- Plant on a cloudy day or in the late evening. Watch the weather forecast for predictions of a cool down to plan your transplanting.

- Shade newly transplanted perennials for a few days if they are in a sunny exposure and subject to high winds.

- Delay planting until the heat breaks and temperatures are lower.

- Cut back the foliage by one-third to one-half to minimize moisture loss through transpiration.

- Water and mulch new plantings to assure sufficient soil moisture during establishment of the root system.

CARE

ANNUALS

If you didn't mulch prior to planting your annual bedding plants, now is the time to do so. Compost, pine needles, shredded pole peelings, shredded cedar, and other organic materials will help to maintain uniform moisture and reduce evaporation of water.

Stake taller annual and biennial flowers including foxglove, sunflower, larkspur, hollyhock, and castor bean. This will prevent them from blowing over in a high wind. I like to use bamboo stakes that are about a foot taller than the expected height of the plant. Insert the stakes to a depth of 1 foot next to the plants while they are still young transplants. Tie or secure the plants to the stakes with twine or other soft string; loop the tie around the plant stem, then loop the tie around the stake, tying it loosely so there is room for the stem to grow.

Do not disturb the soil in the flowerbeds during the hot, dry weather. Loosening the soil by cultivation can damage the surface roots and increase water loss from the soil. Inspect the mulch around flowers and replenish as necessary to a level of 2 to 3 inches.

As the summer heat turns on, some annuals will benefit from thinning and cleanup. Deadheading the spent flowers and clipping back leggy stems will help promote more vigorous growth and new flower buds. Pinch back stems a few inches. You can do this chore before going on vacation, and the plants will be blooming again with a flush of new growth when you return.

Pinch the tips of coleus every month to keep the plants dense and compact. Since the flowers are insignificant to most of us, pinch them off too. This will promote more colorful foliage.

BULBS

Check taller-growing summer-blooming bulbs to make sure their supports or stakes are sturdy. Strong winds can topple the stems and break off flowers. If you need to add more bamboo stakes around plants, do this with care. The soil should be slightly moistened so they will insert into the ground easily. Then tie the stems with a "twist 'em" or twine.

Add more mulch around the base of bulbs if it is decomposing or settling down. I like to use pine needles when they are available, but you can mulch with shredded cedar, dried grass clippings, pole peelings, or compost. Mulch keeps the soil from drying out so rapidly in the heat of summer and keeps the roots cool. It also discourages weed growth.

■ *Bark mulch*

■ *Gravel mulch*

■ *Pine straw*

■ *Coleus is a popular annual plant with brightly colored leaves. Pinch off coleus flower stalks when they sprout so that the plant stays neat and tidy. If coleus gets too large, just cut off the top half of the plant stems. They will resprout.*

Continue to remove or deadhead faded or spent flowers as needed to keep the garden tidy and fresh.

To encourage more branching of dahlias, pinch the terminal growth so more lateral branching will occur. This will keep the plants more compact if you wish. If you are growing large decorative dahlias, you don't need to do this. However, pinching out the small cluster of buds, but leaving the center bud, will result in a larger, dinner plate-sized bloom. Experiment to see how you can train and manipulate blooming and growth.

EDIBLES

Early in the month, apply a sidedressing of vegetable fertilizer around crops to give them a summer boost.

Apply a 2- to 3-inch layer of mulch around the plants, leaving space for air circulation to discourage pests from nesting at the base of the plants. Organic mulches preserve soil moisture, discourage weed growth, and keep foliage, fruit, and vegetables clean.

Harvest maturing vegetables and fruit at their peak to stimulate more growth. This will also prevent the vegetables from overmaturing and rotting. Sweet corn can mature quite quickly, so pick it after the milk squirts from the top row of kernels. Have a pot of boiling water ready so you can enjoy this sweet harvest right from your own garden—immediately!

Dig early onions if the tops have naturally dried and flopped over. Let them dry for a day or two, then store in a cool, dry spot.

Pinch and prune herbs to delay flowering and loss of flavor. You can use fresh herbs at twice the amounts recommended for dried, bottled ones. If you have time and space, freeze or dry extra herbs.

My Italian grandmother used cheesecloth to shade the herb garden during prolonged periods of heat and drought. She set sturdy wooden poles in the ground and stretched the cheesecloth over the crops so they would continue to grow and flourish.

Check the fruit of tomato and pepper plants for blackened bottoms. Blossom end rot is caused when fruit forms during cool weather and periods of erratic watering. Apply mulch around plants and water as needed.

Some fruit trees like cherries and apricots may be about to produce fruit. Check daily, and harvest the ripening fruit. It is best not to allow over-ripened fruit to fall to the ground and rot. This invites bees, wasps, and other critters into your home orchard.

Use wooden 2 × 4s with a V-notch in one end to support fruit-laden branches of apples, peaches, pears, plums, and others so branches won't break from the weight of the ripening fruit.

■ *Apply a sidedressing of compost, manure, or granular fertilizer to give vegetables a midseason boost.*

As the fall crop of carrots and beets are growing, thin the plants to the correct spacing as indicated on the seed packets. Pinch suckers off indeterminate tomato plants if you are training them on a support. Once the stem is sufficiently strong and securely attached to the support, you can leave some to encourage additional side branches that will develop flowers and fruit.

You can cut out the old fruiting canes of bramble fruits such as raspberries and blackberries as soon as the fruit is harvested. The older canes will not bear much fruit again. This will promote better air circulation, reduce leaf diseases, and discourage stem borers. Pinch back the tips of small fruits to reduce their overall height, if desired.

LAWNS
Mow the lawn every seven to ten days, or as needed. This is a good time to sharpen your lawn mower blade again or to switch it out with a new one. A sharp blade prevents fraying of the leaf blades where diseases can enter.

Continue to mow often enough to remove one-third of the leaf blade each time. Keep the mower blade set at 2½ to 3 inches to help grass plants withstand the summer heat and possible extended drought conditions.

Leave the grass clippings on the lawn when you mow (unless you have waited too long and the grass clippings are so abundant that they clump together). Mulching mowers will cut the grass clippings fine enough that they will filter down into the soil and decompose.

Warm-season grasses including bentgrass, zoysia, and buffalograss can be maintained at 1 to 2 inches tall.

PERENNIALS
Check perennials for signs of heat stress: wilting leaves, flower buds that "blast" (fail to open), and scorch on the leaf margins. These could indicate lack of available subsoil moisture. Check the soil moisture every few days to prevent severe stress to the plants.

Organic mulches around plants will begin to break down with summer heat and moisture, so replenish it around plants as needed. Spread a fresh layer of compost or pine needles to maintain a 2-inch layer around the root zone. Pull any weeds that may have popped up through the mulch.

Continue to cut off any broken, insect-infested, or diseased stems and foliage.

Deadhead spent blooms to promote new buds for future flowers. Some perennials that need deadheading include daylilies, perennial salvia, phlox, coneflowers, rudbeckia, beebalm, coreopsis, Stokes' aster, and yarrow.

■ *Onions for storage should be "cured." Do this by removing their stalks and air-drying them at warm temperatures for several days.*

■ *Blossom end rot on tomatoes*

TO MOW THE LAWN

1. Set the mower height so that you're mowing at the tallest recommended height for your grass type. Most mower adjustment brackets are next to the front wheels, but consult your mower manual for specific instructions for setting your mower height.

2. Prime and choke the mower. The primer button is a small, soft plastic button on the top of the mower. Push it five or six times. Set the choke to the "cold" engine setting. If your mower doesn't have a choke, consult your manual for instructions.

3. While the mower is still on the sidewalk or driveway, hold down the safety lever at the top of the mower, set the throttle, and grab the starter cord. Pull the starter cord in a jerking motion three or four times, until the mower starts. Once running, roll it over to the grass, slowly move the choke lever back to "warm," and begin mowing.

4. Start by mowing around the edge of the lawn first. This will give you somewhere to turn the mower at each corner. If you're using a bagging mower, move the mower back to the concrete or sidewalk and empty the bag. If you're using a mower with a side discharge, point the discharge toward the area you have not yet mowed, so that you can chop the grass clippings as you continue to mow.

5. Continue mowing the rest of the lawn. One trick to making sure that your lawn remains green and smooth is to change the direction you mow. One week, mow parallel to your driveway, the next week, mow perpendicular to the driveway. This prevents the mower's wheels from making deep ruts in the lawn.

6. While mowing each new row, place your mower so that it overlaps the previous row by 25 percent. By doing this, your'e sure to cut the entire lawn evenly.

Make the last pinch of hardy garden chrysanthemums by July 4. This encourages additional shoots, more compact growth and more flowers in autumn.

ROSES

Roses can tolerate summer's heat, but they suffer in prolonged periods of extreme heat and drought. When temperatures reach and stay above 90 degrees Fahrenheit, foliage and flowers will wilt and may scorch. The root system can't keep up with the rapid loss of moisture from the top growth. Daily misting can help cool the environment, but don't do this in the evening.

Spread new or refresh old mulch over the soil beneath your rose bushes to maintain uniform soil moisture and reduce weed invasions. If weeds do sprout up, they are easier to pull out from an airy mulch.

Landscape, shrub, species, and old-fashioned roses are generally much hardier than many classic hybrid tea roses. Most are on their own rootstock, have a freer growth habit, are more adapted to a wide range of soils, and can handle varied climatic situations and elevations.

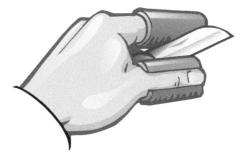

■ *Protect fingers from cuts with short pieces of old garden hose slipped over thumb and forefinger.*

One of the most useful tools for routine summer pruning is a sharp pocket knife. To protect your thumb from cuts and index finger from thorns, use two short pieces of old garden hose. Slice them down them the middle so that you can slip your thumb and index finger over them. When you make a pruning cut, you simply hold the stems between the thumb and finger of one hand and make the cut.

If you want bigger blooms, disbud the sideshoots from larger-blooming varieties to encourage larger flowers. Routinely check bushes for damaged or broken canes and faded flowers. Remove them to keep the garden clean and reduce disease problems. Pick up dead and fallen leaves and other debris on the ground to prevent splashing of soilborne fungus disease spores onto the lower leaves of the bushes.

Prune spring- and early-flowering rose varieties, including early-blooming climbers, shrub roses, some rambling roses, and perpetual hybrids shortly after they've flowered. This will help to shape the plants and give them ample time to set buds on new wood for next growing season.

SHRUBS

Discourage birds from eating the berries of raspberries and other small fruits by draping netting over these shrubs.

Check the organic mulch spread over the root zone of shrubs. It may be settling or need replenishment. As summer's heat and frequent watering accelerates decomposition of mulch, the layers begin to get thinner and gradually help enrich the soil—a good thing. To work at its best, organic mulches need to be 2 to 3 inches thick. This will help to hold in moisture and discourage the invasion of weeds. Avoid piling it higher than 3 inches, however, as too thick a mulch can deprive roots of oxygen, impede drainage, and invite rodents. Note: Never apply mulch directly against the stems or canes of shrubs. It can result in crown rot and possible rodent damage. The stems need proper air circulation.

Limit pruning to removing dead, diseased, storm-injured, or insect-ridden branches and stems. Do not shear shrubs unless you prefer this look. Shearing too late in summer results in dieback, scorch to the lower foliage, and browning of evergreens. It is best done in the cooler weather of spring.

TREES

Prune off dead and damaged branches as you discover them. Save large pruning jobs for professionals. They are insured and have the proper equipment and training to do the job safely.

Remove weeds and other unwanted plants from the base of young trees. Replenish mulch that is disintegrating.

Continue to cut away water sprouts and suckers that originate around the base of the trunk or in adjacent lawn areas. Except for removing broken or diseased branches, delay major pruning until the trees are dormant to avoid stimulating yet more new growth that will be vulnerable to frost or storm damage.

VINES, GROUNDCOVERS & ORNAMENTAL GRASSES

You can still plant container-grown plants from the nursery, but special precautions are urged. Choose a cloudy, cool day to plant, as heat discourages root growth and wilts top-growth. Shade new plants with cardboard boxes or burlap for a few days after transplanting to help them acclimate to the hot weather. Spread organic mulch around the root zone to keep the soil cool and reduce evaporation.

Be prepared to water as the soil dries out and mist the foliage on hot days to cool the plants and reduce scorch and wilting. A fine mist nozzle that attaches to the garden hose is a handy tool for this purpose.

Once the large-flowered clematis have finished blooming, you may cut them back by 30 to 50 percent to stimulate repeat bloom later in the summer. Even a light clipping will tidy up the vines and leave some handsome seedpods for summer and fall interest.

Cut back the branches of climbing hydrangea that extend more than a foot from the main stem.

■ *After planting a tree, apply 2 to 3 inches of organic mulch such as shredded bark or wood chips, keeping the mulch a few inches away from the trunk.*

Otherwise, this vine can become top-heavy and pull itself away from its support. Snip the overgrown branching stems individually back to a point where some leaves are emerging.

Annual groundcovers may begin to get leggy and will benefit from a light pruning to stimulate more side branching. They will resume blooming in a few short weeks. This works well on trailing petunias, impatiens, creeping zinnia, and other annuals used as groundcover.

WATER

ANNUALS

Remember to check the soil *before* you water. Annuals that are mulched will have to be watered less frequently than plants without mulch. Pull away the mulch and dig down to a depth of 3 to 4 inches to see how moist the soil is. If it is beginning to dry out, it's time to give the plants a good, deep drink.

Use drip irrigation tubes or a soaker hose to water slowly and deeply. This will encourage more drought-enduring plants. If you find the soil moist, avoid overwatering. Leaves will remain wilted and will not perk up in the evening or when temperatures cool down.

BULBS

Keep the bulb garden moist during the heat of summer with regular watering. Apply enough water—about an inch a week—to maintain healthy and vigorous growth. This will also allow the buds to fully develop and open. Check the soil moisture by probing into the ground with a garden trowel and if it is beginning to dry out to a depth of 2 inches or more, give the garden a good drink. Bulbs that are mulched will need less frequent watering.

Bulbs growing in containers will need more attention to watering as they dry out faster. Water thoroughly as needed and allow the excess water to drain out. Pour the excess out of the drainage saucer.

EDIBLES

This is the time of year that plants use more moisture to sustain growth and develop fruit and vegetables. Water when the soil underneath the layers of mulch is beginning to dry out. Check moisture levels with a garden trowel or shovel to customize your own watering schedule. Gardens need 1 inch of water a week to keep growing and producing. Uniform moisture is a must for peppers, tomatoes, and cucumbers.

Water container gardens that are in full sun daily, unless you have incorporated moisture-holding polymers into the soil mix (then water as the soil begins to dry out). You need to customize a watering schedule to fit *your* garden's exposure, soil type, wind, and various other environmental factors.

I like to water early in the morning to give the plants a good start for the day. Avoid overhead watering at night since this allows moisture to stay on the foliage and encourage mildew diseases. Vegetables that touch wet ground are more prone to rot.

LAWNS

Water cool-season grasses such as Kentucky bluegrass, fescue, and ryegrass every five to seven days if it does not rain. To encourage grass plants to root down deeply and develop drought endurance, water deeply, soaking the soil to a depth of 4 inches or more. Then don't water for another seven days. Compacted or clay soils may require a pause between watering sessions to allow the water to percolate into the soil and to prevent runoff.

Only in sandy soils do you need to water more frequently, but set the sprinkler for shorter durations. Even sandy soils will compact and will benefit from cyclic watering.

Resist the temptation to lightly sprinkle the grass daily just because it feels good to you. This encourages the grass roots to stay shallow and they dry out more quickly.

PERENNIALS

If the summer has prolonged periods of drought, it is important to check the watering needs of both established and newly transplanted perennials. Dig down around the root zone to a depth of 4 inches or more. If the soil is beginning to dry out, it's time to give the perennials a deep watering.

Perennials that are mulched are better able to withstand short periods of drought than those that are not mulched and are exposed to sun and wind. Shade perennials should be checked periodically, too. Even though shade cools the soil, tree and shrub roots compete for soil moisture and can stress the plants. Check the soil by probing an inch or two down and under the mulch layer. If the soil is dry, apply water.

ROSES

Without sufficient water during the heat of summer roses will become stunted, blooms are smaller, and flowering may cease. Monitor the soil by checking it to see how fast it dries out. Use a garden trowel and dig down a few inches; as the soil begins to dry out, it's time to apply water. Apply an inch or more of water weekly or at the first signs of wilting. Use an organic mulch to help maintain soil moisture and conserve during water restrictions.

Monitor soil moisture of container-growing roses by digging down or inserting a long screwdriver into the pot a few inches. If the soil is beginning to dry out, water pots thoroughly until water comes out the drainage hole. Discard excess drainage water after an hour or so.

SHRUBS

Make sure your shrubs get adequate water in the hot, dry periods of summer. If we are experiencing a period of drought, water shrubs deeply at least once a week or as often as your water provider will allow. This will reduce severe stress and dieback.

Give shrubs a deep drink by using a soaker hose around the root zone or placing a frog-eye sprinkler in the vicinity of the root area. Allow the water to run slowly until you notice it beginning to run off. Leaky (soaker) hoses or pipes that sweat water through their pores can be positioned throughout a shrub border so all of them can be watered at one time. Organic mulches will help to conserve the water you apply during the hot summer period. Use them judiciously.

TREES

When rain showers are scarce, check soil moisture under the mulch around newly transplanted trees at least weekly. If the soil is beginning to dry out

to a depth of 6 inches or more, it's time to give the tree a good, deep drink. Mulch will effectively cool the soil and deter runoff of valuable moisture when the rain does come.

VINES, GROUNDCOVERS & ORNAMENTAL GRASSES

During the summer as temperatures rise and humidity is low, the stress on plants increases. Vines, groundcovers, and ornamental grasses will appreciate a deep watering every week or two. Mulched plantings can go longer between waterings as the mulch cools the soil and reduces evaporation.

FERTILIZE

ANNUALS

If you applied a slow-acting fertilizer during the planting process, it is generally sufficient for most plants for six to ten weeks, depending on the product. Check the label to determine if it's time to apply more fertilizer. If foliar plant fertilizer is used, apply it during the cool part of the day, early morning or late evening, to avoid burning the roots.

Avoid the application of high-nitrogen fertilizer. This stimulates plants to produce excess foliage, which can be more susceptible to insects and diseases. Also, too much nitrogen reduces flower development.

Never fertilize annual flowers that are under stress from drought or extreme heat.

BULBS

Bulbs that were planted with a slow-release granular fertilizer will not need any additional fertilizer at this time. If the plants show signs of nutrient deficiency or a soil test indicates the need for more nutrients, you can apply granular fertilizer at the base of the plants. Lightly cultivate it into the soil and water the fertilizer in.

Soil that is covered by organic mulches will eventually gain nutrients as the materials break down, plus the organic amendments improve the soil's structure.

EDIBLES

Most vegetables and herbs that were fertilized earlier will not need additional applications now. For new plants, apply a water-soluble plant fertilizer to the foliage in early morning or late evening. Organic fertilizers such as fish emulsion or liquid kelp may prove helpful. If you are doing successive planting, mix compost or sphagnum peat moss into the empty spots before planting the next round of fall crops. This will ensure they get off to a good start.

LAWNS

Only highly managed and irrigated lawns should be fertilized this month. Use a low-nitrogen, slow-release fertilizer to avoid burning the grass. Semi-dormant lawns or non-irrigated lawns do not need fertilizer now. This could damage and even kill the grass.

PERENNIALS

All that organic mulch and compost you place around perennials will eventually decompose and slowly release nutrients to the plants. The humus will also encourage beneficial organisms such as earthworms to till the soil naturally and release nutrients.

Slow-release fertilizers are much more available to plants in soils enriched with organic matter. Microbes in the soil will make the nutrients more readily available.

If it's been more than six weeks since you added a slow-release fertilizer to the soil, late summer-blooming perennials will benefit from another dose of granular fertilizer. Some slow-acting fertilizers can last for the entire growing season, so read the label to determine if you need to apply more.

ROSES

It's best not to fertilize roses in the extreme heat or during extended drought periods. If you applied a slow-release fertilizer earlier in the season, it should sustain the plants until later in the month. However, you may have to fertilize roses that are susceptible to iron deficiency; yellowing foliage and lack of vigor are indicators. Use a granular or wettable powder form of chelated iron.

Wait for weather to cool before applying the homemade rose tonic in late July. Apply to the soil, not to the foliage.

SHRUBS

Shrubs generally do not benefit from additional fertilizer in the heat of summer.

TREES

It is getting too late to fertilize trees in July. They will soon be making a transition for fall dormancy, and there is no benefit of applying fertilizer to stimulate late succulent growth.

VINES, GROUNDCOVERS & ORNAMENTAL GRASSES

Fertilizer is not needed now, with the exception of potted vines that are flowering on the patio or deck. Use a water-soluble plant fertilizer diluted to half-strength, and apply to a moistened potting mixture every other week.

PROBLEM-SOLVE

ANNUALS

Watch for spider mites on marigolds and zinnias. They will cause the foliage to have a dingy, salt-and-pepper appearance. There may be signs of fine webbing weaving throughout the foliage and stems. Mites can be washed off the plants with a strong stream of water; direct the water to both the upper and lower portions of the leaves.

Insecticidal soap sprays or a homemade soap spray and miticides will also keep pests in check. Read and follow label directions.

Pest problems tend to proliferate if we kill beneficial predators by spraying with insecticides. Before resorting to insecticides, try to wash the pests off plant surfaces every few days. Aphids will continue to proliferate on the new, succulent foliage of annuals. Wash them off with a forceful spray of water from the garden hose.

BULBS

Earwigs are fond of the blooms of dahlias. They can nibble at the petals, thus destroying the symmetry of the bloom. Place earwig traps made from rolled-up, moistened newspaper in the flower bed to capture these little beasties. Also see the homemade remedies for controls of earwigs on page 221.

Be on the watch for foliar diseases including powdery mildew. It will show up as grayish white patches on the leaves. Increase air circulation by thinning the plants a bit and avoid watering the garden at night. Water early in the day so the foliage goes into the night dry. If you wish, use homemade mildew control to keep infections at a minimum.

Spider mites can be a problem in the heat of summer. If detected early, wash them off the foliage with a strong water spray or use a homemade soap solution.

Keep your summer bulb plants healthy and stress-free by providing proper watering techniques, nutrition, uniform light, and air circulation.

EDIBLES

Continue to monitor insect pests including squash bugs, cucumber beetles, aphids, whiteflies, and a variety of caterpillars. You can control most pests early in the game by washing them off with a forceful spray of water from the hose. If this doesn't get them all, use a homemade soap spray (see page 220) in early morning or evening. Insecticidal soaps are also labeled for vegetables and herbs.

Squash bugs, cucumber beetles, slugs, weevils, and asparagus beetles can be handpicked if you're not squeamish about this kind of control. Just drop them into a bucket of soapy water. Read and follow label directions when using any kind of pesticide and observe waiting periods before harvest time.

Powdery mildew disease can appear almost overnight. Use the homemade mildew prevention controls. Pick off the heavily infected leaves and discard them. Do not compost diseased or insect-ridden plant parts.

Use bird netting if needed, and thwart rabbits by putting up a critter barrier. Don't let weeds go to seed. Keep hoeing and cultivating as needed.

LAWNS

Weeds are opportunistic and will continue to pop up when there are bare spots in the lawn. You can spot-spray the tough perennial weeds with a herbicide as needed. Shield nearby desirable plants to avoid herbicide drift. Place a plastic milk jug with the bottom cut out over the offending weed and spray through the top opening.

If you see lots of small moths fluttering around in your lawn, this may indicate the presence of sod webworms. They are laying eggs that will soon hatch into larvae (caterpillars). Birds can be helpful in controlling these pests. If infestations are severe, consult a professional for soil insecticide treatments. Otherwise, a few sod webworms can be tolerated in most vigorously growing lawns.

Watch for the onset of powdery mildew in shady regions of your lawn. Increase air circulation by pruning low-lying branches from trees to allow more light penetration. You can overseed with mildew-resistant turf varieties.

PERENNIALS

Check perennials daily for invasions of insect pests. Aphids, whiteflies, caterpillars, and spider mites continue to be on the prowl in summer. Most can be controlled by washing them off the stems and foliage with a forceful spray of water. Homemade soap sprays, insecticidal soap, and miticides can also be used to keep their numbers in check. Read and follow label directions when applying any insecticide or miticide.

Leaf diseases may be showing up on perennials growing in the shade or those that are too crowded. Watch for the signs of powdery mildew; a grayish white coating on the leaves is a classic symptom of mildew.

Continue to pull, dig, or spot-treat weeds as they appear. Don't let them grow so fast that they produce seeds. With proper spacing of perennials, there should be minimal weed invasions since the soil will be shaded naturally to keep weeds from germinating.

ROSES

Monitor the rose garden every few days for summer insect pests. Leaf cutter bees leave very noticeable

■ *Earwig*　　　■ *Squash bug*　　　■ *Slugs*　　　■ *Whiteflies*

damage by cutting out very precise ovals and circles from the leaves. These pollinators are beneficial and use the leaf sections for nesting. No controls are warranted. If you desire to stop leaf cutter bee damage, cover your prized plants with netting.

Rose midge larvae will cause deformed buds and dead stem tips. They can quickly infest and devastate the rose garden if left uncontrolled. Prune off and destroy infested buds and stem tips. Treat the soil with a proper insecticide, and spray buds and new growth with a systemic. Read and follow label directions.

Spider mites wreak havoc in the summer rose garden. Stippled leaves, dusty-looking foliage, webbing, and premature leaf drop are indicators. Keep the plants adequately watered, and routinely spray the underside of the leaves with forceful water pressure. You can place a frog-eye sprinkler under the plants and turn it on occasionally to thwart mites. If necessary, use the homemade soap spray or a proper miticide. Read and follow label directions.

SHRUBS

Continue your garden watch for summer insect pests and late-summer diseases. Keep pests at bay by periodic handpicking and washing them off with a forceful stream of water from the garden hose.

Large caterpillars may be discovered nibbling on the foliage. The larvae of the *Cecropia* and hawk moths can grow to colossal size if left undisturbed. Use the handpicking method of control or spray heavily infested plants with B.t. (*Bacillus thuringiensis*)—a microbial insecticide. Caterpillars that ingest the B.t. will soon become lethargic, sicken, and die. It is very safe, people- and wildlife-friendly. Read and follow label directions.

Encourage the beneficial insects to your landscape to keep the bad bugs under control. You can purchase ladybugs and praying mantises at some local garden stores or via mail order. Birds are also helpful in eating bugs that invade the landscape; more of a reason to avoid using toxic insecticides in your yard.

TREES

Blister beetles and others may arrive in hoards to attack tree foliage. These pests can cause considerable damage by stripping the leaves from branches. Control these pests by hosing them down or knocking them into a jar of soapy water.

Caterpillars of certain butterflies and moths may feed on some of the foliage of specific trees, but it is often not necessary to control them since damage is nominal. If infestations are severe, apply B.t. (*Bacillus thuringiensis*). If you have a butterfly-friendly landscape, it is perfectly acceptable to allow these caterpillars to feed so you can enjoy the metamorphosis of various winged beauties in your landscape.

VINES, GROUNDCOVERS & ORNAMENTAL GRASSES

Spider mites can wreak havoc in the garden during hot, dry spells. They target stressed plants, including ivies, creeping junipers, and Virginia creeper. Mites cause a pale yellow or tan stippling on the leaves; sometimes you can detect a fine webbing among the stems and branches. Disrupt the mites' life cycle by hosing down the upper and lower surfaces of the foliage. Insecticidal soap sprays and homemade soap sprays are effective for heavy infestations. Read and follow label directions.

August

During early August we can experience hot weather with extended drought periods, and watering is critical to sustain plants and keep them growing. You may need to adjust watering practices and top off mulches to conserve water and suppress late weed growth. Dig down into the soil (pull the mulch away as needed) to a depth of 2 to 4 inches and check to see how moist the soil is. If it is becoming dry, it is time to do some deep watering.

Summer-flowering bulbs will soon be approaching the end of their season, but there is still time to enjoy some little gems that bloom in the autumn. Autumn crocus and colchicum are among my favorites. They have already produced their foliage in the spring and die back in summer. Then in the fall, the flowers poke through to provide a burst of color when you thought the garden was finished.

Garden centers and greenhouses will have a supply of late-flowering perennials including asters, chrysanthemums, new arrivals of pansies and violas, and various others. It's a good time to plant these as season extenders to fill in empty spots. Plus, they will return for next season.

Having spent a good part of my youth on a farm, I'm reminded that many perennial weeds can be effectively controlled in late summer. My uncle would tell me that weeds are preparing for winter and storing up energy. Controlling them by removing flower heads, chopping off the tall stems, and spot-treating with an appropriate herbicide will starve the plant to death.

It's a good time to harvest flowers and herbs for drying. Remove the leaves and combine in small bundles. Use rubber bands to hold the stems together. As the stems dry and shrink, rubber bands will contract and hold stems tight. Use a spring-type clothespin to attach drying flowers to a nail or other support. Dry in a dark, warm, and airy location.

Later in the month, temperatures begin to cool down and the yard is returning to its glory. The entire landscape is maturing with subtle colors, textures, and form.

PLAN

ANNUALS

If you have garden spaces that are looking empty or less colorful, plan to buy some of the late-summer annuals such as zinnias, marigolds, and salvia at garden centers and greenhouse sales. They can be quickly added to the garden. It is a good opportunity to get a bargain and still add color.

BULBS

Plan to renovate some of the older spring-flowering bulb beds that are losing vigor. As bulbs grow and multiply, the bed can become overcrowded and bulbs run out of energy to produce blooms. As landscapes mature, the shade cast by maturing shade trees may create a site with insufficient sunlight for the bulbs to grow. Now is a time to do some relocating, if needed. Plan to do this chore as the temperatures cool down and prior to bulb-planting time.

Enjoy the surprise blooms from the resurrection lily, *Lycoris squamigera*, that pop up without leaves. Plan to add them to your garden if you're wishing for mid- to late August color.

REGIONAL BOTANICAL GARDENS

If you're planning a vacation, visit some of the public gardens where you travel to for inspiration. Some regional botanical gardens or arboreta feature plants that thrive and have wonderful color and features are:

Betty Ford Alpine Gardens (Vail, CO)

Denver Botanic Gardens (Denver, CO)

Hudson Gardens (Littleton, CO)

Western Colorado Botanical Gardens (Grand Junction, CO)

Idaho Botanical Garden (Boise, ID)

International Peace Gardens (Salt Lake City, UT)

Cheyenne Botanic Gardens (Cheyenne, WY)

Montana Arboretum and Gardens (Missoula, MT)

HERE'S HOW

TO HARVEST FLOWERS FOR FRESH USE OR DRYING

1. Cut flowers and opening buds early in the morning for the best quality. Use a sharp knife or garden shears to cut the stem above a set of healthy leaves.

2. Recut the stems just prior to placing the flowers in the vase.

3. Wait until midday to harvest flowers for drying. Pick flowers at their peak. Remove the leaves and gather a few stems into a bundle. Tie together with rubber bands. As the stems shrink, the rubber bands will hold the bundle together.

4. Use a spring-type clothespin to hang the bundle from a line, rack, or nail in a dry, dark location.

EDIBLES

It's time to update your garden journal or notebook as the garden grows on. Take notes on which vegetables and herbs are performing well, and note those that are not living up to your expectations.

Plan on harvesting vegetables, fruits, and herbs regularly so you can enjoy them at their peak. Pick cucumbers when they reach their mature size. Don't leave them on the vines too long or they will turn yellow, develop seeds, and get bitter. Summer squash should be harvested daily while they are still immature and tender. Nothing tastes better than a

6-inch zucchini fried in garlic butter. But if you like, let a zucchini grow bigger, scoop out the seed cavity, and stuff with a filling of your choice.

LAWNS

As temperatures begin to cool down, lawns will return to their glory. Plan ahead for fall core-aeration and overseeding, if needed. This will fill in thinning areas of the lawn. Plan to buy a quality grass seed to match the light requirements.

Inspect your lawn regularly to identify problem spots. This will help you plan your fall strategy for making repairs or planting a new lawn. The earlier you can identify problems and prepare, the more time the lawn will have to get established before the hard frost in November. Cool-season lawn grasses do best as the weather cools down and will grow vigorous and healthy root systems to survive the winter.

PERENNIALS

August is a good time to evaluate your perennial garden and make more notes on what did best and what didn't do so well. You can plan to make improvements in the garden in early fall. Many garden retailers will be putting their plants on sale in mid- to late August and you can acquire some good bargains for autumn planting. Perhaps it's time to dig out older plants for replacement this fall.

Note the perennials that really shined in your garden, despite possible drought conditions. Which

■ Aster × frikartii *'Jungfrau'*

ones took the least amount of attention? Make these notations in your notebook or journal.

If you have space and want your perennials to naturalize, plan on letting some of them go to seed. Rudbeckias, coneflowers, hellebores, Shasta daisies, monarda, asters, and others self-sow their seeds. Otherwise, you'll want to thin out or remove unwanted seedlings to prevent overcrowding.

While some gardeners welcome self-sowing of perennials, others do not want to deal with all the tiny seedlings next season. The choice is yours. Young seedlings can be dug up and transplanted

SOME LATE-FLOWERING PERENNIALS TO PLANT NOW

Asters (*Aster × frikartii* and *A. novae-angliae*)

Chrysanthemums (*C. × rubellum* —'Clara Curtis' is bright pink)

Rudbeckia (*Rudbeckia fulgida* 'Goldsturm')

Blanket Flower (*Gaillardia × grandiflora*)

Sneezeweed (*Helenium* hybrids)

Sedums (*Sedum spectabile*)

Wince Cups (*Callirhoe involucrata*)

■ *Attract songbirds to your garden with sunflowers.*

to more desirable locations or share them with garden friends.

Another benefit for leaving some seedheads is to create a wildlife-friendly garden. Visiting birds such as finches love the seeds of coneflowers and black-eyed Susans.

Plan to visit public and private gardens to see what perennials are showing their stuff. Make notes in your garden journal so you can act on them next growing season, if not this autumn.

ROSES

Monitor soil moisture by probing down a few inches with a garden trowel, and determine a watering schedule. Also, think about adding an automatic drip irrigation system. Gather information to find out which kind would suit your needs.

Take note of roses throughout your region as you travel. You many discover some to add to your landscape next year. Typically, the informal landscape roses catch my eye. They produce colorful, simple flowers and some—like *Rosa glauca,* the red-leaf rose—not only have handsome foliage but produce drooping, orange-red rose hips that persist into winter. A good groundcover rose is *R. nitida*, which has stunning reddish orange fall foliage and is loaded with small, bright rose hips for winter interest.

When you go on vacation, regular watering will be a concern if we're experiencing a drought period. Make plans to have a friend or neighbor check the garden and water as needed. This is where that drip irrigation system would come in handy.

SHRUBS

If you are planning a summer vacation now, established shrubs should do fine as long as you give them a deep watering before you leave and have them properly mulched. During an extended period of heat and drought, make arrangements with someone to check your landscape while your gone.

An automatic sprinkler system and drip irrigation would be most valuable at this time. In the long run it can save you money, water, and time. Drip

systems are not that difficult to install, but if you don't feel comfortable doing it yourself, consult a sprinkler contractor. Get several bids before you make a decision.

Shrubs are excellent plants to attract birds to your landscape. They not only provide some shelter, but many produce edible fruit for the late summer and into the autumn and winter months. If you don't have shrubs that invite wildlife, now is a good time to plan to add some. Find out what kinds of birds visit your area and make a list of shrubs that will attract them. Some of my favorites are serviceberry, cotoneaster, snowberry, and sea buckthorn. Look over your landscape, and see what areas would benefit from new shrubs, and mark these spots with stakes. You can plant the shrubs for a permanent addition. Try to plant by mid-October.

TREES

Now is the time to start planning for autumn planting. Keep in mind the naturescape or xeriscape principle: choose appropriate trees that are adapted to your area. Select plants thoughtfully, and plant them in an environment that is closely matched to each tree's native habitat. Some trees are quite adaptable and will perform well in a variety of situations. If you need to replace aging and diseased aspen trees, consider river birch that are well-suited to low, moist areas but can also grow in well-drained soils on higher ground.

Plan to replace trees that did not survive transplanting or that suffered injury from storms, drought, poor pruning, or compacted soils. As the fall sales arrive, take advantage of early fall planting.

Perhaps it's time to retrofit your landscape. Think about how trees would contribute diversity and functionality. How would they affect both the outdoor and indoor climate of your home? Would the tree shade afternoon sun in summer, but still allow solar radiation in winter? Do you need to create a windbreak to block the wind?

If you are thinking about cutting down an old, maturing tree to make room for construction or reduce shade, think twice. Healthy, mature trees add value to the property. If it is necessary to remove the tree, consult with local arborists and nurseries that may have tree spades large enough to relocate the tree. Professional tree spades can dig up large trees and a good portion of the rootball, then transport them to a new site.

Plan to transplant new trees in late August through mid-October. Get the planting area prepared in advance to save time when the tree arrives. Gather mulch for use after transplanting. See the information on planting trees on page 76.

Research tree species that interest you to determine their requirements for light, soil, and moisture. Check out the *Rocky Mountain Getting Started Garden Guide* for ideas. Get to know their growth habits, mature sizes, and shapes. This way, you can make sure you have the appropriate site on your property for a tree's mature height and spread.

VINES, GROUNDCOVERS & ORNAMENTAL GRASSES

August is a bouquet of infinite variety of color and form in the landscape. Groundcovers, vines, and ornamental grasses are perhaps at their finest now. These plants are reliable and once established, are quite drought tolerant. Enjoy their beauty.

Take photographs of how these plants accentuate specific areas with their colorful foliage, flowers, fruits and berries, form, and texture. Continue ordering hardy bulbs to plant among groundcovers and around ornamental grasses.

The heat of summer can take its toll on plants. Now would be a good time to evaluate changes that may be necessary to fill in gaps. Consider soil conditions, wind, exposure to sunlight or shade, and other variables that affect plant growth and performance. Watch the ornamental grasses as they unfold their seedheads. It's a great time to pick a bouquet of feathery grass tassels to dry for winter-long indoor arrangements.

PLANT

ANNUALS

This is a hot month to sow seeds or transplant seedlings or annuals. It is not unusual for an annual to succumb to stress or to be crowded out by other plants. So, if you need to replace the occasional dead or pooped-out annual in your container gardens, choose a cloudy, cool day. Carefully dig the plant out and replace with a new addition to keep color appearing through the late summer into fall. Check with your local garden center for sales or closeouts on annuals and perennials.

When transplanting small seedlings, water the new plants thoroughly, and mist occasionally with a fine spray of water to keep them cool. This will lessen transplant shock. Young seedlings from self-sowing annuals will sprout here and there in the garden. When they are about 2 to 3 inches tall, thin them to the correct spacing so they can grow more vigorously.

BULBS

In some parts of the region, pre-ordered hardy bulbs will be arriving in the mail. It will be time to start planting them, or if you must store them, keep them in a cool location in the basement or garage. Don't forget about them; mark your calendar to remind you to plant them before the ground freezes.

You can dig individual planting holes in a random pattern to plant bulbs, or dig an entire bed and plant them in masses for a more bold display. Plant at the depth recommended for each type.

If you have space, naturalizing is a way to create an informal display in the same manner as nature

■ *Plant garlic in the fall to harvest next summer.*

HERE'S HOW

TO DIVIDE BULBS

Want to divide and conquer bulbs that have become overcrowded or that have lost their vigor? Then follow these steps:

1. Carefully dig up existing plants and bulbs with a heavy-duty spading fork to lift out the clumps of hardy bulbs without doing a lot of injury to the bulbs. Shake the soil from the bulbs and set them aside in a cool spot. I like to put them in a burlap sack, but you can also use paper bags.

2. Dig the soil deeply or rototill the new planting area and add a generous supply of compost or sphagnum peat moss to improve soil structure and drainage. Remove any stones, old roots, and other plants debris.

3. Now would be a good time to work in slow-release granular fertilizer before replanting the bulbs.

4. Rake the loosened soil to level the area and you will be ready to start planting. Dig holes or planting areas to reset the bulbs and any companion perennials.

5. After planting, set out the frog-eye sprinkler and water the area thoroughly. Mulch to maintain uniform soil moisture and reduce frequency of watering. Mulches will also suppress weed growth.

might plant flowers in a woodland or forest setting. This is effective in groundcovers or certain lawn areas where you might want to create a meadow effect.

EDIBLES

Early in August, there is still time for a second planting of radishes, turnips, spinach, leaf lettuce, chard, and winter onions. Be sure to check the maturity dates on the seed packets and count *back* from the first expected frost in your area. It's a good idea to sow the seeds a bit deeper during the heat of summer and sow them a little more generously so you get good germination. Keep the seedbed moist so it will have the opportunity to get started. A light misting two or three times

a day may be needed for the first week or so after planting.

Sow garlic cloves so they can start growing. Once the ground has frosted, apply mulch for the winter. Garlic will overwinter, start growing again next spring, and are ready to harvest by next summer.

LAWNS

As the end of the month approaches you can start seeding or installing new sod. It's a good time to overseed lawns that are thinning due to drought stress or weed invasions. Since weeds are tapering down their activity now, it's an ideal time to seed a lawn or patch bare spots with sod.

With less weed competition, grass can get a head start and grow thickly before winter. Kentucky bluegrass, turf-type fescue, and ryegrass can be seeded starting in mid- to late August. Prepare the soil ahead of time to create a good soil foundation for vigorous, strong, healthy root growth.

PERENNIALS

See "Here's How to Propagate Perennials from Softwood Cuttings" below.

ROSES

Later in the month and through mid-October as the heat subsides, you can plant container-grown roses that are usually on sale at garden retailers. Since they've been sitting at the store in a container all summer, it's best to get them planted right away so they can acclimate before the soil freezes. Select roses with healthy green foliage and strong stems; carefully slide the rootball out of the container to check for good root growth.

Follow the guidelines on planting container-grown roses in the April "Plant" section (page 74). Untangle or lightly prune off matted roots and circling roots caused by the confinement of the pot their stay in the nursery. This will help them transplant more successfully.

Prepare the soil by adding compost to your native soil; use one-third compost to two-thirds native soil. Throw a handful of high-phosphorus granular

HERE'S HOW

TO PROPAGATE PERENNIALS FROM SOFTWOOD CUTTINGS

This is a good month to propagate or start new perennials from softwood cuttings. This can be done at almost any time during the active growing season.

- Cut stem sections that have become somewhat mature; cut 6 to 8 inches back from the tip just above a node at the point where the leaves emerge. Select stems that are tipped with healthy foliage, or pinch off any flowers.

- Remove the lowest leaves so that an inch of so of the stem is bare. Dip or dust the cut end with a rooting powder (rooting hormone).

- Insert a pencil or dibble into a pot filled with moistened vermiculite or a sterilized growing medium to make a hole for the stem cutting.

- Then, stick the treated end of the cutting into the moistened rooting medium.

- Water in well and cover the container with a clear plastic bag to maintain humidity around the cutting.

- Place the containers in light, but not direct sun. Make sure the rooting medium does not dry out. The emergence of small leaves is a good sign that roots are establishing on the cutting.

- Remove the plastic cover and increase sunlight gradually. Water in with a soluble plant fertilizer diluted to half-strength.

- Transplant into larger containers if desired and place in the cold frame for overwintering, or plant directly into a prepared perennial bed. Shelter the young plants from harsh winds.

- Mulch with a few inches of compost or other organic material. Water as needed when the soil begins to dry out.

fertilizer into the bottom of the planting hole and lightly mix. If you like, prune off any flower buds so the plant can divert its energy on establishing new roots to withstand the fall and winter.

SHRUBS

Early August is not a good time to plant shrubs, particularly if there are high soil temperatures. This will only inhibit root growth and stress new plants. If you desire to plant, plan to spend extra time attending to their basic needs for establishment. Follow the guidelines for planting container-grown shrubs on page 96.

But as temperatures begin to fall later in the month, or during extended periods of rain and cooler days, you can transplant container-grown shrubs to their permanent locations. Remember to dig the planting hole two to three times wider to encourage strong root development, which allows them to become acclimated by winter.

As Labor Day approaches, many garden stores will promote sales for their overstock of shrubs. It is a good time to take advantage of the bargains and make new additions to your landscape. Purchase

■ *Columbine seedpods*

healthy, disease-free shrubs. Avoid stressed plants that will just sulk and be slow to start off.

TREES

Delay the purchase of balled-and-burlapped trees for several more weeks, until the weather is cool. As temperatures cool down, growers will dig and wrap new trees to sell. These are much better than those heeled in during the heat of summer with their rootballs exposed to the heat and drying conditions.

Container-grown trees can be planted now. This will allow them adequate time to get established before the ground freezes. See instructions for planting container-grown trees on pages 76–77. Pay attention to regular watering during the first few weeks after planting. Check soil moisture with a garden trowel to a depth of 6 inches or more, and if it is beginning to dry out, apply water to the water-holding dam surrounding the rootball.

VINES, GROUNDCOVERS & ORNAMENTAL GRASSES

As the weather begins to cool down in mid- to late August, you can start to plant container-grown plants again. Prepare the planting site by adding some compost or sphagnum peat moss. Incorporate at least one-third by volume into your native soil. This will help improve drainage, hold nutrients, and enhance root development.

Dig the planting holes two to three times wider than the container, and only as deep as the pot is high. Set the plants in the planting hole at the same depth as they were originally growing. If the roots have become potbound, tease them apart so they will intermingle with your native soil and start growing.

CARE

ANNUALS

Protect the annual and biennial garden from the heat and a prolonged drought period. Hopefully, most of our flowerbeds have been mulched.

As mulches tend to break down with microbial activity, it may be necessary to add more around the exposed areas of the flowerbeds. It is a good idea to maintain a 2- to 3-inch layer of mulch over bare soil. Mulch will suppress late weed growth and will ultimately enrich the soil with slow-acting nutrients as it decomposes.

The maturing heads of sunflowers may need protection from birds and squirrels if you intend to harvest them later. Cover the maturing heads with cheesecloth to prevent birds and other critters from removing the seeds.

Keep flowerbeds tidy by deadheading faded flowers, picking off dead leaves and pruning away injured stems. This will help to reduce the spread of diseases.

Do not allow the accumulation of dead or rotted plant debris to sit around in the flowerbeds, as this will attract slugs and often fosters disease spores.

If you like to collect flower seeds, now is the time to allow some flowers to mature so the seed will ripen. Columbine, bachelor's buttons, calendula, hollyhock, and four-o-clocks produce viable seed for future planting. Once the flower heads are dried, take a small paper bag outdoors and place the seedhead within the bag. Label the variety and color. Seeds will disperse into the bag and can be collected later and stored for future use.

BULBS

As the weather turns cooler, summer-blooming bulbs will start to wane a bit. Deadhead the faded flowers on dahlias, gladiolus, begonias, and lilies. Clip or pinch off yellow or brown foliage to keep the garden looking tidy. Don't pull as this often will yank the bulb out of the ground.

If the mulch in bulb beds has began to settle and decompose, topdress with new mulch to keep the soil cool and moist.

Be prepared for unexpected storms including hail that can shred the foliage and flowers. Have cardboard boxes or netting handy to cover plants prior to a predicted storm.

Pick some of the flowers that are beginning to open to enjoy in fresh bouquets.

■ *Mulching tomato plants*

■ *Place netting over your blueberries to protect them from the birds.*

EDIBLES

Topdress the vegetable garden with fresh compost as needed to maintain soil moisture and suppress weed growth. Mulching around tomatoes will keep the fruit from contacting the ground and rotting or getting invaded by earwigs and other pests.

Gather bundles of herbs, tie them together with rubber bands, and hang upside down in a warm, dark, dry garage or garden shed. You can start to harvest last year's crop of garlic when the tops turn yellow and flop over. Lift out the entire bulb and dry the garlic in a well-ventilated shed or garage.

To protect pumpkins and winter squash from rot, slip a roof shingle or a fragment of outdoor carpeting under ripening fruits to lift them off the moist soil.

Temperatures above 90 degrees Fahrenheit can slow tomato production. You can shade them with cheesecloth, but patience will pay off and they will start producing again as the weather begins to cool down.

Blackberries and raspberries are producing a good crop by now. Harvest them daily before the birds beat you to them. You can also cover vulnerable fruit with bird netting. Support the netting with stakes taller than the canes to prevent birds from perching on the netting and sneaking out exposed fruit.

Clean up plants that have stopped producing, including bush and pole beans, early cucumbers, summer squash, and peppers. If the plant debris is insect- and disease-free, chop or grind it up and add it to the compost pile. Cover the bare soil where plants were removed to keep it from baking and to reduce weed invasions.

Start harvesting early apples, pears, and peaches from your home orchard as soon as they ripen. Keep them off the ground to avoid rotten fruit that invites yellow jackets, earwigs, and diseases.

Harvest grapes in late August or early September.

LAWNS

If during the heat of summer your cool-season grasses, such as Kentucky bluegrass, have gone dormant, do not fear. It is perfectly natural for cool-season grasses to deal with the heat and water deprivation by turning brown, or shutting down the top growth. Instead of pumping more water to the lawn, allow the lawn to do its natural thing.

Warm-season turfgrasses will do just fine, but will require periodic watering to survive and look good. They are genetically equipped to handle the heat and drought better, though their leaf texture may be a bit rougher.

Check for insect pests that may be residing in the soil. Heavy bird activity in the yard may be an indication of larvae of sod webworms or grubs. Let the birds have at them and consume massive quantities.

Continue to mow both cool- and warm-season turfgrasses as needed. Remember the rule of mowing one-third of the leaf blade at each mowing. Avoid scalping (mowing too short) the lawn as this will stress the grass and cause it to dry out even faster. Leave the grass clippings to slowly fertilize the lawn.

■ *Scalping is a result of mowing too close.*

■ *If it's dead, clean it up.*

PERENNIALS

As the summer wanes, the perennial garden may begin to look a little shabby. Regular deadheading and cutting back spent flowers and dried foliage will tidy up the garden. Thin out crowded perennials to improve air circulation and reduce the incidence of leaf diseases.

Cut off diseased or insect-infested stems or foliage. If you haven't already staked late-season perennials such as Japanese anemone, hibiscus, moonflower, and asters, do so before they are subject to toppling over.

Inspect the mulch layer around perennials. If wind and natural decay have reduced its thickness to an inch or less, apply more mulch to raise the level to 2 to 3 inches. Leave only about a ½-inch-thick layer around the base of the crowns. This will discourage rodents from setting up home and will also prevent rot diseases.

ROSES

Continue to maintain a 2- to 3-inch layer of clean organic mulch over the soil in the rose garden. Old pine needles are one of my favorite mulches; if they are available in your landscape or neighborhood, use them, as they hold together nicely and provide a natural look.

Pick up fallen leaves to prevent the incidence of leaf diseases.

Some rose varieties are grown for their handsome rose hips as the flowers fade on the stem. By midmonth, stop deadheading spent flowers, and allow the rose hips to form. This practice, combined with shorter daylight hours, will signal the plant to slow its growth and prepare for fall and winter. Later in the season the rose hips will provide winter interest and a nutritious food source for birds and other visiting wildlife.

Check climbing and rambling roses to make sure that new growth is securely fastened to their supports. Winds that accompany late summer storms can loosen the canes, resulting in breakage and a ragged look.

Continue to remove any dead, diseased, and dying branches from your roses as needed. Dispose of any debris in the trash, as composting methods usually do not get hot enough to kill disease spores and weed seeds. Carefully inspect for any signs of pests or disease problems. Rust, a leaf disease that causes orange-red pustules on the underside of the leaves,

■ *Rose hips*

may start to show up on hybrid tea roses. Prune out infected canes and pick up fallen leaves.

Prune out suckers that may have sprouted from below the graft union of hybrid tea roses. This sucker growth has a different look from the original rose variety—faster-growing, heavier-leaved foliage. It generally produces no flowers or very tiny blooms.

SHRUBS

Shrubs require minimal care this month. Just be sure to water deeply during extended periods of drought and heat. Water when the top inch of soil starts to dry out. Newly planted shrubs benefit from some temporary shading if they show signs of scorch on hot exposures to the south or west. You can construct a lean-to onto which burlap or shade cloth can be stapled. Also, misting the foliage will help reduce severe stress to newly planted shrubs.

Make sure shrubs receive adequate air circulation to minimize the incidence of powdery mildew disease on the foliage. This may require selective pruning of the older stems that are crowded in the center of the shrubs.

Pay attention to those shrubs recently planted in the heat of summer. They still have a limited root system and will require proper watering to get established. Mist their foliage as needed to cool them down and spread mulch around the root zone if you didn't earlier.

Keep weeds from invading the shrub border. Weeds are in seed-making mode now and this will just add to the weed population next season. Dig, handpull, or hoe weeds as soon as you spot them. Dispose of weeds that have started seedheads as they continue to ripen and disperse if left in the garden. Do not compost weeds with seeds; throw them in the trash.

TREES

To lengthen the life of your trees, try as much as possible to duplicate their native conditions. In the wild, trees grow in communities and their soil is not compacted. Organic matter is continually being replaced by decomposing leaves and twigs on the forest floor. They generally do not have to compete with lawn grasses for water and nutrients. Trying to reproduce similar conditions will reduce stress to your trees and increase their life spans.

Prune only to maintain shape or for topiary or espalier training of trees. Remove broken branches as needed, and watch for diseased branches. Prune out water sprouts and suckers anytime they emerge. Suckers that arise from the base of the trunk should be removed at the point of origin below the knobby place where a tree may have been grafted to a specific rootstock.

VINES, GROUNDCOVERS & ORNAMENTAL GRASSES

Refresh the mulch under vines if it has dwindled. Fluff up the mulch with a rake where it has become compacted. This will allow air, water, and nutrients to reach the root zone.

Secure vine stems and branches that are growing out of bounds, being careful not to damage the plants. Training wayward vines now will save you time later. Boston and English ivies are notorious for growing along the ground when there is no support. Train them as you desire.

If your ornamental grasses are beginning to topple over, they may be getting too much nitrogen or water, or not enough sun. Give them support, such as a tomato cage, to keep standing tall, and plan to treat them differently next year. Relocate them to a sunnier location if light is the problem.

Continue to cut back the faster-growing vines to direct their growth and control their spread. Vines are resilient and can recover from several light prunings throughout the year. Keep them from pulling down gutters and covering the windows. Prune out dead, damaged, or overly long twigs that are rambling aimlessly.

Annual groundcovers such as impatiens and creeping zinnias continue to bloom until the first hard frost. You can stimulate more flower buds and new branching if you deadhead or pinch off the old flowers. After cutting them back, fertilize these annuals with a water-soluble plant fertilizer sprayed on the foliage.

WATER

ANNUALS

Water early in the day or late in the afternoon to allow water to percolate into the soil and to allow the foliage to dry out before nightfall.

Drip irrigation systems will soak the soil deeply and keep moisture from splashing upon the foliage, preventing foliar diseases. Otherwise, water with a frog-eye sprinkler that delivers water at a low angle in droplets that will soak down into the soil.

■ *To see if your container plants need water, stick your index finger in the pot. If the soil is dry down to your second knuckle of your index finger, water the pot.*

Flowers in containers dry out faster. Clay and terracotta pots tend to dry out even faster if they are placed in full sun. The plants have filled in the container with extensive root systems, leaving less room for soil. Keep an eye on them.

BULBS

If we experience a period of heat and drought, be sure to water summer-flowering bulbs so they can produce food energy and finish up their blooming cycle. Dig down into the soil and if it is beginning to dry out to a depth of 2 to 3 inches, turn on the sprinkler or drip irrigation system. Try to avoid overhead watering, particularly at night, as this will encourage foliar diseases.

Water container-grown bulbs regularly, as the potting mixture will tend to dry out faster. Don't let the plants wilt.

EDIBLES

Keep monitoring the water needs of edible plants. Hot weather can deplete plants of needed energy and delay or stunt production. If it doesn't rain for a week or more, water an inch or so, and let it soak in. This is where mulches are helpful to maintain the plants throughout the remainder of the growing season. Invest in soaker hoses and drip irrigation if time and water conservation are high on your garden wish list.

Regular watering is necessary to prevent tomatoes from splitting and cracking and will reduce the onset of blossom-end rot. Keep the bare soil mulched around the plants.

Keep newly planted seeds moist to ensure a vigorous root system. You may have to water both morning and early evening with a light sprinkling. Never allow the soil to get bone-dry, as this will surely kill newly germinating seeds or emerging seedlings.

Container gardens will require more attention in hot, windy weather. Reflecting heat from masonry walls, paved walkways, and driveways all contribute to faster drying of soilless mixtures. Check the soil regularly to customize your watering schedule.

LAWNS

Continue to water newly planted or sodded lawns if there is no significant rainfall for ten days or more. You will note drought stress by a bluish gray tinge and curled leaf blades throughout the lawn. This means it is time to water. Prolonged drought can kill clump grasses including turf-type fescue and perennial ryegrass.

Water deeply, but try to extend the time between waterings to conserve water and make the turf tougher. The soil underfoot will determine how long grass can go between waterings. In a well-prepared soil, grass plants develop deep roots that can capture water deeper in the subsoil, thus being capable of surviving drought. In poor soils, grass roots have no choice but to grow near the surface and will dry out quickly.

PERENNIALS

Continue to water new transplants as the soil begins to dry out.

Established perennials can survive with supplemental water for a week to ten days if they are properly mulched and watered deeply. During periods of little or no rainfall, be sure to water new plants when they need it, and not by the calendar or a water provider's calendar. Check the subsoil moisture by digging down a few inches and inspecting underneath the mulch. If the soil is beginning to dry out, it's time to apply a deep watering.

ROSES

Continue to water weekly, especially if rainfall is not adequate. Usually an inch of water a week is sufficient.

SHRUBS

Be sure to monitor soil moisture around newly planted shrubs, particularly during hot periods. Dig down several inches; if the soil is becoming dry to the touch, it's time to water deeply. Proper mulch around shrubs will also retain soil moisture and help keep the soil from baking.

Established shrubs should be just fine with a deep watering every seven to ten days, depending upon weather and soil conditions. Mulch over the root zone will reduce the frequency of watering, plus discourage weeds from invading.

TREES

If it has been a droughty summer and you are under water restrictions, then implement a triage system for watering your valuable trees.

VINES, GROUNDCOVERS & ORNAMENTAL GRASSES

Water plants as needed to prevent wilting. Early August can be hot and dry, so water deeply but not frequently. Take advantage of mulching to help conserve water, keep the soil from baking, and suppress weed growth.

Groundcover plants can be watered efficiently with a drip irrigation system. It's best to install the system before newly transplanted groundcovers intertwine, but soaker hoses can be placed throughout established plants with patience.

If you are growing hardy ferns as groundcover in shady exposures, the summer heat can be harsh on them. They prefer cool, moist conditions and will often show signs of scorch during heat and extended drought. Water them weekly to maintain more uniform moisture, and add organic matter to bare areas to enrich the soil and help retain moisture.

FERTILIZE

ANNUALS

Most annual flowers do not need additional fertilizer if you applied a slow-release form earlier in the season. The only exceptions are flowers planted in containers. Since they are watered more often, nutrients leach away more rapidly. Use a water-soluble plant fertilizer. I prefer to dilute the mixture to half-strength and apply at every other watering. If it has been over six to eight weeks since a slow-release fertilizer was applied, feed more to finish off the season. Lightly scratch the fertilizer into the mulch or soil and water in thoroughly.

BULBS

Summer-flowering bulbs will not benefit from fertilizer at this time of the year. They need to complete their flowering cycle.

If you are preparing flowerbeds for new plantings of hardy bulbs, incorporate a slow-release granular fertilizer while you add organic matter to the planting areas.

EDIBLES

Younger plants that were seeded for a successive crop will benefit from a sidedressing of granular fertilizer such as a 5-10-5. Lightly rake the fertilizer into the soil, and water it in. If you prefer, an application of soluble plant fertilizer can be sprayed on the foliage early in the morning or evening.

Herbs should be fertilized with a soluble plant fertilizer diluted at half-strength. Too much fertilizer will stimulate lush, succulent top growth that lacks flavor.

LAWNS

Delay fertilizing cool-season grasses until the first part of September (around Labor Day). If you are growing warm-season grasses, you can apply one last fertilizer application by mid-August. After that, warm-season grasses begin to go dormant with the arrival of cool weather and will not benefit from fertilizer.

PERENNIALS

You do not need to apply fertilizer after mid-August. Except for those perennials that bloom in the fall, most plants are already preparing to enter dormancy.

Unless you have six weeks or more before the first frost arrives in your area, any new growth stimulated by late fertilizer applications is likely to be killed by the frost.

ROSES

One last application of the homemade rose tonic (see page 222) can be made the first week of the month, but it's wise to finish up any fertilizing by mid-month. Again, we want the roses to harden up before winter, and feeding them too late in the season encourages softer, more frost-sensitive stems. It is important for roses to spend this time storing energy in their root system to prepare for fall and winter.

SHRUBS

Do not fertilize shrubs now. This is the time shrubs are acclimating for their winter rest period. The stems and branches will need to harden off so they won't be susceptible to frost injury. New growth that is induced now will usually not have adequate time to harden off. Don't think that fertilizing a stressed shrub will save it. Applying soluble salts to a stressed root system will only add insult to injury. Wait to fertilize in the early spring as the growth begins to expand.

TREES

Trees do not require fertilizing at this time of year. If anything, apply an organic mulch or compost around the root zone to renew decaying mulch applied in the spring.

VINES, GROUNDCOVERS & ORNAMENTAL GRASSES

There is no need to fertilize vines, groundcovers, and ornamental grasses this month. If you incorporated a slow-release granular fertilizer at planting time, it is likely that it is still providing some nutrition to the plants.

PROBLEM-SOLVE

ANNUALS

Powdery mildew is a foliage disease that rears its head at this time of year. It is often prevalent during warm days and cool evenings. Zinnias, annual phlox, some petunias, and filler plants in containers will show symptoms of a grayish white residue on the leaves. The best defense is prevention. Increase air circulation so plants are far enough apart to discourage this disease. Pinch or prune plants as needed to achieve this.

Powdery mildew is not life threatening to plants, but can weaken them by destroying healthy foliage that is the lifeline of more blooms. It can be treated with the homemade mildew control on page 220.

If you prefer, ignore this foliar disease since many annuals will be pulled up after the first hard frost. You can determine what is best according to the length of your growing season.

When watering the flower garden, water the *soil*. Try to avoid wetting the foliage, particularly at night.

Wind, heavy rainstorms, or hailstorms may occur during the month. When possible, you can protect plants with rigid cardboard boxes or netting. Have some handy in the garage or garden shed. Annuals that have been staked will be better protected against high winds.

PLANT SYMPTOMS, CAUSES, AND CURES

If you were frustrated by a variety of insect and disease problems in your annuals this year, here are some tips to remember to prevent serious problems next growing season:

- Look for signs of sticky sap on the stems and foliage that indicate that aphids are starting to attack the plants. Wash them off the plant with a forceful spray of water or use a homemade soap spray.

- A fine webbing near the main stems and around the leaf stems usually indicates that spider mites are a problem. Wash both the tops and undersides of the leaves with soapy water. See the homemade remedies on page 220. You may need to use a miticide. Read and follow label directions.

- If the leaves are beginning to turn yellow but the veins are remaining a bright green, this indicates a lack of available iron. Fertilize with a chelated iron.

- Leaves that develop a grayish white coating on their surface indicate powdery mildew. Handpick the worst leaves; treat minor mildew problems with the homemade mildew control.

- When the tender growth of annuals and foliage is twisted and turning yellow or brown, there could be possible herbicide injury. Did some of the herbicide you or a neighbor sprayed on weeds drift to the flower garden?

- Plants that develop lower leaves that turn yellow and begin to drop off indicate something is going on in the root system. Could it be overwatering or the soil not draining properly?

■ *Iron chlorosis means your plants need some iron in the soil in a form that is available to them.*

BULBS

Be on the watch for insect pests as they make their last efforts to feed on succulent foliage. Aphids can cluster in masses on the stems. Wash them off with a forceful spray of water or use a homemade soap spray to get rid of them.

Mildew may show up on the foliage since warm days and cool nights favor this disease. Remove severely infected leaves and dispose in the trash. Spraying with the homemade mildew control can prevent severe infections from occurring. Repeat sprays as new leaves emerge.

EDIBLES

Watch for spider mites and whiteflies. Mites cause the leaves to look a sickly brown or silvery gray. Pinch off and discard the badly infested leaves. Spraying the upper and lower surfaces of the leaves with water will keep mites at bay temporarily. You must be persistent with natural controls. Natural populations of ladybugs will consume large quantities of aphids.

If virus diseases attack tomatoes and peppers in your garden, the best control is to remove and dispose of infected plants. There are no miracle treatments for viruses. Choose disease-resistant varieties for next year; and make a note in your garden journal to indicate which plants were infected the worst.

Tomato leaves that are curled and have purple leaf veins may be infested with tiny insects called psyllids. Dust the plants with sulfur to control this problem.

Powdery mildew is a sure bet this month and will show up on melons, cucumbers, summer squash, and other vegetables. Warm days and cool nights favor this disease. You can choose to ignore it on maturing plants or those that are nearing the end of the growing season. On newly planted fall vegetables, you can prevent mildew by applying the homemade mildew recipe on page 220. It will protect the plants from a severe infection so they can continue to produce foliage and a late crop.

Continue to pull or dig weeds before they have the opportunity to produce seeds.

To exclude wildlife including rabbits, raccoons, deer, and mice, fencing is the best defense, but in some cases, you can try repellents.

LAWNS

Eliminate weeds early in the month if you plan to reseed or sod a new lawn in early September. It will take two to three weeks to get rid of the most stubborn weeds, roots and all. Use a herbicide that contains glyphosate since this targets all weeds, but allows you to plant within a few weeks after application.

One way to sample areas of the lawn for soil insects is to mix 2 to 3 tablespoons of liquid detergent in 1 gallon of warm water. Pour this solution over a 1- to 2-square-foot area. The detergent will irritate soil-inhabiting insects and drive them to the surface. If there are more than five caterpillars per square foot, it may be necessary to treat the lawn with an

HERE'S HOW

TO SPOT-TREAT WEEDS

1. Remove the top and bottom of a 1-gallon plastic milk jug.

2. Cover the weed with the plastic milk jug.

3. Spray the herbicide on the weed inside the milk jug. The jug protects any surrounding plants from the harmful weed-killer. Remove the jug after the herbicide on the weed dries.

■ *You can easily make a weed guard to spot-treat weeds, if you need to protect nearby plantings.*

appropriate soil insecticide. Keep the pets and birds off the lawn if you decide to treat with an insecticide. Read and follow label directions carefully.

PERENNIALS

Continue to be on the watch for pests in the perennial garden. Plants that are infested with mites will have pale, faded, or stippled leaves. Remove these tiny pests with a strong stream of water from the garden hose. You can also apply a homemade soap spray if their numbers are high and damage is significant. Hosing down, too, can control aphids. Let the natural predators like ladybird beetles visit your garden to feast on aphids.

Fungal diseases can start to show up with warm days and cool nights. Powdery mildew can be controlled with better air circulation, the homemade remedy on page 220, or appropriate fungicides. Read and follow label directions.

Weeds should be controlled before they go to seed. Handpull or dig as needed. Dispose in the trash; never put seedheads in the compost pile as they are likely to survive to invade the garden another day.

■ *Spider mites can do quite a lot of damage.*

watch for these problems and take appropriate action. Use a preventative such as the homemade powdery mildew control on page 220. If diseases are a major concern, have them properly identified before using a fungicide. Read and follow label directions when applying any pesticide.

A virus disease known as rose mosaic will sometimes show up in the rose garden. Infections are systemic, working their way throughout the plant. Plant growth may be stunted, and foliage will develop a splotchy pattern of light green or yellow. There is no cure for plant viruses, so you may want to remove infected plants or stems. But since there is no adverse effect on actual flowering, you may choose to leave the bush alone and ignore the virus if it doesn't seem to be moving through the entire plant.

Spider mites and aphids may still be a problem on rose foliage this month. These pests will target plants that are stressed or weak. Consider their appearance as an alert, and try to discover why the bush is struggling. It may be in an improper location; if so, you can make plans to move it next spring. Prevention, early detection, and proper treatment are your best defenses.

■ *Blackspot on rose leaves*

ROSES

Powdery mildew, rust, and blackspot are a few foliar diseases that may show up this month. Be on the

SHRUBS

Some insect activity continues this month. Be on the watch for pest infestations. Aphids, spider mites, and eriophyid mites may be a problem. Keeping the shrub stress-free can prevent a severe problem. Hosing down infested plants will help, as will the application of insecticidal soap sprays. Do not apply insecticides during the heat of the day; apply very early in the day or in the evening as temperatures fall.

Powdery mildew disease is common by now on lilac, dogwood, honeysuckle and other shrubs that experience shade or poor air movement. You will notice a whitish gray coating on the leaves and new growth. While it looks ugly, it is generally not fatal to the plant. In a few weeks the foliage will be dropping anyway. If you are concerned about mildew and want some kind of control measure, try my homemade remedy on page 220.

Good air circulation goes a long way to control many leaf diseases. Spider mites can be a problem on evergreen shrubs that are stressed by heat and drought. Look for signs of sickly, yellowish foliage and a thin webbing among the branches and needles. Use a strong stream of water from the garden hose to wash them off and discourage a repeat attack. Repeat this every few days for a couple of weeks. Light horticultural oils can also be used against mites. Use as directed on the product label. Avoid insecticides that kill the beneficial bugs that are predators of mites.

TREES

Spider mites are very active during hot, dry weather, especially on evergreens and many ornamental trees. Symptoms of mite invasions include salt-and-pepper or bronze-colored foliage. You may often see a network of tiny webs forming a highway for mites to travel from one branch to another. Tap a suspect branch over a white sheet of paper, and look for moving specks. See the homemade remedies on page 220 for a safe control.

Natural mite predators can control mite populations. A strong spray of water from the garden hose applied to the undersides of the leaves will dislodge many adult mites throughout the growing season. Insecticidal soap sprays, homemade soap spray, (see page 220), or a miticide can help. Read and follow label directions when using pesticides.

Powdery mildew diseases can be most prevalent now with cooler night temperatures. Prevention is the best defense. Grow powdery mildew-resistant varieties whenever you have a choice. Prune the tree for better air circulation and sunlight penetration. Also, reduce the use of high-nitrogen fertilizers to avoid late-season succulent growth that is more susceptible to mildew.

Cercospora leaf spot is a common disease on aspens and poplars. It causes brown lesions on the leaves, and foliage will eventually turn yellow or brown and shed from the trees. Maintain good air circulation in the trees by proper pruning practices.

VINES, GROUNDCOVERS & ORNAMENTAL GRASSES

Wilting is not always an indication that plants are thirsty. If the foliage recovers when evening arrives, the problem is just plain heat. Water plants only if wilted foliage does not recover in the cool of evening. If watering does not do the trick, it may be a sign of a virus or wilt disease. In this situation, pull the infected plant and discard it in the trash. Do not compost diseased plant materials.

Foliar diseases, including leaf spot and powdery mildew, may show up this month. You can prevent many of these fungal diseases by providing good air circulation around vines and groundcovers. This is where pruning is necessary to thin out crowded and crossing branches. For powdery mildew, try using the homemade mildew control to prevent a severe outbreak of this disease. See page 220 for the recipe.

Insect invasions may still be evident on groundcovers and vines. Be on the watch for mites, aphids, and caterpillars. These pests can be controlled by hosing them down with a forceful spray of water.

September

Although the gardening season is beginning to wind down, September still has many warm days to allow some annuals and perennials to finish off in glory. The rich yellow-and-golden marigolds bloom with gusto until a hard frost. Petunias and geraniums still provide plenty of color.

Labor Day weekend traditionally marks the unofficial end of summer, even though there are several weeks before fall officially arrives. This can be a glorious time in the perennial garden. Lower temperatures tend to intensify colors in the garden and crisp the foliage. The changing angle of the sun casts a different light and creates warm hues throughout the landscape.

Take time to enjoy roses in bloom. You may find that the plants will respond with more intense blooms with the break from the heat.

Cooler weather is a welcome change from summer's heat. It also signals that it's time to get things done before the ground freezes solid. There will be opportunities to plant new shrubs offered for sale at local garden retailers. Check plants carefully before purchasing; the healthiest specimens are the best candidates for fall transplanting.

Jack Frost is lurking behind the corner waiting to finish off the annuals and give the signal for autumn to arrive. Have plant protectors handy (cardboard boxes, 5-gallon plastic buckets, frost blankets, and the like) if you desire to extend the growing season.

Photograph plants in your landscape to capture their subtle changes. Make notes in your journal of vines, groundcovers, and ornamental grasses that did especially well, and note those that may need rejuvenating. Maybe you could change an area from lawn to groundcover if the light conditions make it difficult for turf to grow. Note this now, so you can sketch plans and prepare to do the project next spring.

Early fall is an acceptable planting season in the Rockies. Waiting too late in the season can jeopardize a plant's ability to transplant successfully. For most parts of the region, get fall planting completed by mid-October or sooner. I recommend planting evergreen shrubs in the spring instead of the fall.

SEPTEMBER

■ *Though this shows an African violet being propagated from leaf cuttings, the process for propagating other plants from tip cuttings is the same.*

PLAN

ANNUALS

If you have time and space to overwinter some of your favorite annuals, plan to take cuttings of geraniums, verbena, coleus, impatiens, begonias, and others. Root the tip cuttings in a sterilized potting mixture. They will usually root within four to six weeks and can be potted indoors for winter color.

Plan to condition or move tropical plants growing in containers to an inside porch or patio to protect them from the colder nights. Many filler plants are tropicals and cannot withstand the cool nights, so you must decide to either keep them or let them die at the end of the growing season.

BULBS

Sketch out a garden plan to mark areas in the landscape where bulb plantings are located. Consider the view from your home's windows, the height of the bulbs, bloom times and sequence, and colors on the plan. Consider companion perennials to interplant with the bulbs to help camouflage the ripening foliage as the bulbs die back.

Make plans to dig up the summer-flowering bulbs that are not winter hardy. These include dahlias, cannas, begonias, gladioli, and caladiums. Store in a cool, frost-free area in the basement or garage.

When autumn arrives, and before the first frost, bring your amaryllis indoors and place in a sunny window. It will bloom again when the time is right.

EDIBLES

With some planning, you can devise protective covers and extend the garden season, even after the first frost in September. Covers can be made from 5-gallon buckets, large fiber nursery pots, plastic or spun fabric tunnels, or cold frames. With this extra protection, cool-weather crops can continue to grow and produce for several weeks more.

As time permits, plan to prepare the soil in the garden for next year's crops. If the weather remains mild for several weeks, you might consider planting a "green manure" or cover crop such as winter rye grass, winter wheat, or oats in early September. This will grow through the fall and can be turned under in the spring to improve soil fertility and structure. It will also hold topsoil in place, improve water retention, and suppress annual winter weeds.

LAWNS

This is a wonderful month for cool-season grasses as they display their full potential and emerald green color against the beauty of a cobalt blue Rocky Mountain sky. Cool nights and warm days make it ideal to plan on reseeding bare spots, plugging in new sod if needed, or starting a new lawn from seed or sod. Plan to have any seeding complete by late September to ensure good germination and root establishment before the ground freezes. Adjust planting times according to your specific elevation and growing season.

Before you plant, add organic amendments (a minimum of 3 cubic yards of organic amendment per 1,000 square feet); rototill or disk to a depth of 4 to 6 inches. This is the time to plan to upgrade or amend lousy soils with a quality organic amendment such as sphagnum peat moss or compost.

PERENNIALS

Many of the earlier blooming perennials have set seedheads or seedpods that accent the garden. Black-eyed Susans, datura, turtlehead, tall sedums, asters, and others sport interesting textures amidst their late-summer foliage. You can either deadhead these or leave them for fall and winter interest. Remember, some will self-sow seeds as well.

GREEN TOMATO ROUNDUP

If a hard freeze is on its way, you can either pick all your tomatoes or, if you have space, pull entire plants. If you harvest the whole plants, hang them upside down in a garage or basement, and let the tomatoes ripen gradually. Check them frequently to get the ripe ones before they hit the floor and go splat!

If you pick green tomatoes, sort them by size. Use the smaller ones in recipes that call for green tomatoes. Those about ¾ of full size will ripen. Place them in a shallow cardboard box, stem-end facing upwards, and cover them with newspaper. You don't need to wrap each fruit individually. Store in the basement or warm area of the garage. Lift the newspaper cover every day, and check for ripe tomatoes. Remove any that show signs of rotting.

■ *If you buy cover crop seeds in individual packages (particularly peas), instead of by the pound, dump all of the seed packages into a big bowl to save time opening packages later. Planting will go faster!*

■ *Use a hoe to dig rows that are 6 inches apart. Then, plant the seeds and cover them with 1 inch of soil. Cover cropping works best if you can plant a large section of the garden or an entire 4 × 4 raised bed with the same type of seeds. Water the seeds daily until they sprout, then water every four or five days.*

Continue to add to your garden journal. Make notes on what's blooming this month as the garden season winds down. If you notice large gaps in the blooming sequence, times when nothing is flowering or the foliage is boring, think about acquiring plants that will add blooms during these times. Check with local nurseries or visit public gardens to see what they use to fill in the gaps.

Refer to the *Rocky Mountain Getting Started Garden Guide* for suggestions on perennials that bloom at various times to extend the flowering season. Some autumn-blooming perennials include mums, coneflowers, asters, blanket flowers, coreopsis, and sneezeweed. One of my favorite bulbs is the resurrection lily, *Lycoris squamigera*. It magically sends up blooming flower stalks amidst waning perennials.

See "Here's How to Create a New Garden Bed" on page 168.

ROSES

If this was your first season growing roses, you have gained valuable experience. You may have discovered that some roses are easier to grow than others. The keys to success are proper location and care. Roses do best if you meet these following requirements:

- Site in at least 6 hours of full sunlight; roses seem to prefer more sun in the morning and some shade in the afternoon to cool them down.

- Provide good air circulation.

- Have excellent soil drainage.

- Water at least 1 inch of water weekly.

- Allow at least 18 inches of distance from walls and fences.

- Use an organic mulch to conserve water and maintain uniform moisture.

- Monitor for insect pests and diseases.

Now is the time to check clearance sales for rose plants and garden accessories. You will find container-grown rose bushes, trellises, arbors, benches, gazing balls, decorative containers, pruning tools, and much more—all marked down.

SHRUBS

Plan to take time to enjoy this slower time of year. Jot down notes of how your shrubs change color with the season; accentuate the positive as well as noting the not-so-desirable attributes. It will help you in changing your landscape when spring arrives next year.

TREES

This autumn, plan to recycle your fallen leaves for mulch or add them to the compost pile. Leaves are a *great* source of free organic mulch for use under trees or in shrub borders. If you do not have a compost pile, use the leaves to start one. See "Here's How to Build a Compost Pile" on page 170.

Shop for new tools, if needed. A new, durable rake will help with leaf cleanup. Invest in a compost thermometer, a chipper/shredder, hardware cloth to protect tree trunks, and quality birdseed.

VINES, GROUNDCOVERS & ORNAMENTAL GRASSES

Make plans to get garden projects underway before the snow flies. Trellises may need repair or painting. Reinforce trellises and fences if the vines are pulling them down or sideways. In larger masses of groundcovers, steppingstones for a walkway will make it easier to maintain the plants and lead you through the garden. Add more compost to bare spots to improve soil structure and drainage.

American bittersweet and euonymus should be loaded with colorful fruit. Plan to harvest some of the branches for indoor fall arrangements. If they are not yet fully dry, hang them upside down in a cool, dry place for a few weeks. Once thoroughly dry, they will last a long time as unique accents.

PLANT

ANNUALS

It is getting too late in the season to plant new annuals. However, some will self-sow where they grow and new seedlings will emerge next spring.

■ *Ornamental cabbages and kale will survive light frosts and look great in a container.*

Snapdragons self-sow freely in my garden and even germinate if the soil remains somewhat warm. Next spring they will continue to grow and flower.

For autumn color and texture in the flower garden, plant ornamental cabbage and kale, violas, and pansies. These are cold hardy and can withstand a light frost.

Containers of flowering annuals may be found on sale at some garden retailers. They are good fillers for the end of the season and will provide color for fall gatherings or outdoor events.

BULBS
Though spring-flowering bulbs do best in sunshine, that doesn't mean you can't plant them near trees and around shrub borders. The leaves on deciduous trees and shrubs usually don't emerge until many spring-flowering bulbs have finished blooming. Avoid the deep shade of tall evergreens, as growing bulbs need to utilize sunshine to manufacture food reserves before going dormant.

Plant daffodil bulbs as early as you can get them since they need more time to develop roots before the ground freezes. Tulips can be delayed for a few weeks if you don't have enough time to plant all your bulbs this month. They do not need to root right away and seem to be less susceptible to rot if they can be delayed from sitting in warm soil. So let the soil temperature cool down a bit if it's been hot and dry.

Plant fall-flowering bulbs as soon as you can get them. These include autumn crocus (*Crocus speciosus* and *C. kotschyanus*) and meadow saffron (*Colchicum* spp. and hybrids). You may often find *Colchicum* bulbs blooming in the storage bins at garden stores.

If you have space in the garage, window well, or cold frame, pot some spring-flowering bulbs to force into bloom. Use a good potting mixture and containers that have drainage holes. Depending on the type of bulbs you're forcing, it will take up to sixteen weeks of chilling for root growth and dormancy before they will initiate bloom. Paperwhite narcissus does not require a cold treatment to bloom.

See "Here's How to Plant Bulbs for Maximum Effect" on page 171.

EDIBLES
You can get a head-start on spring spinach if you plant seeds in a prepared bed early this month. Sow the seeds and keep the bed watered to allow them to germinate. The new young plants will overwinter in a mulched bed and resume growth in the spring.

There is not adequate time to plant cool-weather crops, unless you grow them under protection (like a cold frame). However, you can increase your collection of indoor herbs by taking stem cuttings from outdoor plants.

Plant cover crops for "green manure" at least a month before the first killing frost. Annual rye grass, oats, buckwheat, and crimson clover can be planted in late August to early September.

LAWNS
This is the best time to seed a new lawn or overseed thin, bare spots in cool-season lawns. It is too late to plant warm-season grasses, unless you intend to do a dormant seeding. See "Here's How to Fix Bald Spots in the Lawns" on page 172.

Spot-treat weeds ten to fourteen days before seeding. If the weeds are going to seed, snip off seedheads to prevent their dispersal throughout the yard and garden. Leave the foliage intact so you can spray the leaves with an appropriate herbicide. Read and follow label directions carefully.

HERE'S HOW

TO CREATE A NEW GARDEN BED

Chances are there is already something growing where you want to install your new garden. And chances are it's not desirable vegetation. As tempting as it is, do not just jump right in and start planting, figuring it will be easy to just pull the weeds as you go. Proper site preparation is the key to success. Take the time to get rid of existing vegetation and improve the soil before you start putting plants in the ground. This preparation will pay significant dividends.

1. Use a sun-warmed garden hose to lay out your proposed garden, following the topography of the site. Most gardens look best with gentle curves rather than straight lines.

2. Remove existing vegetation.

   There are several ways to get rid of existing vegetation. Which way you choose depends on how much time you have and how you feel about using herbicides.

   Option 1: The most natural way to create a new garden bed is to dig it up manually. Just be sure to get rid of all the existing plant roots. Even tiny pieces of tough perennial-weed roots can grow into big bad weeds in no time. A major disadvantage with this method is that you lose substantial amounts of topsoil. To avoid this, if you have the time, you can simply turn the sod over and allow it to decay on site. This will take at least one growing season.

Option 2: You can also smother the existing vegetation with about 6 inches of organic mulch such as straw, shredded bark, or compost. Mow closely in spring, cover with a thick layer of newspaper (ten sheets or so) and the organic mulch, and let it stand all summer. Replenish the mulch in fall, and by the next spring your garden should be ready for planting. This method works best on lawn areas rather than areas with lots of deep-rooted perennial weeds.

2 (Option 2)

Option 3: If you don't have a year to prepare the soil or the manual method doesn't appeal to you, you can use a nonselective glycophosphate-based herbicide such as Roundup, which kills tops and roots of herbaceous plants. If you follow directions exactly, aim carefully, and use only when necessary, these products should kill unwanted

2 (Option 1)

plants without causing undue harm to the environment. Allow at least two weeks for all the vegetation to die after spraying. Tough perennial weeds may require a second application.

2 (Option 3)

3. Turn in soil amendments to a depth of 6 to 10 inches. Once the existing vegetation is dead or removed, turn the soil by hand or with a tiller, and add soil amendments.

Do not use a tiller without killing all existing vegetation first—it may look like you've created a bare planting area, but all you've done is grind the roots into smaller pieces that will sprout into more plants than you started with. Even after multiple tillings spaced weeks apart, you'll be haunted by these root pieces.

3

4. Edge the garden. Install edging to keep lawn grasses from invading your garden. The best option is to install a barrier of some type. When it comes to barriers, it's worth paying more for a quality material. Metal edging buried 4 inches or more into the soil effectively keeps turf from sneaking in. If you go with black plastic edging, use contractor grade to avoid having to replace it in a few years.

4

5. Cover the new garden with mulch.

Mulching your new garden will not only help keep the weeds from settling in, it will also help maintain soil moisture and prevent the soil from washing away until you can get the plants established. Cover the entire prepared garden bed with 2 to 3 inches of an organic mulch such as shredded bark, pine bark nuggets, cocoa bean hulls, and shredded leaves. Avoid using grass clippings; they tend to mat down and become smelly.

5

HERE'S HOW

TO BUILD A COMPOST PILE

- Find an area in your landscape that is out of plain sight and receives at least a half-day of sun. This is the spot where you will be depositing lawn and garden waste.

- Collect herbicide-free grass clippings, prunings, weeds without seeds, disease-free annuals, and fallen leaves. Throw them into a pit or a heap. Do not add meat, bones, or pet waste to a compost pile.

- Rent a shredder/chipper to chop coarse organic materials into smaller pieces so they will decompose more rapidly. You can chip small branches and twigs into wood waste that will break down into an earthy compost.

- If you have a lot of garden waste, consider enclosing the compost with fencing, wood pallets, cinder blocks, or use a commercial compost bin.

- Spread yard waste into 4- to 6-inch layers; add 1 inch of soil between layers to introduce microbes that will aid in the digestion of the organic materials. Keep the compost lightly moist to hasten decomposition.

- Turn the compost pile frequently, as soon as the interior of the pile heats up to 150 degrees Fahrenheit.

- You can speed up the decomposition process by adding special composting worms called "red wigglers." These are available through mail-order or online.

- Next spring to early summer, you can begin to harvest the finishing compost at the bottom of the pile or pit. This organic amendment will crumble in your hands and have an earthy aroma.

Plant a premium lawn seed with a hand or mechanical spreader onto the prepared soil.

If you like, cover the seedbed with clean wheat straw or a thin layer of sphagnum peat moss (⅛ to ¼ inch deep). This will help conserve water and hasten germination.

Install sod for an instant lawn or to replace bare spots. See page 94 for instructions.

PERENNIALS

Late summer and early autumn is a good time to plant perennials, either the ones you started from stem cuttings, or plants that are available locally. Just be careful about purchasing plants in containers. They may not look great at this time of year because they, too, are getting ready for the winter. Some may have already become rootbound and need immediate transplanting.

Plant them as early as you can so they can establish a vigorous, hardy root system before the ground

HERE'S HOW

TO PLANT BULBS FOR MAXIMUM EFFECT

1. Dig informal planting beds in the shapes of circles, squares, triangles, or irregular shapes that create the effect you desire. Mass displays are much more appealing than bulbs lined up in rows. Prepare an area as wide and long as the intended bulb bed. Reserve the backfill soil nearby.

2. Work compost, about one-third by volume, into the bottom of the bulb bed and then level the bottom of the bed with the back end of a rake.

3. Plant the bulbs, pointed side up, spaced equidistant, or as you prefer.

4. Sprinkle some slow-release granular fertilizer over the backfill soil and mix it in. If the soil is heavy clay or extremely sandy, this is also a good time to add compost.

5. Refill the designated bulb bed, being careful not to disturb the bulbs.

6. Firm the soil gently over the bulbs, and water in thoroughly.

7. Mulch the area with a few inches of pine needles, wood chips, or shredded cedar mulch.

TO FIX BALD SPOTS IN THE LAWN

1. Start by using a hard rake to spread compost, topsoil, or garden soil in a ½-inch layer covering the bald spot. While you can sow seeds directly in the bare spots, the grass will sprout more quickly and won't dry out as easily if it can start growing in loose, fresh soil.

2. Use a hand spreader to spread grass seed thickly and evenly over the entire area, slightly overlapping the edges of the grass that isn't covered with soil. When you're done seeding, the ground should look like it snowed lightly.

3. Sprinkle wheat straw, which you can get at garden centers and home-improvement stores, over the newly seeded area. This will help the seeds stay moist until they sprout. It's easy to grow new grass seed as long as you keep it moist. The biggest problem that people have when overseeding or replanting lawns is that they don't keep the grass seed moist while sprouting. The straw mulch helps eliminate that problem.

4. Grass seed must stay moist until it sprouts. Watering once a day for a couple of minutes isn't enough. Water the newly seeded area twice a day for ten minutes until the grass is at least an inch tall. Then water the newly seeded area three times a week for ten minutes. Don't mow the newly seeded area for at least two months. Newly growing grass is fragile, and foot traffic or mower blades could rip the new grass seedlings out of the ground.

freezes. They do not have to produce foliage and flowers at this time of year, so the plants put their energy into expanding their root systems.

Take special care if plant roots are matted and wrapped around themselves from being confined in the containers for such a long time. Tease apart the roots, or gently pry them loose so that they can expand and grow into your native soil.

Dig and divide overgrown irises, poppies, peonies, and other spring-blooming perennials. This will provide more plants to add to your garden or share with friends.

ROSES

Even though it's fall, you can still plant container-grown roses if you do it soon. This will allow proper root development before the ground freezes. Follow the planting guidelines in April "Plant" on page 74. You can add a handful of granular phosphate fertilizer (0-20-0) into the bottom of the planting hole but don't add a rose fertilizer that contains nitrogen. Water newly planted roses thoroughly, and continue as the long as the weather remains dry and the soil is unfrozen.

Miniature roses can be planted outdoors (as described for container-grown roses), or you can repot them in fresh potting soil and bring them indoors for the winter. Provide bright light and relatively cool temperatures, 65 to 70 degrees Fahrenheit.

SHRUBS

The shrubs you purchase now are not in bloom; hopefully the tag-along plant labels are still in place. You need this information to ascertain light and soil needs, height and spread, flower color, and any special requirements.

This is not a good time to relocate your established shrubs to new locations in your landscape; wait until spring. In the interim, insert a sharp shovel into the soil around the root zone to prune roots. This will stimulate more fibrous root growth, which makes the shrub easier to move next year.

TREES

Labor Day is a traditional time to plant new trees to replace ones that have died or if you just need or want more trees. Container-grown trees are still readily available and can often be purchased at sale prices. Follow the tree-planting guidelines on page 76.

VINES, GROUNDCOVERS & ORNAMENTAL GRASSES

This is the time to plant spring-flowering bulbs. They make wonderful groundcovers by themselves or can be underplanted with perennial groundcovers. Once the bulbs have finished blooming, the groundcovers help mask the ripening bulb foliage. Use a bulb planter to set bulbs within groundcovers. Plant the bulbs at the appropriate depth and water in well. Miniature daffodils, crocus, snowdrops, wood hyacinths, dwarf irises (*Iris reticulata*), grape hyacinths, and others are good to plant among established ground covers. Study the bulb catalogs and experiment with different kinds.

You can still plant container-grown groundcovers and vines while the soil remains unfrozen. Ornamental grasses, however, are best planted in the spring and early summer.

Prepare the planting sites with a generous supply of compost or a mix of compost and sphagnum peat moss. I like to use a 50/50 blend at the rate of one-third by volume to my native soil.

CARE

ANNUALS

Monitor the nighttime temperatures during the month, as evenings are getting cooler. When the night temperatures drop to 55 degrees Fahrenheit, it's time to bring in tropical plants that you desire to keep as houseplants. Wash the foliage and stems to remove any aphids and mites that can piggyback indoors. You can spray the foliage and stems with the homemade soap spray, then rinse the plant with water. This will help to dislodge many pests and remove the dust and grime from the foliage.

Clip off broken or diseased leaves and stems from annuals as soon as you spot them. This will reduce the onset of diseases. Pinch off or deadhead old faded flowers to keep the garden looking fresh and tidy. Those annuals that are obviously exhausted and not blooming should be pulled and discarded. Once the annuals are out, spread organic mulch over the bare spots to suppress winter weeds from germinating. Cut back the seedheads of annuals that you do not want to self-sow for next year. When the first frost blackens or kills the tenderest annuals, pull them as soon as possible.

BULBS

When digging or planting new bulbs or perennials, be careful not to dig or injure already-planted

TO OVERWINTER GERANIUMS

If you like to overwinter your favorite geraniums, it's time to make them ready for the transition to the indoors.

- Cut back the leggy stems, dig the plants up, and pot them up in a quality potting mixture.

- Add a teaspoon of slow-release granular fertilizer, and mix into the soil. Water the new transplants in well.

- If you don't want to keep the entire geranium plant, take 4-inch stem cuttings from the tips. Insert the cuttings in moistened vermiculite or perlite, and cover with a plastic bag to create a mini-greenhouse effect so the cuttings root more quickly. The cuttings should root within four to six weeks.

- Once rooted, transplant into potting soil.

- Place in bright light to encourage healthy stems and foliage.

hardy bulbs. This is why it is important to mark bulb beds with permanent labels.

If an early frost kills back the tops of summer-flowering bulbs, it is time to make plans to dig them and place them in cool storage. Otherwise, treat them as annuals and discard them on the compost pile as you clean up the garden.

Clean up summer-flowering bulbs by cutting off the ripening foliage with scissors. Deadhead faded flowers. Remove dead, fallen leaves that can harbor diseases and insects.

EDIBLES

Harvest young broccoli, cabbage, and other cool-weather crops planted in July or early August. If they are not quite ready, mulch them so they can continue to grow through a light frost. Root crops can be left in the ground until after the first hard frost. This will actually sweeten their flavor. Try this with carrots, turnips, and parsnips.

Harvest winter squash and pumpkins as they mature later in the month. The outer skin will be too hard to penetrate with your thumbnail. If left in the garden and hit by a frost, the outer skin will decay. Cut the pumpkins and winter squash from the vines, leaving a short piece of stem on

the vegetable. They will last for several months in cool, dry storage.

Harvest any remaining onions and garlic when the tops turn yellow or brown and flop over. Cure, or dry, the bulbs for a few weeks in a warm, dry, shady, airy place. Then store them in a cool, dry location.

If tomatoes have not been killed by the first frost, you can encourage more fruit to ripen by covering the plants at night with a frost blanket. Remove the cover during the warmth of the day. Also, try pulling the indeterminate tomato plants that still have clusters of green tomatoes attached and hang them upside down in a garage or garden shed where they won't freeze. These will eventually ripen.

Some gardeners harvest the last of green tomatoes and place them in single layers in cardboard boxes in a warm room. Do not place them in direct sunlight, or they will sunscald. Over a period of weeks, the green tomatoes will ripen.

LAWNS

If your lawn experienced heavy foot traffic over the summer, this is a great time to core-aerate your lawn prior to the application of lawn fertilizer.

After core-aeration, topdress your lawn with pulverized or fine compost that will filter down into the soil through the holes created from aeration. This will also encourage microbial activity to help decompose thatch. (Note, you can screen purchased compost for topdressing or screen your own homemade compost.)

You may leave the cores remaining from the aeration on the soil surface and they will eventually break down by irrigation and rainfall. If you wish, rake up the plugs and recycle to the compost pile. Some prefer to mow after aeration, but mowing over the cores will dull your lawn mower blade, so remember to sharpen the blade if you don't rake the cores.

■ *If your lawn has worn spots from heavy foot traffic, this is a good month to treat that by core-aerating.*

HERE'S HOW

TO OVERWINTER FROST-TENDER TROPICALS

Banana plants, hibiscus, oleander, lantana, bougainvillea, and other tropical plants need to be moved indoors before a hard frost if you want to carry them over for next season.

1. Bring the plants into a garage, sunroom, or other protected area. Keep them isolated for two weeks. Monitor for insects and other pests and use an insecticidal soap to treat aphids and spider mites. Handpick and destroy slugs, earwigs, beetles, and caterpillars.

2. Move plants indoors to a sunny location. A south- or southwest-facing window or sunroom would be ideal. If you don't have a sunny room, artificial lights will enhance light conditions in most homes.

3. Continue to water the soil mix thoroughly whenever the top few inches start to dry out. Do not fertilize until the plant has time to adjust to its new location and shows signs of growth.

4. Prune or shape the plant to fit into its winter location. It is normal for leaves to drop; up to one-third of the leaves may shed. The plant will replace fallen leaves as it adjusts to the new environment.

5. Continue to monitor for pests and water as needed.

6. Prune overgrown plants in late February or March. Pruning too late will delay summer bloom.

7. Wait until late February or early March to start fertilizing with a diluted solution of flowering houseplant food.

Continue to mow cool-season grasses at a height of 2 to 3 inches. Be sure the blade is sharp.

When you mow the lawn in autumn, use a mulching mower that will finely cut the grass blades. The finely cut leaf fragments will filter down between the grass blades to decompose and enrich the soil. You are, in effect, mulching the grass plants, just as you would other landscape plants to conserve water and keep the soil cool. If you collect clippings, put them in the compost pile. Be sure the clippings are not contaminated with weed seeds or pesticide residues.

PERENNIALS

Keep perennial beds tidy and weed-free by regular deadheading and digging or pulling out weeds that have snuck into the garden before they go to seed. If plants in certain parts of the landscape have not performed well, there could be a problem with the soil. Look for symptoms of yellowing foliage, stunted growth, and lack of vigor. These could also be signs of a pest invasion. Consider having a soil test performed to determine if there is a lack of available nutrients.

When the birds have had their fill of seedheads from coneflowers and black-eyed Susans, you can cut back the old stems to the ground. To maintain a tidy garden, continue to prune out dead and dying stems and foliage. Deadhead spent flowers to keep perennials and their foliage appealing.

■ *Once seedheads from black-eyed Susans, coneflowers, and sunflowers have been picked clean by the birds, like this nuthatch, you can cut down the stalks.*

ROSES

Avoid the urge to prune back roses in September, as it can stimulate new growth that won't have time to harden off for winter. Remember, rose bushes need to utilize as much foliage as possible to produce the stored energy that helps them survive the winter.

Continue to deadhead hybrid tea roses, and there may still be time for late buds to open. Discard fallen leaves and other debris that may be harboring insects, their eggs, or plant diseases.

Topdressing the soil around your roses with compost or composted manure is not essential, but it is a good way to improve the soil. As it breaks down, it will provide some slow-release nutrients come springtime. You can combine this task with season-end cleanup.

Delay piling mulch up over the crowns and lower stems of roses for winter protection. It's still too early. Wait until the plants have become more dormant and there is frost in the ground.

Continue to deadhead spent blooms and to pick up fallen leaves. Remove damaged or broken canes as soon as you discover them. Delay structural pruning until spring. The more healthy canes that remain, the better the chances for winter survival.

SHRUBS

Continue to care for newly planted shrubs by watering deeply as soon as the soil begins to dry out. This is especially important during periods when rainfall is scarce. Replace mulch over the root zone if it is beginning to diminish. Mulches help to maintain uniform moisture in the soil and discourage weeds. Established shrubs need attention too. Water at least once a month to allow them to properly harden off (prepare for winter) before frost arrives.

Frost-sensitive plants such as citrus, fig, Norfolk pine, bougainvillea, fuchsia, and others that have been spending the summer outdoors will need to come indoors before frost. Now is the time to check whether they need repotting; if so, increase the size of the container an inch or two and make sure the container has drainage. Use a good potting mixture

TO PREPARE MINIATURE ROSES TO GROW INDOORS

1. Wash mini roses' leaves and stems with soapy water, then rinse with clear water.

2. Lightly prune the roots to remove any circling around the container.

3. Repot into fresh potting mixture if the plants have become rootbound.

4. If needed, spray the foliage with Neem oil or insecticidal soap to eliminate any residual aphids or spider mites, including the egg stages.

5. Bring the potted roses indoors so they can adjust to the indoor environment.

Note that reduced light will cause some leaf drop. Locate them in the sunniest area, a western or southern exposure. Eventually, your miniature rose will acclimate to the indoors. They grow best with bright light and cool temperatures of 65 to 70 degrees Fahrenheit.

to which you can add slow-release granular fertilizer. Set the plant at the same depth in the new container that it was in its previous pot. Lightly firm the potting mixture to fill in spaces, and water in well.

Check plants for any signs of insect pests. Wash their foliage with water or use the homemade soap spray on page 220. Rinse the leaves, allow to dry, and then bring indoors. If you have a serious pest problem, you may spray the foliage and stems with a light horticultural oil. This will suffocate most pests and their eggs. Read and follow label directions on the product package.

Limit pruning to insect-infested stems, storm-damaged branches, and dead wood. Use sharp pruning equipment to make clean cuts.

TREES

Delay refreshing the mulch around trees until after the ground freezes to keep rodents from setting up house. Make them choose other areas for their cozy winter nests. Thin or remove groundcover plantings to within a foot of the tree's trunk. Protect trunks of young trees by encasing them in hardware cloth to keep critters from nibbling the tender bark over the fall and winter.

Delay most pruning until late winter or early spring when the trees are leafless. You can prune out dead, dying, or diseased branches anytime. Use sharp and clean pruning tools to make clean cuts.

VINES, GROUNDCOVERS & ORNAMENTAL GRASSES

Bring in the tender vines that were summering out on the patio or deck as night temperatures get too cold. Check these plants for insects and spider mites that would have a field day if they piggyback inside. If you discover any pests, wash them off with a forceful spray of water, or use the homemade soap spray (see page 220).

When Jack Frost leaves his calling card, it's time to clean up the garden. Remove frost-blackened annual vines from their trellises or other supports. As the foliage of some groundcovers matures and ripens, snip off the dead leaves, and put them in the compost pile. This will help improve the appearance of the bed and reduce the areas where insects and diseases may spend the winter.

Unless vines are extremely top-heavy or damaged by wind and storms, delay pruning until late winter or early spring. Pruning can stimulate latent growth during a possible Indian summer. This tender new growth is vulnerable to frost injury, which stresses the plant. It is okay to prune off dead, dying, or damaged branches or stems.

WATER

ANNUALS

Continue to water the annual flower garden if rainfall is scarce. With cooler weather and shorter days approaching, you don't need to water as often. Remember to check the soil moisture in the flowerbed by digging down with a garden trowel. If the soil is beginning to dry out to a depth of 3 to 4 inches, it's time to water.

Annuals in containers will need more constant attention, as they will dry out faster.

Use a trowel to dig down into the soil, under any mulch, to test soil moisture. If it's dry several inches down, it's time to water.

BULBS

During prolonged hot, dry periods of three weeks or more, water new hardy bulb plantings as the soil dries out. Fall winds and high temperatures can dry the soil out quickly. Dig down underneath the mulch, and check to see how the moisture is holding up. If it is beginning to get dry to a depth of 4 inches or more, it's time to set out a sprinkler to water.

EDIBLES

Unless the autumn is extremely dry, there is no need to water the garden if cool-weather vegetables have been properly mulched. If you're uncertain, check underneath the mulch with a garden trowel or shovel to see what the soil moisture is like. Cool weather is a time to wean the garden off frequent waterings.

During dry spells, continue to water perennial vegetables, including asparagus and rhubarb.

Keep the compost pile moist to help speed up the process of decomposition. The microorganisms will continue to work on warm days, and the pile may emit steam in the early morning, meaning things are in balance. Composting can continue deep in the pile even after the first few frosts.

LAWNS

Water established lawns deeply and infrequently when rainfall is scarce. I usually water the lawn once a week during the fall months. This will encourage strong root and rhizome growth of cool-season grasses such as Kentucky bluegrass. Test for soil moisture by probing the soil with a heavy-duty screwdriver or garden trowel. When the soil is moist to a depth of 4 inches, you don't need to water. If the soil is beginning to dry out, give the lawn a deep watering.

Keep newly seeded areas continuously moist to ensure healthy establishment. As sprouts grow into seedlings, water deeply, but less often, to encourage the roots to grow downward for drought endurance.

PERENNIALS

Monitor watering of newly set perennials so they can establish a healthy root system. New transplants need the most attention before the soil freezes. If the plants are well-mulched, they need moisture less frequently. Dig down several inches underneath the mulch to see the depth of subsoil moisture. When the soil begins to dry out, it's time to water.

Cooler weather generally means less watering. During a prolonged drought and a hotter-than-usual month, however, the rules may change. This is why you need to check the soil regularly to develop a proper watering schedule for your particular soil conditions.

ROSES

If natural precipitation is limited, continue to water roses both in the garden and containers. Water deeply every two weeks, depending upon weather conditions and how fast the soil dries out. Monitor soil moisture with a soil probe or dig down with a garden trowel. Proper watering during this season will help the roses get ready for winter conditions as they gradually harden off their canes. Keep them healthy and they will continue to reward you for years to come.

SHRUBS

When natural precipitation is lacking and during prolonged periods of drought, water shrubs if the soil is becoming dry. Check underneath the mulch to determine if the soil is drying out.

TREES

Continue to water newly planted trees as needed. Check the soil moisture by probing into the root zone to a depth of 4 to 6 inches. If the soil is becoming dry, give the tree a good watering to maintain subsoil moisture before the ground freezes. Water established trees during prolonged periods of drought. Use a frog-eye sprinkler or soaker hose to water deeply and keep the subsoil charged with adequate moisture. This is generally needed every five to six weeks, depending upon weather conditions.

VINES, GROUNDCOVERS & ORNAMENTAL GRASSES

If you are experiencing prolonged periods of dry, windy conditions, water new plants at least every two weeks. This will protect your investment and ensure root survival. Established plantings can get along with a deep watering once a month. Mulched areas will not need to be watered as frequently because the mulch helps to maintain soil moisture and reduce evaporation.

Check the soil around ornamental grasses. If it is beginning to dry out, give it a deep watering about once a month. The same goes for perennial vines. The soil should be watered thoroughly before it freezes.

FERTILIZE

ANNUALS

There is no need to fertilize annuals in the garden this month. If you have containers you intend to bring in for the winter as houseplants, you can add some slow-release granular fertilizer into the potting mixture. This will provide the plants with nutrients over the next several months.

BULBS

Fertilizing should be done at the time of planting hardy bulbs. The easiest way is to sprinkle a slow-release granular fertilizer into the backfill soil and then cover the bulbs with the prepared soil. Never let fertilizer directly touch the bulbs as the salts may damage the bulb and impede root development.

EDIBLES

No fertilizer is needed at this time of year.

LAWNS

For cool-season grasses, apply a complete lawn fertilizer that contains iron and sulfur during the first part of the month (around Labor Day). This will be the first of the autumn lawn fertilizer applications. It is helpful to core-aerate the lawn prior to putting down the fertilizer. Water the lawn after the fertilizer is applied.

PERENNIALS

Fertilizing is not necessary this late in the season. Allow the perennials to initialize their dormancy cycle so they are well-equipped to tolerate the winter weather.

ROSES

Outdoor roses do not need supplemental fertilizer applications at this time, but topdressing with compost or aged manure can condition the soil.

SHRUBS

Delay fertilizing newly planted and established shrubs until next spring.

TREES, VINES, GROUNDCOVERS & ORNAMENTAL GRASSES

No fertilizer applications needed this month.

PROBLEM-SOLVE

ANNUALS

Insects and other critters are getting ready for fall and winter. They will seek out nesting sites to spend the cool nights. To reduce pest problems, promptly pull up dead and dying plants and discard them in the trash. If dead or frosted plants are healthy, retire them to the compost pile. They can be shredded or chopped to hasten decomposition.

Deer, rabbits, meadow mice, chipmunks, and other critters can make sneak attacks in the flower garden as they browse about. To repel them, spray the homemade critter repellent (see page 221). This will temporarily keep them at bay. Repeat as needed.

Rust (orange powdery spots on the leaves) may appear on snapdragons, hollyhocks, and other plants. Rake up fallen leaves and dispose. Do *not* compost.

BULBS

HERE'S HOW

TO SCREEN BULBS FROM PREDATORS

To protect hardy, spring-flowering bulbs from voles and pocket gophers, cover the newly planted bulbs with a heavy mesh screening that will allow the shoots to grow through. Dig a planting bed or trench about 10 inches deep and spread a ½-inch mesh across the bottom and up the sides of the hole. Plant the bulbs at the proper depth and then finally cover the top with more wire mesh screening.

EDIBLES

Insects will be looking for winter quarters this month. Cultivating the soil and exposing their eggs or other overwintering stages will keep bugs from becoming a problem.

Rodents may try to overwinter in the compost pile or mulched areas. Check for signs of their activity. To deter mice, voles, chipmunks, and other critters, delay spreading mulch until the ground has frozen hard. By this time, they will have found homes.

LAWNS

Broadleaf and grassy weeds continue to grow until a hard frost. Take advantage of the warm days to spot-treat with an appropriate herbicide. Read and follow label directions. Controlling weeds in the autumn gives you a head start on next season.

By all means take time to pick the seedheads off maturing weeds, put them in a big plastic bag, and dispose in the trash. Don't let weed seeds disperse everywhere this fall.

White grubs may continue to harm lawns in the early fall. Dead patches may appear throughout the lawn or at the edges of sidewalks or driveways.

Flocks of black birds feeding on the lawn generally indicate that soil insects are present. Even skunks will find grubs a food source and will dig holes in the lawn seeking these delectable morsels. As long as the soil temperatures remain in the 65- to 75-degree Fahrenheit range, you can treat grub problems. Grubs begin to migrate deeper in the soil below the frost line to overwinter. A long-term biological approach to managing grubs and larvae in the soil is with milky spore disease, a naturally occurring bacterium (*Bacillus popilliae*). It will infect many types of beetle grubs including white grubs.

Weeds will continue to grow and produce seedheads, so keep pulling them. Remove dead and dying plants from the garden, and recycle disease- and insect-free plant debris to the compost pile. Do not compost weeds that have seedheads. The compost pile usually does not get hot enough to kill weed seeds, and you will be plagued by their growth next year. Clean out container gardens after herbs and vegetables are finished producing. This will remove nesting areas for insect pests and disease organisms.

PERENNIALS

Continue to wash aphids and spider mites off plants that are infested. It's getting late enough in the season that knocking these pests off the foliage and stems will soon do them in.

■ *If you see skunks digging in your yard, they are likely looking for grubs to eat. Treat the lawns for the grubs and the skunks should go away.*

Remove infected leaves that have mildew or rust and dispose of them in the garbage. Do not add diseased plant debris to the compost pile.

Don't turn your back on weeds. Summer annuals including goosegrass and crabgrass are going to seed now. Get rid of them before they disperse their seeds everywhere you don't want them.

ROSES

If your roses continue to show signs of leaf diseases such as mildew or blackspot, cut off infected portions and discard in the trash. Preventative sprays of baking soda and horticultural oil can also be helpful. See homemade remedies on page 220. Soon the leaves will drop and you can clean them up to remove disease spores.

If weeds have popped up, handpull or dig them out so they won't get a chance to go to seed. It's much easier to pull weeds when the soil is moist after a rain or routine watering. If summer's mulch has decomposed or thinned out, refresh it with new mulch to keep weeds at bay. Keep mulches a few inches away from the canes to discourage rodents like voles and meadow mice from nesting there and chewing the stems.

SHRUBS

Insect problems should be slowing down by now. If there are late outbreaks of aphids, hose them down with a forceful stream of water from the hose. Homemade soap spray can be used too. Frost will soon arrive and wipe out a good majority of the wimpy bugs.

Mildew continues to show itself on shrub foliage. It is primarily unsightly and does not need to be sprayed. Leaves will soon be shedding; plan to clean up and discard diseased leaves that drop to the base of the shrub. This will help reduce the spread of this disease next season.

Continue to pull or dig weeds; don't let them go to seed. Prevention of weed seed dispersal will cut back a bad invasion next year.

Protect new shrubs from possible damage from wildlife and rodents. Have repellents ready to use; build wire cages to erect around vulnerable shrubs.

These will reduce severe gnawing damage from deer and elk. You can make homemade collars to protect stems from the ravages of rabbits, mice, and voles. Do not place mulches right around the base of stems as this often encourages rodents to nest.

TREES

Prepare now to protect trees from deer, elk, and rodents that like to feed on the bark. Protect trees from deer and elk with fencing that encloses the trunk. Keep the fencing 2 feet away from the trunk by using stakes to create an encasement around the trunk.

Smaller animals such as rabbits and voles can be deterred by installing hardware cloth or plastic guards around the trunks of young shade and fruit trees. To discourage voles and meadow mice, pull the mulch away from the trunk about a foot.

Hardware cloth cylinders can be constructed to keep rabbits and voles from chewing the bark. Use a shovel to cut the ground around the tree just enough to insert the wire cylinder. The bottom edge of the cylinder should be at least 6 inches below the ground level. To avoid future injury to the trunk, move the hardware cloth cylinder farther away from the trunk after one or two years.

VINES, GROUNDCOVERS & ORNAMENTAL GRASSES

It's the season for critters to scout out winter nesting sites, and rodents like to construct winter homes in heavily mulched areas. Keep mulch away from the base of vines and ornamental grasses. A good rule of thumb is to wait to apply more mulch around plants until after the ground freezes. By then, meadow mice, voles, chipmunks, and other critters will have already nested elsewhere.

Continue to pull up weeds or dig them out before they go to seed. It can be challenging to get weeds out of groundcovers, but after a good rain or irrigation, slip on a pair of leather gloves and start pulling. Otherwise, you may need to spot-treat weeds. Remember to shield groundcovers before spraying a weed's foliage.

October

October is one of my favorite months. Cool nights, crisp mornings, and comfortable days make it an ideal time to enjoy your landscape. Take time to travel. There are so many beautiful sights, sounds, and aromas to be discovered in our region. In the High Country, frost may have already ended the season for many flowering annuals and perennials. However, in the lower elevations frost may not yet have arrived.

Cool-season grasses including Kentucky bluegrass, turf-type fescue, and perennial ryegrass perform at their best in autumn. They take advantage of the cooler weather to store energy from the leaf blades to the root system. Soil temperatures are ideal for vigorous root growth, and rhizome root systems make the lawn grow thicker.

Many ornamental trees and shrubs brighten autumn skies with an assortment of colors ranging from fiery reds, oranges, and yellows. This coloration occurs naturally as days grow shorter and the pigments become unmasked. Yellow xanthophylls, orange carotenoids, and red anthocyanins are present in foliage. The anthocyanins are manufactured by the conversion of sugars in autumn; the other pigments have been there all along, but are not visible until the masking green chlorophyll breaks down in fall.

When other perennials are finished, fall bulbs such as meadow saffron (*Colchicum autumnale*) bloom with wonderful lavender to purple blossoms. Look for the bulbs at local garden stores or nurseries, and plant some now for next season. They grow their foliage in spring, die back in summer, and emerge with flowers in autumn.

If you have a slope and want to design and install a stone wall, this would be a good time. It's fun to plant and watch plants grow and develop among native rocks. Stack the lower layer of rocks on a solid foundation of sand and make it level. Then work your way upwards with more rocks to the desired height.

PLAN

ANNUALS

Plan to salvage annuals that you wish to keep as houseplants. These might include geraniums, coleus, impatiens, and begonias. Take 4- to 6-inch cuttings from the terminal growth and root in moistened vermiculite, perlite, or sterilized potting mix.

Note when the first frost arrives. In most regions, it occurs about the same time every year, give or take a week. In the coldest parts of the region, and higher elevations, frost can arrive sooner, so be ready to move container-grown annuals indoors or to protected areas.

BULBS

Bulb-planting season continues while the weather remains mild and the ground gets a chill. Plan to try something new. There are so many kinds of tulips, daffodils, and the minor bulbs that can brighten areas of the landscape in spring.

If you are planning to overwinter tender summer-flowering bulbs, locate a spot where the temperatures are about 45 to 55 degrees Fahrenheit. An old root cellar would be ideal, but most of us don't have that option. So pick a spot in the basement, a window well that can be insulated, or an attached garage. An old refrigerator that is still in good working order will do nicely too.

Plan an area to "naturalize" with the minor bulbs such as crocus, winter aconite, miniature narcissus, grape hyacinths, and glory-of-the-snow. You might consider planting a slope with these minor bulbs for a real impact and then interplant with a companion groundcover to conserve water (as a living mulch).

EDIBLES

This is the month to amend the bare garden soil, so make plans to stockpile some well-rotted manure, compost, shredded leaves, or dried grass clippings. Leaves that have waxy cuticles should be shredded or sent through a grinder before adding to the garden soil. Otherwise, you'll have a mucky mess come spring.

■ *Composting can be a challenge for small-space and city gardeners, but it is worth it. An ideal location for a compost bin is one hidden from view but close enough for you to easily bring stuff to it and haul the finished compost away. It is also nice to have the compost pile near a water source so you can add water during dry spells, but it's not necessary. Some type of creative screening is usually necessary.*

LAWNS

If you seeded or sodded a lawn in September, plan to maintain a uniform watering schedule to ensure the grass plants are deeply rooted before the ground freezes in November or December.

If your underground sprinkler system pipes are shallow (4 to 6 inches) plan to have them blown out (winterized) to prevent freeze damage. Contact a reputable sprinkler service for this chore. Protect the aboveground backflow preventer and above ground parts by wrapping with a blanket or insulation, then a plastic bag to keep it from getting wet. Secure with duct tape.

PERENNIALS

Plan to expand a perennial bed or maybe reduce the size of one that is getting out of hand.

Take time to prepare the soil before planting a new perennial bed. The key to success is in a well-drained soil that is enriched with humus.

ROSES

Plan to visit public and neighborhood gardens to see what roses are growing and how they are sited in the landscape. It has been tradition to plant roses in beds where they show off their stunning blooms. In their own beds, they are easy to prune, water, fertilize, and maintain. One of my favorite ways to accentuate a rose bed is to plant hybrid tea, grandiflora, or floribunda roses in an actual antique iron bed frame. When sited in full sun, the roses grow and bloom to create a colorful tapestry.

October is a good time to design a rose garden, either a separate bed or a section in your landscape, to accommodate roses of your liking. Be picky about the location to provide optimum growing conditions.

SHRUBS

Cooler weather and bright sunny days make October in the Rockies a real pleasure. This is when we appreciate the last colors of autumn. Some shrubs not only show colorful fall foliage but also yield berries to feed the birds in winter.

HERE'S HOW

TO OVERWINTER TREES IN CONTAINERS

It's not too early to plan how you will overwinter small trees in their pots. You can choose one of three ways, and some early preparation is necessary. So this is a good time to decide, based on your landscape, which method will work best for you:

1. Place the tree in a cold frame or unheated garage or garden shed if the ground is frozen solid.

2. Bury the tree, pot and all, in the ground, and mulch with compost or shredded wood chips.

3. Partially bury the tree in a sheltered place in the yard with shredded wood chips and compost piled generously over the pot.

Whichever method you choose, you'll need to water periodically, every three to four weeks if the winter is dry.

TREES

Photograph the trees in their autumn glory, and decide which colors you would like in your landscape. This will help you plan your tree plantings next spring.

VINES, GROUNDCOVERS & ORNAMENTAL GRASSES

If the first fall frost has not visited your garden, it won't be long. Enjoy the mild autumn days, and photograph your landscape to capture the essence of fall. Make notes in your garden journal as the season winds down, and note the date when the first frost arrives for future reference. October is the time to plan the color of your next year's autumn if it is lacking.

If your landscape lacks red fall foliage, consider planting Virginia creeper next spring. Its leaves transform to shades of purple, red, and scarlet. Most other vines display yellow fall color. The many types of sumac can also add flaming red to the autumn landscape.

There are a few evergreen groundcovers that transform from green to purplish red in fall. One of my favorites that I've planted for many years is *Juniperus horizontalis* 'Wiltonii'. A deciduous groundcover that holds its foliage through the fall and winter remarkably well is *Ajuga* 'Burgundy Glow'.

Cranberry cotoneaster is a hardy deciduous shrub that works well as groundcover as it spills over rocks and retaining walls. The foliage turns a plum purple in fall, covered with bright red berries. The seed capsules on vines such as bittersweet and euonymus can be quite outstanding, so if you have an appropriate location, plan to add these colorful touches to your landscape for next fall.

PLANT

ANNUALS

Continue to plant ornamental cabbage and kale as they are available in nurseries. These plants will add color and texture to the flower garden. They can fill in the bare spots and accent the rock garden or terraces. Many that I've planted have tolerated light frosts and will last well into December.

BULBS

As long as the weather permits and the ground is not frozen, continue to plant spring-blooming bulbs. Plant *en masse* to create more dramatic effects, or if space is limited, dig a trench at the proper depth for the specific bulb and plant a row along the driveway or sidewalk. Bright colors are always a welcoming beacon.

Mix bulb plantings into perennial flowerbeds or groundcovers. You can plant under trees whose shallow roots will not be disturbed by the shallow planting depth. This is a form of naturalizing an area under the canopy of deciduous shade trees.

To protect hardy, spring-flowering bulbs from voles and pocket gophers, cover the newly planted bulbs with a heavy mesh screening that will allow the shoots to grow through. Dig a planting bed or trench about 10 inches deep and spread a ½-inch mesh across the bottom and up the sides of the hole. Plant the bulbs at the proper depth and then finally cover the top with more wire mesh screening. Also see page 180.

■ *Pansies and violas are great late fall annual additions to the garden.*

EDIBLES

There is very little planting to do in October. Plants growing in cold frames are the exception as you control the environment. Prop open the lid on warm sunny days and cover the cold frame in the evening. You can grow leaf lettuce, endive, escarole, and radishes for several weeks by this method.

HERE'S HOW

TO PATCH A BARE SPOT WITH SOD

1. Use a spade to cut a square or rectangle shape around the damaged or bare patch. This will make it easier to snugly fit the sod patch in place.

2. Break up the soil with a garden fork and mix in compost or a similar amendment. Level the patch area to about 1 inch below the surrounding turf. Lightly tamp the soil down with a scrap 4 × 4 or metal tamper.

3. Measure the patch area; cut a piece of sod to fit snugly. It's better to cut it slightly larger and then trim it to fit as necessary. Use a large, sharp knife to cut the sod.

4. Settle the patch with the back of a garden rake to ensure good contact with the soil below. Water well, keeping the patch moist until it is well-established.

If frost has not killed back all the herbs in your garden, you can still dig up viable plants and pot them up in a soilless potting mixture or take cuttings to root indoors.

Herbs can be grown on a sunny windowsill or under bright artificial lights on a plant stand. Watch for insects that may piggyback indoors. Control the pests by washing them off the foliage and stems.

If the weather remains mild and the soil is workable, plant a crop of fall garlic if the bulbs are available at your local garden store. After the soil freezes, mulch the garlic with straw.

LAWNS

In most parts of the region, it is getting too late to plant new grass seed. If you have experience, you can try dormant seeding, but remember that birds, other critters, and the wind may be factors that will affect successful germination. Dormant-seeded lawns in areas without snow cover are exposed to winter winds, strong sunlight, and drought.

Soil conditions are ideal for sodding. You can sod a new lawn, or replant bare spots with new sod pieces.

■ *Other than overwintering herbs to grow indoors on sunny windowsills, there's not much planting going on in the edible garden.*

PERENNIALS

You can continue to plant perennials practically anytime the ground is not frozen. It is much better to plant them than to store them in their cramped containers over the winter. The earlier you plant, the better head start the plants will have to establish roots before the ground freezes.

ROSES

Although it's pushing the envelope to plant roses now, you can gamble and plant container-grown roses that you find on sale. Dig the planting hole two to three times as wide as the container, and prepare the soil with compost or sphagnum peat moss.

SHRUBS

Plant evergreen shrubs no later than mid-October to help ensure their survival before the soil freezes hard. You can safely plant shrubs till mid-month, but waiting too late can jeopardize root growth if the soil freezes suddenly. Mulch around newly planted shrubs to keep the ground from freezing. This will give extra time for root growth, and it helps retain more uniform moisture.

TREES

You still have the opportunity to plant new deciduous trees provided you get it accomplished by mid-month. Waiting too late is a gamble and may result in transplant shock and tree losses. Trees that are planted earlier in the fall will have a better chance of acclimating before the ground freezes solid. Remember to dig the planting hole two to three times wider than the rootball to allow for strong and healthy root establishment. Dig the hole only as deep as the rootball.

VINES, GROUNDCOVERS & ORNAMENTAL GRASSES

If planting must be done this month, get container-grown nursery stock in the ground by mid-month. After that, you are gambling with nature. Plants need at least four to six weeks in unfrozen ground to establish a strong root system. Keep them watered as the soil dries out, and mulch around the plants (not directly at the base of the vine or groundcover), to help maintain soil moisture and prevent the soil from freezing early.

Snow cover will help insulate the soil in some parts of the region, but on the High Plains, snow is not a long-lasting commodity in the autumn landscape.

CARE

ANNUALS

Continue to monitor the flower garden and pull out annuals that have succumbed to frost damage. To encourage copious numbers of free seedlings next spring, disturb the soil as little as possible while removing the dead and dying plants.

Some garden flowers including cleome, four o'clocks, and love-in-the-mist will produce many seedpods or capsules and self-sow into the surrounding soil. So to discourage too many seedlings, rake up the remaining summer mulch and replace it with a fresh layer of chopped wood shavings, pine needles, chopped leaves, or compost.

Non-diseased plants can be placed in the compost pile. Cover up the bare spots with a 3- to 4-inch layer of mulch such as compost, shredded leaves, cedar mulch, pine needles, or evergreen boughs. This will protect the soil over the winter and suppress winter annual weeds from germinating.

Remember to collect the seeds from any annuals you would like to grow again next year. Cut off the ripening seedheads or capsules prior to throwing the spent flowers into the compost pile or the trash. Store the seeds in brown paper bags in a cool, dry spot. Just as a reminder, if you collect seed from hybrid flowers and fruits, the offspring will be variable in color and size.

Clean up flowerbeds, and get the soil ready for next year by allowing the chopped leaves from the mulching mower to cover the bare spots. This material will eventually break down and provide organic matter. Mulch the bare soil.

BULBS

Once frost has killed back the tops of gladiolus and dahlias and other tender bulbs, it's time to dig them up. They can be stored over the winter in a cool spot. Inspect the bulbs, tubers, or corms for signs of disease or insect damage. Discard any that are suspect. Many will have developed offshoots or new bulblets. I prefer to store the entire clump and separate the new segments in the spring.

Shake the excess soil from the bulbs; store in old wooden crates or Styrofoam coolers filled with slightly moistened sphagnum peat moss or sawdust. Place in an area where temperatures are between 45 to 55 degrees Fahrenheit. Check monthly for signs of rot (too moist) or shriveling (too dry).

EDIBLES

Some years, we experience an Indian summer, and pumpkins, winter squash, and ornamental gourds

HERE'S HOW

TO OVERWINTER TENDER BULBS

Carefully dig up the tender bulbs with a spading fork. Allow plenty of digging room for additional bulbs that may have multiplied over the summer.

Cure (dry) the bulbs for storage by letting them dry out of the direct sunlight. See suggested curing times in this chart:

Bulb	Cure Time	Storage Material	Storage Temperature
Tuberous begonia	several days	dry peat moss	50 degrees Fahrenheit
Caladium	several days	dry peat moss	50 degrees Fahrenheit
Calla lily	one to two days	peat moss or perlite	50 degrees Fahrenheit
Canna	overnight	peat moss	45 to 50 degrees Fahrenheit
Dahlia	several hours	dry peat or sawdust	45 degrees Fahrenheit
Gladiolus	two weeks	dry/in mesh bags	40 degrees Fahrenheit

Place the tender bulbs in a box or wooden flat filled with peat moss, sawdust, or other storage material. Gladioli prefer to be stored dry and uncovered. Label the type and color of the bulb. Move to a cool, dark location for the winter.

Check monthly for signs of mold (which indicates there is too much moisture) and discard any bad bulbs. If they shrivel, a light misting is all that's needed. If mold becomes a problem, increase air circulation.

can continue to mature in the garden. Once a hard frost arrives, harvest them right away so they won't rot. When the pumpkins turn a solid orange, cut their stems with a knife. Cure them in a warm, dry location for a week or so. Then store in a cool, dry garage or barn at 55 to 60 degrees Fahrenheit.

Do you still have green tomatoes? They require temperatures of 65 degrees Fahrenheit to ripen. Harvest unblemished green fruits, set them in shallow cardboard boxes shoulder to shoulder, and store them in a cool spot to ripen. Bring the pinkish ones inside to ripen more quickly in the warmth of the kitchen. Enjoy!

Collect and grind or shred leaves and other garden debris that may blow in. Add to the compost pile. Keep weeds pulled or dug to prevent seed dispersal. Throw away plants that are suspect for diseases. Squash vine borers can overwinter in plant debris, so dispose of any plants that are likely to harbor these pests.

LAWNS
Keep new grass seedlings thriving by regular watering. This is when the plants need to establish a vigorous, strong root system to survive the winter.

■ (Top) *A leaf blower can make quick work out of clearing the lawn of leaves, especially if your town has curbside pickup. The blowing action also clears organic debris down to the soil, helping ready the lawn for winter.* (Bottom) *Using a blower/vac to pick up leaves is a quick way to gather them for your own compost pile.*

STORING ROOT CROPS AFTER THE FIRST FREEZE

Even when the weather turns frosty, root crops can be stored in place if you know how. Cover carrots and parsnips with straw or compost up to 6 inches deep. This will protect the roots and make them even sweeter. When you need to harvest some, just pull away some of the mulch, and dig down to harvest what you need. Replace the mulch to protect the remainder from constant freezing.

An alternative to storing root crops in the ground is to bury a 5-gallon bucket in the soil, harvest the root crops, and place them in moistened sand in the bucket. Put the lid on the bucket, and set a bale of straw as mulch on top of the lid. You can access the bucket when you need to harvest vegetables for the kitchen.

Fertilize cool-season lawns such as bluegrass, tall fescue, and ryegrass in late October (Halloween). This should be the fourth and final application. Water the lawn thoroughly after application.

Rake or blow excessive amounts of fallen leaves from newly seeded lawns so the grass plants receive proper light, water, and air movement.

Older lawns benefit from topdressing with organic matter to condition the soil underfoot. Core-aerate the lawn prior to applying the topdressing.

In warmer areas, lawn mowing will continue until the grass begins to go dormant. Do not scalp, or mow the lawn too short. Lawn grasses that are cut too short are more subject to wind desiccation and the soil will dry out more rapidly. Keep the mowing height at 2½ to 3 inches to encourage good root growth.

Toward the end of leaf-fall, when the layers of leaves become thinner, mow the lawn and leaves with a mulching mower. This will chop the leaves into finer fragments that will fall between the grass blades and mulch the soil for the winter.

PERENNIALS

Herbaceous perennials will soon die back with the arrival of Jack Frost, although their roots still grow underground. Clean up dried, dead leaves and dried stems that have flopped over. Some of the more rigid stems can be left upright for fall and winter interest. They can be removed later next spring.

Avoid mulching perennials until the ground freezes. Mulching too heavily in the fall is an invitation for rodents to nest at the crown of our perennials.

■ *The semi-evergreen foliage of hellebores is attractive even if the flowers are not in bloom.*

Some perennials will keep green foliage over the winter. Hellebores provide attractive semi-evergreen leaves year-round if it is not a drought year.

Biennials are plants that require two growing seasons to complete their life cycle, such as hollyhocks, foxglove, and Canterbury bells. They will remain green late into the fall and send up their flower spikes next year. If this is the first autumn for biennials, mulch them well for the winter. If this is the second fall, the plants will die by the hard frost, and you can pull them out. However, watch for new seedlings that may have self-sown in areas where they were cleaned out.

The first hard-killing frost is a signal to clean up the blackened foliage and stems. Cut back soggy, water-soaked stems and dried, broken plant debris. Leaves that were infected with powdery mildew should be raked up and collected, then discarded to the trash. Pull or cut back weeds. Be sure to get all the seedheads to reduce seed dispersal.

Finish getting winter-ready. Clean up old pots, twigs fallen from trees, and other wind-blown debris. Pull out garden supports and stakes, and put them back in storage. Bring in decorative containers that are subject to freeze damage. This includes statuary, birdbaths, and garden decorations that are not constructed to withstand freezing and thawing.

Mow leaves with a mulching mower as they lie on the lawn, and then bag them up with grass clippings for use as mulch. You can also compost them.

Dig new beds, add organic matter, and let them sit for the winter. Rains and snow will moisten the beds and they will be ready to plant next spring.

ROSES

It still can be too early to apply winter mulch to protect grafted roses, except at higher elevations. Wait until there is frost in the ground. Winter mulch is meant to keep the bush dormant, not to pamper it with a warm collar that can stimulate growth. Winter mulches also prevent the alternating thawing and freezing that causes plants to heave out of the ground and become more vulnerable to winter damage.

Rose winter mulch

TO PREPARE TREE ROSES FOR WINTER

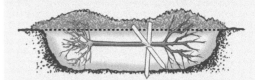

Rose trees are difficult to overwinter in our region. Tree roses have two graft unions and are therefore doubly vulnerable to weather fluctuations and temperature extremes. To protect them over the winter, pot the plant up in a large container and store in an unheated garage where temperatures are between 35 to 50 degrees Fahrenheit. Another, more time-consuming method is to dig a long trench (the height of the rose tree) 2 feet deep. Then, lay the entire rose tree horizontally in the trench. For rose trees planted directly in the ground, loosen the earth around the crown and roots so it is easier to tip the tree into the trench.

TO PROTECT CONTAINER-GROWN AND CLIMBING ROSES IN WINTER

Roses growing in containers need to be heeled into the ground or planted so they will successfully overwinter. To heel them in: Dig a hole that is two to three times wider than the container and about an inch deeper. Set the containerized rose bush into the hole with the rim of the pot below ground level. Once in place, line the sides of the hole with shredded wood mulch or compost. Cover the base of the rose bush with soil. Keep the soil in the container watered at least monthly during extended dry periods. Water when air temperatures are above 45 degrees Fahrenheit and when the soil is not frozen.

To protect climbing roses: Dig a trench deep enough to accommodate the canes. Tip the plant over and lay in the trench. Cover the canes with soil. Once the soil freezes, mulch with a thick layer of clean straw. You can use chicken wire to keep the mulch from blowing away. Start removing this protection in April.

No major pruning is needed now. Extremely long stems or canes that are subject to wind damage can be secured to supports or lightly pruned at the top to prevent them from whipping in the winds. Keep deadheading faded blooms. Cut about midway down the stem, leaving half the leaves to store energy. Clean up fallen leaves that may mat together and impede moisture and air movement to the root system. Put fallen leaves to use by shredding and adding to a compost pile.

SHRUBS

As the leaves fall, collect and discard those that are infected with diseases such as mildew. Other leaves can be collected and put in the compost pile. Add more mulch over the root zone of shrubs if needed, but do not place the mulch against the stems. To do so may invite gnawing critters to nest for winter.

Limit pruning to removal of diseased, damaged, dead, or broken branches and stems. Trim back overgrown branches if they are prone to whip in winter winds.

TREES

When adding new or more mulch around trees, keep the material a few inches *away* from the base of the trunk to discourage rodents such as field mice and voles from nesting there.

This is the time of year when many evergreens shed their older needles. If you see this happening with needle shed occurring from the inside of the tree towards the outside, it is a natural phenomenon. Do not try to fix this by giving the tree more water and please do not add fertilizer; this will only add insult to injury.

While you can still identify them easily, continue to prune out dead and diseased branches and twigs from your trees.

VINES, GROUNDCOVERS & ORNAMENTAL GRASSES

Mulch newly set plants after the ground freezes. Voles and meadow mice will get into heavy mulch now and nest around the plants, eventually feeding on the bark and roots, so keep mulch away from the plant bases and stems. After the ground freezes, these critters will have already found winter quarters elsewhere, and there will be less chance that they will come back to live next to your plants.

As leaves fall from deciduous trees, you might find it handy to lay wire or nylon netting over ground covers to catch the leaves that often mat together

■ *Leave ornamental grass plumes and seedheads so you can enjoy their fall show.*

and get stuck among the plants. Once leaf fall is over, just roll up the leaf-laden netting and carry the accumulated leaves to the compost pile. Store the netting until it's time to protect the strawberry and raspberry patch from the birds next year.

Leave ornamental grasses in their full-grown glory. Their mature seedheads and bleached stems provide form and structure in the landscape both fall and into winter.

Clean up the frosted annuals, remove other plant debris, and build your compost pile. Tidying up the garden will remove nesting areas for insects, diseases, and rodents.

Cut back dead or damaged branches or stems. Otherwise, delay pruning until late winter or early spring. Secure stems of vines that have been loosened by the wind or ties that have disintegrated.

WATER

ANNUALS

When rainfall is scarce, water any annuals and biennials that are still growing strong. In cooler weather they do not require as much frequent irrigation as they did during the hot summer months. Flowers that are mulched will require less watering and the mulch prevents the water from slashing on the foliage. This can greatly reduce foliar diseases.

Keep container-grown annuals watered as the soilless mix begins to dry.

BULBS

If the autumn is dry without significant rain or snow, water newly planted bulb beds to ensure good root development.

EDIBLES

Make sure that perennial vegetables (asparagus, for example) are deeply watered before the ground freezes solid. Do this on a warm sunny day when temperatures are in the 50s or higher. Once a month is usually all that is needed during prolonged dry spells. Water when the soil is unfrozen.

Keep the compost pile moist to keep the micro-organisms working. Check the interior of the pile with a piece of pipe to determine moisture needs. If the plant refuse and other garden debris were wet when added, you may not want to overwater the compost as this will inhibit decomposition. For your holiday wish list, request a compost thermometer to check on how the compost is coming along.

LAWNS

When there is a lack of fall rainfall, continue to water new lawns every seven to ten days, or as determined by moisture in the soil. Newly seeded or sodded lawns need particular attention to proper watering until the ground freezes solid.

PERENNIALS

Water any new transplants as long as the ground remains unfrozen. When there is little or no persistent snow cover, soil moisture is essential to maintain the root system. Make sure that biennials are getting adequate moisture as well.

ROSES

Continue to monitor soil moisture in your landscape. It is especially important to water newly planted roses to ensure good root development. If there is little or no natural precipitation, bring out the hose and frog-eye sprinkler, and do some fall watering every three to four weeks. Don't forget to disconnect and drain the hose by nightfall and put it back into storage. Mulched rose gardens have the advantage of not drying out so quickly and can go longer between waterings than they did in summer.

SHRUBS

Deeply water all shrubs before the ground freezes solid. Shrubs suffer severe desiccation during the winter season. Though the damage is not apparent until next spring, roots are actually killed during prolonged periods of winter drought. Evergreen shrubs continue to lose moisture through their foliage in all seasons, and drying winds exacerbate the problem.

TREES

Water your evergreens deeply as the soil dries out. This should be done before the ground freezes.

Pines, spruces, and firs continue to lose water by transpiration during the fall and winter, but when the ground is frozen they cannot replenish the water if it isn't already there.

In fall and early winter, don't forget to water newly planted trees during extended dry spells (three weeks or more) to help maintain moisture to their roots. Water on an "as-needed" basis by testing the soil around the root zone.

VINES, GROUNDCOVERS & ORNAMENTAL GRASSES

Water new plantings monthly when weather conditions are windy and dry. Mulched plants need less frequent watering than those with bare ground. Check the soil moisture by digging down with a garden trowel. If it is dry to a depth of 4 inches or more, apply water on a warm day. Do not allow your vines, groundcovers, and ornamental grasses to go into winter without a good drink.

FERTILIZE

ANNUALS

No fertilizer is needed at this time.

BULBS

Remember, when planting new bulb beds, avoid scattering a fertilizer layer in the bottom of the planting site. Soluble salts will often burn the root tissues as they emerge. Instead, mix a slow-release fertilizer into the soil when planting.

Sprinkle and lightly cultivate granular fertilizer into established bulb plantings. Water in well.

EDIBLES

No fertilizer is required at this time of year. You can add some well-rotted manure around asparagus plants and rhubarb so it will gradually break down over the winter months.

LAWNS

Apply your second application of fall fertilizer in late October (around Halloween). This fertilization is very important while the grass is still green and growing roots. This application will last throughout the fall and provide slow-release nutrients so that you will not have to apply an early application in the spring.

PERENNIALS

No fertilizers are needed, but now that the leaves are shedding from deciduous trees, it's an excellent time to construct a compost pile. Leaves are a valuable source of organic matter as they break down. Plan to rent a shredder or chopper to grind up the coarser, waxy leaves. This will speed up their decomposition.

ROSES

You don't need to fertilize your outdoor roses. It's even best to delay fertilizing any recently planted roses until next spring. A 2-inch layer of compost spread around the root zone of newly planted roses is all that's needed. Fertilize miniature roses indoors once a month as new growth appears. Use a water-soluble fertilizer, and apply to an already moistened soil.

SHRUBS, TREES, VINES, GROUNDCOVERS & ORNAMENTAL GRASSES

No fertilizer needed at this time of season.

PROBLEM-SOLVE

ANNUALS

Watch for giant conifer aphids as they make their last feeding frenzy on annuals and biennials. To avoid bringing any of these pests indoors, wash plants you're overwintering with a forceful spray of water. Plan to keep the insect watch going every few days to keep the pests at bay before they can get out of hand.

If you want to extend your garden season into the fall and winter, you can still plant pansies in fall. Pansies will develop strong root systems during the mild fall days when the weather suits them perfectly. They will become well-established to survive the winter cold and snow over the fall and winter months. As winter succeeds, and the hardy bulbs start to emerge, the pansies are ready to bloom, providing an undercover to accent the bulbs.

After planting spring-flowering bulbs this autumn, plant violas and pansies throughout the flower bed for spectacular and colorful displays.

BULBS

Be on the watch for emerging weeds, particularly weedy grasses. Many will germinate in the fall. Handpull or hoe out the clumps before they get a stronghold. Pick off seedheads of any weeds that escaped your attention.

EDIBLES

Cultivate the soil to expose the larvae and cocoons of overwintering insect pests. The freezing and thawing effects over the winter will rid the garden of many soil-inhabiting insects and their eggs. Leave the soil roughened so it will take the full brunt of winter freezing, thawing, wetting, and drying. Inspect areas around the compost pile for rodents, and set out traps if necessary.

LAWNS

Continue to watch for white grubs and other causes of thinning of lawn areas. Keep weeds from going to seed by digging them out and disposing.

■ *White grubs are one of the most common lawn pests and one of the most easily eradicated with organic controls.*

PERENNIALS

Rodents will be looking to construct new winter homes; don't let them find them in your perennial garden. Meadow mice, voles, chipmunks, and others like to build nests in a deep, fluffy mulch, so delay the spreading of mulch until the ground freezes. By then, the rodents will have found alternative nesting sites.

Fallen leaves that mat together will prevent moisture and air from getting into the soil. Lightly rake leaves or chop them up to reduce matting. Use a shredder to grind them into smaller pieces, then cover the soil with them.

ROSES

Deer, elk, and rabbits may nibble on rose stems and any remaining foliage if their food sources are scarce. Given alternatives, critters generally avoid plants with thorns, but if there is not much else available, they will feed on rose bushes. If needed, spray with a homemade repellent (see page 221), or construct a cage around your valued rose specimens.

SHRUBS

Most insect problems will cease with the arrival of cooler nights. A hard freeze *is* on its way (if it hasn't already occurred once in your area). Diseases can be reduced by raking and collecting leaves that can carryover the fungus spores. Do not add diseased leaves or plant parts to the compost pile. Continue to hand pull or dig invading weeds before they make seeds.

Bundle upright evergreens and other weak-wooded shrubs that are prone to spread apart under snow loads. Use binder twine, and start at the bottom, pulling the twine upward. The twine should be removed in late spring when the danger of heavy snows has past. Do not cover shrubs with plastic cones or plastic. They will be cooked on sunny days even if temperatures are cold at night.

TREES

Older needles on pine trees turn brown and fall off. This is usually a normal condition. Many evergreens including pines and spruces naturally shed their three- to four-year-old needles. You don't need to do anything unless you want to rake up excess needle-drop and use them as mulch.

Diseased leaves that have fallen at the base of trees should be collected and disposed of. They will harbor disease spores that can infect new foliage next spring. Do not place diseased debris in the compost pile, as compost temperatures rarely get high enough to kill the pathogens.

Swellings or galls (tumor-like growths) caused by insects, mites, or diseases, may become visible as the leaves drop. Most should be left alone or if desired they can be removed during pruning in late winter.

To protect trees against deer damage, there are several deterrents you can try. One of my favorites is a homemade remedy that *really* works (see the homemade critter repellent recipe on page 221). It will need to be reapplied after a heavy rainfall or as the sunlight breaks it down. Some gardeners report success by hanging strong-scented soap bars or mesh bags filled with human hair on the outer branches with no more than 3 feet between them.

Remember, deer soon become accustomed to any object, so alternating repellent items will confuse them and keep them away longer.

VINES, GROUNDCOVERS & ORNAMENTAL GRASSES

As weeds continue to grow despite the cool weather, keep them pulled. Do not let them disperse their seeds. Some weeds are "winter annuals," which germinate in the fall and survive the winter. When spring arrives, they continue to grow and compete with landscape plants. Get rid of these young seedlings while they are vulnerable to hoeing or cultivation.

Rodents are scouting for winter quarters, so be on the watch for their nesting sites. Delay mulching until after the ground freezes. To prevent the spread of diseases and rid the wintering places for insects, rake up and remove fallen leaves.

November

Gardening is not over, though other activities seem to consume our time. It's a good idea to make an end-of-the-season checklist to prepare for winter. Take time to review your growing experiences this season. Write comments in your garden notebook or journal. They will help you assess your landscape and will serve as reminders on what plants may need transplanting or replacing. Which plants performed the best? Were some more disease-prone than others? Was the location right for a designated variety, or is it outgrowing its spot? Maybe you would like to automate watering by installing a drip irrigation system next year.

Few perennials bloom in winter, with the exception of *Erica carnea* (hardy evergreen heath), *Helleborus* (Lenten rose), and some of the minor bulbs, but this is a good time to consider planting some in your landscape. Add notes and suggestions to your garden journal or notebook so you can order plants next spring. Ornamental grasses have multiple uses, and left unpruned in autumn, will provide contrast and form in the winter garden. Our native mountain mahogany *Cercocarpus montanus* is one of the few broadleaf evergreens that will accent the winter landscape.

If your garden has performed poorly over the past few years, it may be time for a soil test. Vegetables, herbs, and fruit will deplete the soil of nutrients more than most ornamental plants or the pH may be affecting the availability of certain nutrients or elements. However, you don't need to have a soil test done every year. The test is only one instrument in the diagnosis of problems. There can be other problems including an increasing amount of shade from maturing trees and shrubs, new buildings, poor soil drainage, chemical residues in the soil, and watering issues.

November can be mild and dry, or it can be cold and snowy. High altitude gardens may already be covered by a blanket of snow. The landscape will have subtle changes in colors against the cobalt blue sky, and vines with berry-laden branches will show off their beauty. Take some time to reflect on this garden season.

PLAN

■ *Starting plants early in a cold frame is a great way to get a head start on the growing season. A cold frame is also a great place for hardening off delicate seedlings to prepare them for transplanting.*

ALL

This is a good time to consider building a cold frame. This handy structure is a great way to harden off seedlings in the spring as they make their transition from the indoor environment to the outside conditions. It's like a miniature unheated greenhouse, but can be transformed into a temporary hotbed if you add heating cables or a heat mat.

ANNUALS

Now is the time to plan the garden for future years. If you really enjoyed this year's crop of annuals, you may want to plant more next year and try them in different places. Make notes in your garden journal or notebook to keep track of what needs doing.

Gather all the old seed packets that are strewn about and store them in a plastic shoebox. Many of the leftover seeds will last another year and can still be sown. Keep track of plant or seed tags that came with your annuals, and keep garden notes. This will help you answer questions about varieties that did best, including colors of the plants and cultural

information. These labels will prove invaluable when it comes time to order more seeds in January or February.

BULBS

Think about buying planting bulb kits from the garden store. These make nice holiday gifts to add a cheerful touch of color to brighten the recipient's home. Paperwhite narcissus and amaryllis bulbs are generally available at local retailers now. You can pot them up yourself, or some of the bulbs may already be potted with sprouts beginning to emerge. Choose those that are barely sprouting; this way the recipient will have a longer time to enjoy their growth and blooms.

Holiday cyclamen (*Cyclamen persicum*) are wonderful holiday gifts. This plant grows from a small corm that produces a mass of foliage with flowers resembling orchids or butterflies, thus the common name "poor man's orchid." It does best in bright light with cool temperatures. Cyclamen have a delicate fragrance; green or silver-mottled green, heart-shaped leaves; and come in a wide range of colors from white, pink, red, lilac, and salmon. They will bloom for several weeks in a cool environment.

Plan to check any bulbs, corms, tubers, and rhizomes you put in storage, be it the basement, garage, or root cellar. If the storing medium is getting a bit too dry, give it a light misting. Do not water too much as this can rot the bulbs.

EDIBLES

Keep adding notes to your garden notebook or journal while things are still fresh in your mind. Remember specific things that happened over the garden season including weather, planting and harvesting dates, insect pests, disease problems, and any other environmental factors that made the gardening year interesting or challenging.

Inventory your garden tools. Clean them up before putting them in storage. A wire brush will scrape off caked soil. Once the metal parts are clean, spray a coating of oil to prevent rust. If you have space, prepare a 5-gallon bucket of sharp or coarse sand, and mix in a quart of motor oil. Then insert the metal parts of rakes, hoes, shovels, trowels, and other tools into the oily sand. This will do a good job of cleaning and coating the metal surfaces. Now they're ready for winter storage.

Keep a hose handy to do some fall and winter watering should we experience prolonged dry spells of three weeks or more. Perennial vegetables and fruits need supplemental moisture if there is little or no snow in your area.

LAWNS

HERE'S HOW

TO REDUCE LAWN CARE

Evaluate the size of your lawn and its function in your landscape. You can reduce lawn maintenance by reducing the size of your yard. Consider removing grass from sloped areas and creating a rock garden. Identify areas where lawn grasses perform poorly. Heavily shaded areas are not the best sites for thick turf. Consider replacing grass under trees with groundcovers or mulch. Other tips include:

- Widen the areas around shrub borders or around perennial flowerbeds. If you've always wanted a deck, gazebo, or patio, plan to build one to replace turf areas.

- Construct a dog run so the dogs have their own space.

- If you have children or grandchildren, create a play area with a swing set or playhouse.

- If your budget allows, how about installing a swimming pool?

- Widen walkways or pathways to eliminate larger turf areas.

- Place a ring of organic mulch under trees to avoid thinning turfgrasses and prevent mower damage to the bark.

- Create a water garden or water feature in your landscape. Re-circulating water is a commonsense way to conserve water. You only need to add water occasionally to keep the water garden functional.

PERENNIALS

HERE'S HOW

TO DESIGN A WINTER GARDEN

With the right planning, it is possible to have a winter perennial garden. The ornamental grasses you planted in the spring will become the highlights of your fall and winter garden. Their mature seedheads add height and form to the landscape, and the rustling of the bleached leaves adds a relaxing sound.

With some careful planning and a judicious selection of plants, you can create a perennial bed that provides winter interest when there is little or no snow cover.

Choose a site that is visible from a window so you can enjoy the tapestry of plants when you are shut in by the cold weather. A winter garden might include:

- Colorful evergreen foliage from hellebores, hardy ferns, hardy evergreen heath, and kinnikinnick.

- The semievergreen foliage of mahonia, barrenwort, and heuchera will have foliage that transform into purplish to red hues. This will last for several weeks when weather conditions are mild to moderate.

- Interesting dried stems of coneflowers, dwarf astilbe, black-eyed Susans, and others provide various textures in the garden.

- The silver foliage that persists on lamb's ears and artemisias are always a welcome sight.

- Dried yarrow stems and seedheads add architectural lines, as do tall sedums and other perennials.

ROSES

Make plans to tuck your roses away for winter. Wait until the weather and soil stays consistently cold.

Wait until the weather is consistently cold and the soil is cold before covering up your rose bushes with soil or mulch.

■ *This rose has been wrapped in landscape fabric to help protect it against winter wind and cold.*

Mound soil or mulch around the base of the rose bush to protect the graft union.

Get on the mailing list for rose specialty catalogs. They serve as a great resource for new and unusual rose varieties, rose gardening accessories, and other unique items that may not be available locally.

SHRUBS

Shrubs will show off their hidden attributes now. Take time to view interesting bark such as that of burning bush, winged euonymus, and red-twig and yellow-twig dogwoods. They make a nice contrast in the landscape.

Plan to set out bird feeders as berries and other natural food sources become scarce. Don't forget to include a birdbath or other source of water for birds too.

Some shrubs in your landscape lend themselves to holiday decorating. Pick a warm day, string your lights, and test them so you can replace burned-out bulbs. Be sure they are low-wattage and UL–approved for outdoor use.

TREES

Trees add winter interest with their form and structure. When planning your landscape or retrofitting to make it seem like new, take advantage of a tree's winter characteristics. The bark, branches, and architectural forms give both deciduous and evergreen trees character. Look for the exfoliating or peeling bark in trees such as birch and sycamore. Located in the proper sites, these trees may add attractive interest to your landscape.

Season's end is a good time to update your tree records. Note major pruning, problems, and observations for trees in your landscape. Jot down the flowering dates or fruiting times as well. This information and a brief summary of the weather conditions over the season may prove helpful in the future when planting more trees of a similar species.

VINES, GROUNDCOVERS & ORNAMENTAL GRASSES

Keep your binoculars handy to watch for wild birds visiting your landscape. They'll be hunting for berries and other seedpods as a food source. Squirrels may visit the garden too.

■ *Burning bush*

Dried seedheads and bleached stems of ornamental grasses hang on through fall and early winter. A light frost on the branches of vines and ornamental grasses gives the landscape a special touch.

Take some time to photograph nature's wonders, take an inventory of the plants that performed well, and make notes in your garden journal. Did that new groundcover fill in as promised? Would you like to add more ornamental grasses to accentuate the landscape and add a vine as a living screen for the summer months? Are there areas in the yard that may need a redesign?

Enjoy the bare branches of vines as they cling to trellises and arbors. Even Boston ivy leaves its tracings of dried stems to stand out on the walls and old tree trunks.

Appreciate the ornamental grasses as they glow in the autumn light and rustle in the wind. There is much to be thankful for when the winter garden glistens with vines, groundcovers, and ornamental grasses.

PLANT

ANNUALS

As long as the ground remains unfrozen, you can still plant pansies and violas for fall and winter color. Experiment with planting them in containers on the patio or windowsill. If they are somewhat protected by an overhang and not exposed to the high winds, these will bloom periodically in the winter to provide some color. Use pine cones and grasses to decorate the containers and help provide some additional winter protection. Don't forget to water any container plantings so they won't dehydrate.

BULBS

It's getting late to plant hardy bulbs in most parts of the region, except where the soil is not yet frozen. So if you find some last-minute bargains, purchase them and get them planted right away.

If you discover some bulbs that you forgot to plant last month, you still have time to get them in the ground. Tulips, daffodils, crocus, and others perform better by planting them in the ground rather than leaving them in their packages to dry out. As long as the ground is not frozen solid, find an area to plant them. Break through a lightly frosted soil with a hoe to get into the ground if necessary.

Consider potting up bulbs for forcing into bloom in the winter. Use bulb pans or shallow clay pots that have drainage holes. Use a quality potting mixture that is well drained.

HERE'S HOW

TO PLANT SPRING-FLOWERING BULBS LATE IN THE SEASON

1. With a heavy-duty shovel or spading fork, break through the frozen soil and outline planting areas.

2. Slide the shovel under one edge of the outlined area and pry off the frozen layer. It will lift off just like a manhole cover.

3. Plant the bulbs at the proper depth and space accordingly.

4. Cover with some loose soil, water in, and replace the 'soil lid'. If squirrels are watching, the frozen soil lid will make it difficult for critters to dig the bulbs.

EDIBLES

Nothing should be planted directly outdoors this month, unless you have a season extender such as a cold frame or hot bed. Many short-season crops such as spinach, leaf lettuce, and endive can be grown with the protection of a cold frame and will provide fresh greens until a hard frost sets them back. A heating mat or cable can help protect plants within the cold frame on very cold nights, or you can cover the top with an insulated blanket or carpeting. Experiment to see what you can grow even though winter is approaching!

LAWNS

It is too late to seed new lawns or overseed dead patches.

TO FORCE OR COAX BULBS TO BLOOM INDOORS

1. Look for bulbs that are labeled good for forcing; there are certain varieties that undergo this process better than others.

2. Choose containers that are good "bulb pots," wide and shallow, 6 to 8 inches deep. Containers should have drainage holes in the bottom.

3. Put a light layer of potting mixture in the bottom of the pot.

4. Set the bulbs in the planting mixture so their tips are even with the rim of the container. Place them shoulder-to-shoulder since it is okay to crowd them at this time.

5. Water the potting mixture thoroughly.

6. Place the planted bulbs in a cool location (40 to 50 degrees Fahrenheit) for several weeks while the roots develop.

7. Around Thanksgiving, put the pots where the bulbs will experience mild winter temperatures (35 to 40 degrees Fahrenheit) so they will start their dormancy period. An old cellar, unheated garage, outdoor cold frame, insulated window well, or old refrigerator are some good cooling-off places.

8. Watch for signs of sprouting within twelve to sixteen weeks, depending on the kinds of bulbs you are forcing.

9. When the green sprouts appear, bring the pots out into a cool room where there is bright light so they will think it is spring.

10. When they are ready to open their flowers, bring them to a spot where everyone can enjoy a spring show even though it's winter!

If the soil remains unfrozen and you have established a good soil foundation, you can still install sod. As long as sod growers are cutting and delivering sod, you can lay it until the ground freezes solid.

PERENNIALS

Outdoor planting is past in most parts of the region. If you purchased perennials too late to plant, you can heel the plants into a trench, pots and all. Cover with protective winter mulch to protect the roots and crowns from a hard freeze. In early spring you can lift them out and plant into the garden. If you're lucky enough to have a cold frame, many perennials will winter there and survive the rigors of temperature fluctuations.

ROSES

Planting and transplanting should not be done during this month, unless you are willing to gamble. Shorter days, cold temperatures, and frost in the ground are not conducive for successful root development. If the weather remains relatively warm, you can experiment and plant some of those bargain rose bushes.

Water newly planted rose bushes thoroughly. In this situation, apply an organic mulch over the root area to keep the soil from freezing so the root system can acclimate before a prolonged cold spell.

Miniature roses are available at garden shops and can be transplanted into decorative containers for gifts or as a future blooming indoor plant. Indoors, locate them in bright light and a cool location. If you have forced-air heat, place a cool mist humidifier near them.

SHRUBS

If you didn't get container-grown shrubs planted, you'd better heel them in a trench before a hard frost visits your area. If stored above ground, freezes will damage their root system. Dig a trench deep enough to place the containers within and fill in the spaces with compost or other organic mulch until they can be planted in spring.

TREES

You can still plant trees if the soil remains unfrozen, but it is becoming more risky this month. If you should acquire a tree, it is better to plant it than to try to store it over the winter.

VINES, GROUNDCOVERS & ORNAMENTAL GRASSES

It's getting too late in the season to plant vines and groundcovers. If you purchase bargain plants now, store them for winter as mentioned in "Shrubs."

You can add bulbs to groundcover plantings until the ground freezes solid. The sooner the better.

Water new plantings to ensure that the roots can start to grow before the bulbs undergo their dormancy. Then, once the water has soaked in, mulch the areas to maintain uniform moisture and protection from fluctuating temperatures.

CARE

ANNUALS

Some of the more cold-tolerant annuals such as ornamental cabbage and kale may have succumbed to a hard frost. It is best to dig these out and send them to the compost pile. Otherwise they will give off a foul odor as they decay.

HERE'S HOW

TO OVERWINTER CONTAINERIZED PLANTS

Outdoors
- Find a vacant planting space in a protected location. Areas near the house—a garden shed or fence—that are sheltered from winter winds and direct sun are suggested sites.

- Dig a trench deep enough to set the pots down to their rims. Fill in around the pots with soil. The soil will insulate the roots and crown.

- Once the ground freezes, protect the tops by covering with evergreen boughs or clean, wheat straw for added insulation.

Indoors
- Store containerized plants in an unheated garage or insulated garden shed. Set the plants on boards and surround the pots with unopened bags of mulch, old blankets, or other items for added insulation.

- Water whenever the soil is starting to dry out. Dig down a couple of inches to check on a monthly basis.

Mulch any bare soil with compost and lightly work it in to improve the soil structure. Young transplants of pansies and violas should be mulched with a few inches of pine needles or shredded cedar for winter protection and to hold in the moisture.

BULBS

Most fall-blooming bulbs such as *Colchicum* and autumn crocus have completed their bloom cycle. Their faded blossoms will collapse to the ground and can remain there, as they will decompose rapidly.

Bulb beds that were planted earlier, but were not mulched, should be mulched after the ground freezes. This winter mulch is not intended to prevent the ground from freezing, but it buffers soil temperatures during the winter to minimize the extremes of our fluctuating temperatures. If bulbs experience alternate freezing and thawing, this will often cause shallow-planted bulbs to heave to the surface. Spread organic mulch to a depth of 2 to 3 inches over the bulb beds. Pine needles are my favorite, but choose from ground bark, shredded cedar or aspen mulch, or chopped leaves.

Finish cutting back the dead lily stalks that have already ripened. When they are completely dry, these old stalks are easy to pull right out of the ground.

Tidy up the garden if weeds and other plant debris have blown in. Discard these materials to the trash to prevent the dispersion of seeds.

EDIBLES

If you haven't done the final garden cleanup, remove the last of the frozen, dead plants. Left in the garden, they can harbor insects and their eggs over the winter. Cut back the tops of maturing asparagus and rhubarb plants. Clean out fallen leaves, weeds, and other plant refuse. Turn the compost every few weeks while the weather remains open and warm. Lightly water the compost pile if rain or snow is scarce to help microorganisms break down the raw materials. You can also get a compost thermometer to monitor the internal temperature of your pile and "keep it cooking." Keep the temperature between 150 to 160 degrees Fahrenheit.

Prepare the soil for next spring by adding compost to the garden before the soil freezes. If you have a source of aged or composted manure available, now is the time to spread it over the vegetable garden to a depth of 6 to 8 inches.

You can add deciduous leaves to the garden soil, but don't overdo the application because it can "gum up" the soil. If you don't already have a compost pile, find an area in the corner of the yard where you can recycle leaves and other disease-free plant refuse. It will take six months to a year to achieve good compost, but who doesn't want to have this "black gold" for augmenting the soil?

LAWNS

Continue to mow the lawn if mild weather allows the turf to grow. Even though grass growth is slower, a light mowing will keep the turf looking neat and healthy. Do not scalp when mowing in autumn. Alternate your mowing patterns to reduce soil compaction. Mow in horizontal rows

■ *Create new raised beds in the fall so they will be ready to plant in the spring.*

one week, in vertical rows the next, then in diagonal rows.

Snow mold is best prevented rather than cured. In the autumn, prepare vulnerable areas by core-aeration to break through heavy thatch layers; hand-rake matted accumulations of dead grass. Avoid the application of high-nitrogen lawn fertilizers in the late season and mow the lawn to a height of 2 inches. During the winter, avoid walking on snow-covered lawns and don't pile the snow into huge mountains in the shaded areas. Snow mold is usually not fatal but can thin out areas; lawns will recover with time with good management practices.

PERENNIALS

Now that the ground has frozen, you can spread winter mulch up to 4 inches deep on the soil over the root zone of perennials. I like to use pine needles, but shredded wood chips, chopped leaves, pole peelings, and shredded cedar will work nicely too.

Applying the mulch after the soil is cold or frozen serves several purposes:

- It protects the soil from compaction by heavy rains or snow.

- It insulates the soil by buffering temperature extremes of the freezing and thawing cycles that often heave soil and plant crowns out of the ground.

- Mulch helps to retain moisture.

- Winter mulch keeps the soil cool in early spring to delay premature emergence of perennials.

- A good mulch suppresses weeds early in the season by inhibiting sunlight to reach the seeds.

ROSES

One of the best management practices to prevent disease problems is routine sanitation in the garden. Continue to clean up fallen leaves that accumulate around the bushes. Disease spores, insect pests, and their eggs can overwinter in plant debris. If you have a compost pile, recycle non-diseased leaves

HERE'S HOW

TO OVERWINTER ROSES IN CONTAINERS

Roses in containers are more difficult to overwinter than plants in the ground. Their roots are above ground and exposed to temperature extremes and drying out. If you must retain them, store the plant, pot and all, in a cold frame. If you have space in your yard, heel them into the ground by digging a hole deep enough to hold the container. Set the pot an inch or two deeper than ground level, and apply protective mulch around the area.

Don't forget to water these potted roses during prolonged dry periods. This may need to be done every three to four weeks, depending upon local weather conditions. Water early in the day when temperatures are above freezing to allow the moisture to soak down.

and other plant debris, but discard disease-infected foliage and seed-producing weeds.

Once all the leaves have fallen from deciduous trees and a hard frost occurs, it's time to winterize roses, especially grafted varieties. They should be dormant by now.

Landscape roses are typically rugged and need only minimal winter protection. Water them deeply if precipitation has been scarce, and mulch around the root zone with compost or shredded wood chips, chopped leaves, or something similar.

Hybrid tea roses and other grafted types need more care and attention. You may cut back any extremely tall canes that will whip around in the winter wind. Canes should be no shorter than 2 feet. Pile up soil, compost, or other mulching material (pine needles, pole peelings, shredded wood chips, or chopped leaves) over the crown, graft union, and lower parts of the canes. Be sure that the knobby graft region is covered with mulch.

Climbing roses benefit from winter protection if winter temperatures dip below zero for extended periods. Unfasten the canes from their supports

HERE'S HOW

TO CLEAN GARDEN TOOLS

- Scrape, wipe, or wash off excess soil and debris. Use a putty knife to remove hardened soil, or soak soil-encrusted tools in a bucket of soapy water, and scrub with a wire brush.

- Remove rust with coarse steel wool or medium-grit sanding paper or cloth. Add a few drops of machine oil to each side of the tool surface. Use a small cloth to spread it over the metal parts. This will protect surfaces against rust.

- Sharpen the soil-cutting edges of shovels, hoes, and trowels to make digging easier. Use a sanding grinder or an 8- or 10-inch mill file to sharpen or restore the cutting edge.

- Check wooden handles for splinters and rough spots. Use 80-grit sandpaper on rough, wooden-handled tools. Coat with linseed oil.

- Make sure the handles are tightly fastened to shovels, spading forks, hoes, and rakes. You may need to reinstall missing pins or bolts, screws, and nails.

■ *Before hanging up garden tools for the winter, clean them to avoid rust.*

and gather them together in a horizontal bundle on the ground. If you desire, dig a shallow trench in which to lay the canes. Cover the crown and canes with a loose soil, finished compost, shredded wood chips, or pine needles. If it is too difficult to remove the canes, make sure they are tied up securely on their supports. Mound soil or mulch as high up as possible on the bush. You can also construct a cage that encircles the climber and fill it with organic mulch.

From now until spring, avoid the urge to prune your roses except to remove storm-injured canes from dormant rose bushes. Canes should remain 18 to 24 inches long because a certain amount of winter damage will occur at the stem tips. Extra length protects healthy wood lower on the cane.

SHRUBS

Delay spreading winter mulch over the root zone of newly planted shrubs. It is best to wait until there is frost on the ground. Layer organic mulch 3 to 4 inches deep, but do not allow the mulch to rest against the bark of stems.

Protect shrubs from winter sun and wind by placing shelters around vulnerable plants. Use burlap, commercial shade cloth, or snow fencing. When the ground freezes, mulch new shrubs planted this fall. Bramble fruits can be mulched as well. Use compost, shredded bark, or other organic materials.

Limit pruning to removing dead and broken branches. If you're pruning to collect berries or short evergreen boughs for decorations, do so selectively to preserve the natural shape of the shrub.

This is a good time to sharpen, clean, and oil pruners. If you don't know how, take them to a professional garden shop that offers this service. See the "Here's How to Clean Garden Tools" above.

TREES

Protect multi-stemmed evergreens by tying up the branches with sisal twine, working the twine up from the bottom of the evergreen in a spiral fashion. This will prevent heavy winds and snow from splitting the leaders apart and resulting limb breakage. Remember to remove the twine in late spring.

Around Thanksgiving, apply reflective tree wrap around the trunk of newly planted trees. Start at the bottom of the trunk, wrapping upward, and secure with duct tape at the first side branch. This helps protect the thin, young bark from sunscald injury (splitting and cracking of the bark).

Check guy or support wires around newly planted trees to be sure the hose sections still shield the wires to prevent girdling the bark. Add additional renewal mulch after the ground freezes. This will help to reduce frost heave at the root zone.

Protect new trees from animal damage by wrapping hardware cloth around the trunk.

The only pruning to do now until year's end is to remove broken or diseased branches. Anytime the protective bark covering is broken open, there is the potential for desiccation. Remove dead, injured, or diseased branches with a smooth cut through healthy tissue just beyond the branch collar. This will remove a source of further infection and help the tree begin to close or "heal" the wound.

VINES, GROUNDCOVERS & ORNAMENTAL GRASSES

Fasten the loose stems of older established perennial vines such as climbing hydrangea, trumpet vine, honeysuckle, and hardy wisteria. Use twine or plant ties to secure to supports. This will prevent them from suffering from winter storm damage.

Remove fallen leaves that accumulate on groundcovers since they can smother the plants and block the passage of air and water to the root zone. As mentioned earlier, you can rig up a nylon or wire netting over groundcovers under trees to capture the falling leaves. Once leaf drop has finished, lift up the netting, carry the leaves to the compost pile, or shred them to make soil amendment. If you prefer, use a power vacuum or blower to dislodge leaves from groundcover foliage.

It is time to do a final cleanup of the yard to prevent overwintering insects and disease spores. Cut back dead plant stems and seedheads. Pull up the support stakes or tomato cages that provided temporary support for new plants, and place them in storage. Limit your pruning to removal of dead, damaged, or overly long branches that pose a hazard to nearby structures.

WATER

ALL

Low precipitation, fluctuating temperatures, dry air, and lack of soil moisture are characteristics of fall and winter in many areas of the Rocky Mountain region. Often there can be little or no snow cover to provide adequate soil moisture from October through March. When these conditions occur, trees, shrubs, lawns, vines, groundcovers, and perennials may be damaged if they do not receive supplemental water.

The result of prolonged, dry periods causes injury or death to plant roots. Affected plants may appear normal and resume growth in spring, using up stored energy. Later in the season, plants may be weakened and parts of the plant may die as temperatures rise. Insects and diseases will attack weakened plants.

ANNUALS

Plants that you decided to overwinter indoors will need to be watered regularly as you turn on the furnace. Check soil moisture by probing the potting mix with your finger. If it is becoming dry to the touch, give the plants a thorough watering. Discard excess water that collects in the drainage saucer to avoid waterlogging the soil, resulting in root rot.

BULBS

If you have potted bulbs for forcing, be sure to keep the potting mixture moist, not soggy. This goes for amaryllis and paperwhite narcissus. Paperwhites in moist gravel just need to have the gravel layer kept moist and they will start sprouting.

Once the sprouts emerge, move to brighter light, but in a cool location.

TO WATER IN THE LATE FALL

- Pick a day when temperatures are above 45 degrees Fahrenheit to water the landscape so it will soak in before possible freezing at night. Caution: A layer of ice on lawns can cause suffocation or result in matting of the grass.

- Water landscape plants receiving reflected heat from buildings, walls, and fences. The low angle of the winter sun causes damage to plants on the south and west exposures and southwest-facing slopes. Windy locations result in faster drying of plants and require special attention. Lawns may be susceptible to grass mite damage. Water is the best treatment to prevent mite damage.

- Use a sprinkler that delivers a low arc of water to cover the root zone of trees and shrubs. Apply water to as much of the root system under the dripline and beyond if possible. If using a deep-root watering needle, insert no deeper than 8 inches into the soil.

- Apply 10 gallons of water for each diameter inch of the tree. Use a ruler to measure a tree's diameter at 6 inches above ground level.

- Shrubs that are mulched may still require winter watering. Apply 5 gallons twice a month for newly planted shrubs. Established shrubs (less than 3 feet) should receive 5 gallons monthly. Larger shrubs (more than 6 feet) benefit from 15 to 20 gallons on a monthly basis. Adjust amounts to account for any natural precipitation.

- Herbaceous perennials can be watered for a period of fifteen to thirty minutes, depending on exposure and soil conditions. Water monthly if dry periods persist for more than three weeks.

- Drain hoses and return to storage for later use.

A frog-eye sprinkler

When the soil outdoors is not frozen, check the soil moisture by digging down with a garden trowel. If rain or snow has been scarce, get out the garden hose and water dry areas, particularly the western and southern exposures. Use a frog-eye sprinkler early in the day when temperatures are above freezing to allow the water to soak in.

Tender bulbs, corms, rhizomes, and tubers that were dug and stored should be checked monthly. Some may need moisture to keep them from shriveling out; this includes dahlias, begonias, and cannas. Keeping them in damp sawdust, sphagnum peat moss, or shredded newspaper in ventilated boxes or bags are some methods for successful storage. Other tender bulbs such as gladiolus, caladium, and tuberose do best in drier storage. Place them in net onion sacks or burlap bags and hang them in the basement or garage. If you kept the bulb packages, check the instructions for storage.

If the fall has been extremely dry without snow or rain, you may need to do some winter watering.

EDIBLES
Very little watering is needed this month. The only exceptions are the perennial asparagus beds and rhubarb. Water them once a month when there is little or no moisture. Apply water early in the day to allow it to soak in. I use a frog-eye sprinkler and allow it to run fifteen to twenty minutes to get needed moisture into dry soils. Once the ground is frozen, it is too late to water.

LAWNS
If there is little rainfall or snow, water newly seeded or sodded lawns, as long as the ground is not frozen. The grass plants need to develop a deep root system before the ground freezes. If you reside in the High Country, you can usually depend on the snow cover during the winter months to protect the grass, and you will not have to worry about winter watering.

PERENNIALS
Late autumn and early winter dry spells are not unusual. There may be little or no snow cover in the Plains, Foothills, or even some parts of the High Country. A prolonged dry winter can be disastrous to some perennials. When this should happen, bring the garden hose and frog-eye sprinkler out from storage. Water early in the day as long as the ground remains unfrozen. Once water starts to run off, move the sprinkler to another area. Disconnect the hose, drain, and return to storage. Pay particular attention to newly planted, transplanted, and divided perennials.

ROSES
If it's been an Indian summer and conditions are dry, water all roses in your landscape before the ground freezes hard. Check your soil moisture by inserting a long screwdriver or soil probe into the ground. Bring out the garden hose and frog-eye sprinkler, and pick a warm sunny day when temperatures are above freezing. Water early in the day to permit the water to soak in, then drain the hose before storing it away.

SHRUBS
Check soil moisture monthly and water heeled in shrubs as needed. Water early in the day when temperatures are 45 degrees Fahrenheit or above. Evergreens are the most susceptible to winter desiccation, so give them a good, deep drink before the ground freezes solid.

TREES
If fall rains or snows are inadequate to keep newly planted trees watered, get out the garden hose and frog-eye sprinkler to do some fall watering. Sending a tree into winter with plenty of moisture reduces the potential for winterkill next year.

Evergreens continue to lose moisture from their foliage all fall and winter, but once the ground is frozen, they will be unable to take up enough water to replace it. Providing a deep watering before the ground freezes will reduce the potential for damaged evergreen needles.

VINES, GROUNDCOVERS & ORNAMENTAL GRASSES
Watering should be done on a limited basis now. However, if it has been a dry fall without snow or rain, new plants will benefit from a deep watering while the ground remains unfrozen. Do not let evergreen groundcovers such as wintercreeper, ground junipers, kinnikinnick, and creeping Oregon grape holly go into the winter with dry soil. This will result in more winter desiccation to their foliage. Some of the broadleaf evergreens such as euonymus will hold on to their foliage and need winter watering when conditions are dry.

Ornamental grasses also suffer from desiccation during prolonged dry periods. Even though the leaves dry up in autumn and winter, the crowns can be killed by continual exposure to drying winds and dry soil. Keep the root systems moist by watering before the ground freezes solid. Apply water early in the day so it can soak down to the root zone. Disconnect the hose and return to storage.

FERTILIZE

ANNUALS
Flowering annuals and herbs that are overwintering indoors will take some time to acclimate to the indoor conditions. The shortened duration and

quality of light is lessened, so expect some yellowed and dropping leaves. They need a few weeks to adjust, and when new growth is evident you can apply soluble plant fertilizer. Dilute to half-strength to avoid building up the salt levels in the soil.

If you added a slow-release granular fertilizer to the soil at transplanting, you don't need to feed a soluble plant food. Many overwintering annuals will begin to bloom again in a few weeks if the right conditions are favorable.

BULBS
No fertilizer is needed during this month.

EDIBLES
No fertilizer applications are recommended now. The addition of organic materials such as compost and manure will provide nutrients as they begin to break down.

LAWNS
There is no need to fertilize lawns at this time. You should have applied the two fall feedings already; one around Labor Day and the second around Halloween.

PERENNIALS
No fertilizing is needed this month.

ROSES
If your indoor miniature roses did not have a slow-release fertilizer added to the potting mixture, fertilize with a soluble plant food once monthly. Read and follow the manufacturer's label directions.

SHRUBS, TREES, VINES, GROUNDCOVERS & ORNAMENTAL GRASSES
Dormant shrubs, trees, vines, groundcovers, and ornamental grasses will not benefit from the application of fertilizers now. Wait until spring.

PROBLEM-SOLVE

ANNUALS
Monitor for pests such as spider mites, aphids, whiteflies and others that may have moved indoors on plants. These pests will suck out plant juices, causing the leaves to yellow and eventually turn brown and drop. Treat with insecticidal soap or homemade remedy on page 220.

BULBS
As you examine the tender bulbs you stored away, be on the watch for rot diseases. If some are getting mushy or show signs of mold, discard them. Keep the storage medium slightly moist, never soggy wet. The temperatures in storage should be between 55 to 65 degrees Fahrenheit. If it's too hot, they will start to sprout prematurely.

If you live in an area where meadow mice, voles, and other critters are a problem, mulch bulb beds only after the ground freezes. This will thwart rodents from trying to set up house for winter in the bulb beds. They will find winter quarters somewhere else, like an open field or in the forest.

EDIBLES
Continue to clean up the garden if you have not already. It's important to remove hiding places for insects and debris that harbor diseases.

If they're within reach, remove all mummified fruit from your fruit trees, and rake up and dispose of any on the ground. Good sanitation practices reduce the reinfestation of insects and disease organisms the following growing season.

Prepare for next year by evaluating the cause of problems in this year's garden. If you had problems with drainage and lousy soil, plan to garden in raised beds or containers. You can create more suitable growing conditions with proper drainage.

LAWNS
Continue to battle the invasion of perennial weeds. Field bindweed, Canada thistle, and dandelions are just a few that persist. Spot-treat with an appropriate herbicide. Read and follow label directions.

PERENNIALS
Drying winter winds and temperature fluctuations can be harmful to a newly planted perennial garden. Until the plants become established within a few years, be sure to provide protective winter mulch. Leave 4- to 6-inch lengths of stems on perennials when cutting them back during garden

TO RECOGNIZE PLANT PEST SYMPTOMS

If you were frustrated by a variety of insect and disease problems in your annuals this year, here are some tips to remember to prevent serious problems next growing season:

- Look for signs of sticky sap on the stems and foliage that indicate that aphids are starting to attack the plants. Wash them off the plant with a forceful spray of water or use a homemade soap spray.

- A fine webbing near the main stems and around the leaf stems usually indicates that spider mites are a problem. Wash both the top and underside of the leaves with soapy water. You may need to use an insecticidal soap or miticide. Read and follow label directions.

- If the leaves are beginning to turn yellow but the veins remain bright green, this indicates a lack of available iron. Fertilize with a chelated iron.

- Leaves that develop a grayish white coating on their surface indicate powdery mildew. Handpick the worst leaves; treat minor mildew problems with the homemade mildew control. See homemade remedies on page 220.

- When the tender growth of annuals and foliage is twisted and turning yellow or brown, there could be possible herbicide injury. Did some of the herbicide you or a neighbor sprayed on weeds drift to the flower garden?

- Plants that develop lower leaves that turn yellow and begin to drop off indicate something is going on in the root system. Could it be overwatering or the soil not draining properly?

cleanup. This will trap and hold compost or chopped leaf mulch so it is less prone to wind erosion. Construct a low windscreen made from landscape fabric or burlap; fasten it to stakes at the front of the wind-blown beds to block the wind.

ROSES

Watch for spider mites and aphids on indoor miniature roses. They tend to proliferate in warm, dry conditions indoors. To catch infestations early, routinely check for signs of pale or dull leaves and fine webs streaming throughout the plant. Wash plants under the faucet every week or so to prevent mites from becoming a problem. If you do get an infestation of spider mites or aphids, control them with the homemade soap spray (see page 220) or Neem oil. Read and follow label directions.

If the leaves develop scorched tips due to lack of humidity, place a cool mist vaporizer near your miniature rose plants. This will also reduce the incidence of spider mites.

SHRUBS

Deer, elk, rabbits, and porcupines may make visits to your landscape and nibble on shrubs. Protect valuable plants by applying a repellent spray, or hang bars of perfumed soap or mesh bags of human hair. Placing wire cages or fencing around individual shrubs is the most reliable way to thwart deer and elk. Use hardware cloth to make collars to protect vulnerable stems from rabbits and mice.

TREES

If you didn't protect trees from animal damage, you still have time during the mild weather. Wrap trunks in hardware cloth to keep critters from nibbling the tender bark.

VINES, GROUNDCOVERS & ORNAMENTAL GRASSES

During the late fall and early winter, deer, elk, rabbits, and other critters feed on landscape plants if they can gain entry to your yard. The best defense against elk and deer is exclusion; construct a deer-proof fence 10 feet high to keep them out. Repellents work temporarily, but must be reapplied after they begin to break down from sunlight, heat, and moisture.

Rabbits and other small rodents can be deterred by placing wire cages (made from hardware cloth) around or over individual plants and groundcovers.

December

December is a month to relax and reflect. Browse nursery catalogs and learn more about shrubs that interest you. Check out climatic zones to select the hardiest plant species for your area. Bring your garden notebook up to date, and decide on your New Year's gardening resolutions. Make lists of groundcovers, vines, and ornamental grasses you would like to try next year. The mail-order catalogs are chock-full of enticing pictures, but study them carefully before making final decisions. Making the right choices saves time, energy, and money.

Milder areas may not freeze until late in December. Take the time to get outdoors and check the lawn and landscape plants. If weather conditions have left little or no moisture for over three weeks, bring out the hose and do some winter watering. Use a low-arc sprinkler (such as the twin-eye or "frog-eye" sprinkler) and set it at the root zone of woody plants. Water early in the day to allow water to soak in and set the sprinkler for twenty-five to thirty minute intervals. Reset the sprinkler to get good overlap and soak the entire root zones.

Watch for visiting wild birds. They are often a welcome addition to the garden. Their movements and antics can be entertaining. Keep birdfeeders filled and winterize a birdbath.

When snow arrives, be careful as you shake off heavy snows from trees and shrubs. This practice is intended to prevent branches from breaking on the weak-wooded landscape plants. *Gently* shake snow off or use a broom and *slowly* lift up snow-laden branches to avoid branch damage. If you're in a windy area, shovel snow onto exposed perennials, especially those planted close to the house. Snow is nature's best winter mulch, and if it stays around, and can be piled over spring-flowering bulb beds, perennial flowers, and around the bases of shrubs and trees.

As the winter solstice approaches, the holiday season begins to take up our time and energy. But if you can find a quiet moment, this is a good time to review the past year and reflect on the beautiful seasons that have just passed.

When there's nothing blooming in the garden, you can use natural materials like pinecones and evergreen boughs as your "container garden."

PLAN

ALL

Winter is a good time to enroll in gardening and landscaping classes at your local library or botanic garden. You can gain more knowledge and experience from local gardeners to become more successful in your perennial gardening endeavors.

Plan your holiday shopping list. Gardeners always appreciate a gift certificate to a special nursery or garden store. For gardening friends who love vines, give the gift of an arbor or pergola. No matter how the season turned out, we gardeners are always optimistic that next year will be even better

ANNUALS

Plan to decorate outdoor containers with bunches of dried ornamental grasses, pinecones, and evergreen boughs for winter interest. Catalogs should be arriving, so order early to get the newest plant introductions. Clean up old containers and store them in the garage or garden shed. Take an inventory of your seed-starting supplies so you'll be ready to order early next year.

BULBS

Study bulb catalogs, which will be touting their spring and summer selections, to see which bulbs will work in your area. It's fun to try hardy new bulbs and even unusual summer-flowering kinds such as tuberose.

Plan holiday gift shopping at your local garden retailers. Buy paperwhite narcissus, bulb planters, or gift certificates for spring bulbs.

EDIBLES

Winter is a cleansing process for the garden. Freezing, thawing, and winter precipitation will mellow the soil to make it easy to work in spring. A long period of freezing weather also rids the soil of pests. Winter gives us pause to reflect.

As snow begins to fly through the air, seed catalogs begin to fly through the mail. Read them as your time permits. Look for new varieties of vegetables and herbs to try the upcoming growing seasons. It's easy to be persuaded by the colorful photographs and plant descriptions, but shop wisely and choose plants that are appropriate for your particular garden site. Add notes to your garden notebook or journal while thoughts are fresh in your mind.

LAWNS

In many years, a properly maintained cool-season lawn will still be green in December. If there hasn't been any snow yet, plan on winter watering. As long as the ground remains unfrozen, the subsoil needs moisture to sustain the grasses' root system.

ROSES

As the year draws to an end, it's a good time to reflect on all the blessings we experienced in our rose garden this season. Continue to make notes in your garden notebook or journal as friendly reminders of what needs doing next year. If you have taken photos of your roses and garden, be sure to label them before you forget.

SHRUBS

If you need to replace shrubs in your landscape, now is the time to plan the installation of new selections that are hardy to your area. Sit by a warm fire and make notes from nursery catalogs.

TREES

If you're planning on a living Christmas tree, get the site ready for planting now. Consider mature height and spread of the evergreen so it is located properly.

PLANT

ANNUALS

Lightly tug at the plant cuttings you started earlier in the fall to see if they are rooting. There should be adequate moisture in the rooting medium. Some plants take longer to root than others, so be patient. Pot up the rooted cuttings into a soilless growing mixture. If you don't have enough sunlight, suspend fluorescent lights by chains so they hang down close to the foliage. This will encourage strong, healthy transplants.

BULBS

Do you have bulbs sitting around that you forgot to plant in October? If the ground is not frozen solid, plant them outdoors now.

If you can't plant them outside, pot them up in containers, and store them in a cool garage or basement. At least they won't dry out, and some may bloom in their pots. You can later transfer them to a permanent location.

EDIBLES

The only planting at this time of year is that of starting herbs indoors, or taking cuttings and rooting them in a sterile growing medium. Keep the seedlings in bright light to prevent them from becoming too leggy. Temperatures should be kept on the low side to discourage pests and diseases.

LAWNS

We don't plant lawns in December, either seeding or sodding. See page 217 for lawn watering advice.

PERENNIALS

As long as the ground remains unfrozen, work some compost into the soil around your perennials to improve the soil structure and drainage. Winter is a good time to add organic amendments; the alternate freezing and thawing will break down organics and mellow the soil for spring planting.

ROSES

This is not the time to plant roses, but if you get some on sale, get them planted before the ground freezes and mulch properly.

SHRUBS

If you've planted new shrubs, check the soil—digging under the mulch if needed—for moisture. Don't let them get too dry if it's an extended dry period. Winter watering monthly will help them survive.

You can decorate outdoor containers with some of your prunings to create seasonal arrangements. Harvest colorful berries and rose hips and include them in fall and winter arrangements.

TREES

If you decided to have a potted, living Christmas tree, keep it indoors for five to seven days, no longer. Otherwise it will break out of dormancy, which makes it difficult to plant directly outside after the holidays. Allow the potted tree to acclimate in an unheated garage or porch for a week or so before you plant it outdoors. Choose a day when temperatures are above freezing to plant. Water in thoroughly after planting and spread a layer of organic mulch over the root zone.

VINES, GROUNDCOVERS & ORNAMENTAL GRASSES

In areas where the ground has not yet frozen, plant container-grown plants that are on final closeout.

Use evergreen boughs to protect tender vines from drying, winter winds. You can use prunings from your Christmas tree to create shade and temporary windbreaks for vines on southern and western exposures.

CARE

ANNUALS

Finish cleanup of your annual beds. Chop or shred disease-free plants for the compost pile. Use compost and fallen leaves to improve the soil.

As annual plants adjust to growing indoors, they will naturally stretch to get more light. You can pinch back the stems of coleus, begonia, impatiens, and geraniums. If you don't have a sunny window or greenhouse, place the plants under artificial lights.

BULBS

Perform your monthly check of stored tender bulbs. If some of the tubers or rhizomes are dry or

■ *If not stored properly, dahlia bulbs can rot. Cut off any rotted sections.*

shriveled, lightly mist the storage medium. Keep them in cool temperatures, but be sure the temperatures do not drop below 35 degrees Fahrenheit.

EDIBLES

Once the ground has frozen, it is time to mulch around perennial vegetables, herbs, and fruits, including strawberries, rhubarb, sage, mint, and chives. Use clean wheat straw, chopped leaves, or pine needles if they are available. Winter mulching helps insulate the plants from the cycles of freezing and thawing that can heave the crowns out of the ground. If you grow fall-bearing raspberries, this is a good time to cut canes back to the ground as a final cleanup.

Harvest herbs as they continue to grow indoors.

LAWNS

Dormant lawn grasses need minimal care in winter. Remember to provide moisture on the open, warm days when there has been little or no snowfall.

PERENNIALS

Finish up any lagging chores and necessary grooming of ripened (mature) perennials. Mulch all perennials that are exposed to winter wind and fluctuations in temperatures to prevent frost heaves. Collect and store perennial plant stakes and supports.

The taller-growing perennials that have attractive seedpods can be left to add winter interest. As long as they remain erect and provide structure and

texture to the garden, don't prune them back quite yet. A heavy snow can flatten these dried stems, so they will have to be cut back eventually. Once the seedheads have been eaten by the birds and other wildlife and lose their winter interest, cut them back to tidy up the perennial bed.

ROSES

If you haven't already provided winter protection, hill up soil and mulch (pine needles, shredded wood chips, pole peelings, chopped leaves) over the crown, graft, and lower canes of hybrid tea and other grafted rose varieties. The grafted region, or bud union, should be planted *below* ground level in most parts of our region. Winter mulch should be piled 4 to 6 inches deep around the rose bush. This will insulate the ground to prevent the alternate freezing and thawing that damages the roots over the winter.

Limit pruning to dead and broken canes.

SHRUBS

Construct windbreaks around sensitive evergreen such as arborvitae, Alberta spruce and yew, and deciduous shrubs that are predisposed to winter damage or winterkill. Safeguard them from sunscald, wind, snow, critters, and desiccation. Protective snow sheds can be temporarily set over foundation plantings that are vulnerable when snow slides off the roof

Some evergreen shrubs tend to flop over or break off in heavy snowfall especially those that have

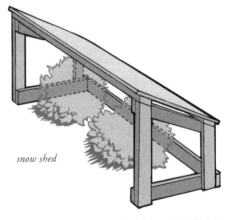

snow shed

■ *Temporary snow sheds can be placed over valuable shrub plantings, especially under roof eaves, to protect against heavy snow.*

multiple stems such as upright junipers and yews. They benefit from tying. Loosely gather the branches against the stems, and loop some binder twine around the entire bundle. Start at the bottom, and wrap the twine upward.

You can selectively prune a few branches from evergreen shrubs to use in holiday decorations. Try to maintain the natural form and beauty of the shrub. If you grow holly, prune some of the branches with red berries to decorate empty outdoor containers. Mix in a few sprigs of juniper or pine, and those outdoor pots won't be so drab looking.

TREES

Limit pruning of evergreens to collecting boughs and cones for holiday decorations. Place the cut ends in tepid water immediately, and keep them in water until it is time to make decorations. Spray evergreen decorations with an anti-desiccant to preserve moisture in the needles and stems. It is better to purchase evergreen boughs from a nursery than to extensively prune your own evergreens.

VINES, GROUNDCOVERS & ORNAMENTAL GRASSES

After the ground freezes, spread a 2- to 3-inch layer of mulch around new plantings to protect them from temperature fluctuations and hold in moisture. For the High Country, a blanket of snow is nature's best insulator to protect plants from wind and winter sun.

WATER

ANNUALS

Water seedlings growing indoors; let the growing mixture dry out slightly between waterings. Check soil moisture of transplants taken from the garden in autumn. If the soil feels dry, water.

Give your houseplants extra humidity especially in homes with forced air heating since it takes natural humidity out of the air. Make a pebble tray. Add a layer of gravel to a waterproof plant saucer and fill it with water to keep the container from sitting directly in the water. The water will evaporate and provide extra humidity around the plant. Refill the gravel layer as needed.

BULBS

Check bulbs in storage. Moisten the sphagnum peat moss, sawdust, or shredded newspaper that's surrounding the tender bulbs for the winter season. A misting will usually freshen the storage medium.

Bulbs potted for forcing will need some moisture even in cold storage. If the potting mixture feels dry to the touch or if the pot feels lighter, give them a drink. Allow the excess water to drain out, and discard water that accumulates in the drainage saucer.

EDIBLES

Indoor herbs need careful watering to avoid saturating the soil, especially those artificial mixes that can stay wet for longer periods. Allow the soil mix to dry out slightly between waterings to prevent root rot.

In warm periods without precipitation, check perennial vegetables and fruits to see if they are dry. Apply water early in the day when air temperatures are in the 45- to 50-degree Fahrenheit range.

LAWNS

Water established lawns, and particularly newly seeded or sodded lawns, during extended dry periods in winter. Winter watering should be done when temperatures are above freezing and the soil is unfrozen. Water early in the day with a frog-eye sprinkler so the water can percolate down to the subsoil where the roots can utilize it.

PERENNIALS

Until there is a major freeze and winter sets in, keep in mind that perennials may need supplemental irrigation during prolonged dry periods. Check the soil moisture underneath the mulch with a garden trowel or hand cultivator. As long as the ground remains unfrozen, apply the water early in the day when temperatures remain above freezing so it can soak in. Winter watering need only be done every four to five weeks during dry spells. Note the dry years and the general weather conditions, which vary from year to year, in your journal or notebook.

Remember that some rock garden perennials such as native penstemons, pussytoes, succulents, and cacti will not appreciate too much water. They will do best in soils that are gritty and well-drained. Native perennials are more adapted to local weather.

ROSES

Monitor soil moisture as needed. During prolonged dry, windy periods, get out the garden hose for winter watering. Water when temperatures are above freezing, early in the day, and when the soil is unfrozen. This will allow the moisture to soak in to where it is needed. Be sure to disconnect, drain, and store the hose away by nightfall.

Water miniature roses indoors as soon as the soil begins to feel dry to the touch. Avoid keeping the potting mixture too soggy—roses don't like wet feet. Provide good drainage by discarding excess water in the bottom saucer after an hour or so. This will prevent fungus gnats.

SHRUBS

There is always a chance that December will be a dry month. Check soil moisture underneath the mulch if three to four weeks pass without appreciable rain or snowfall. During periods of prolonged drought, pick a warm day and water shrubs. As long as the soil is unfrozen and you water early in the day, moisture will soak down so the roots will benefit.

TREES

During extended dry periods, check soil moisture for all your trees by probing the soil around the root zone. If the soil is dry to a depth of 4 to 6 inches, water early in the day when temperatures are above freezing. Drain, disconnect, and store your hose after use.

Once you plant your living Christmas tree in late December or early January, check monthly to see if there's adequate soil moisture. Winter watering may be necessary during extended dry spells.

VINES, GROUNDCOVERS & ORNAMENTAL GRASSES

If you have been watering regularly throughout the fall, vines, groundcovers, and ornamental grasses should be fine. It is important that these plants have adequate moisture before the ground freezes, especially the newly planted ones.

When there's no snow or rain for a prolonged period, you can water on a warm day. Temperatures should be above freezing, and the ground should not be frozen. Otherwise, the water will run off.

FERTILIZE

ALL

There's no need to fertilize anything planted in frozen ground. Store unused fertilizers for winter. Keep the granular forms in a cool, dry place. Store liquid fertilizers in a cool (above freezing), dark location.

Plants brought indoors for overwintering are still acclimating to the indoor conditions, so avoid frequent fertilizer applications. Lower light and low humidity result in poor growth. Wait until the plants start to grow before adding any fertilizer.

Go easy on fertilizing indoor herbs since they are not receiving the quantity and quality of light they were used to outdoors. Use a soluble plant fertilizer, but dilute it to half-strength and apply to a moistened soil. Never apply fertilizer to dried soil as the salts can damage a plant's tender roots.

If you did not apply a granular, slow-release fertilizer to the potting mixture of indoor miniature roses, you can feed your roses a water-soluble fertilizer. Or, if you prefer, sprinkle some granular plant food on the surface of the potting mixture, and lightly scratch it in. Read and follow product labels for frequency of application.

PROBLEM-SOLVE

ANNUALS

Check indoor annuals for pest infestations weekly. Scout for aphids, whiteflies, and spider mites. If you detect them, rinse the foliage with tepid water every few days, and follow up with a spray of homemade soap spray or insecticidal soap. Try trapping whiteflies with homemade or commercial yellow sticky traps. Coat a piece of yellow cardboard with a sticky substance (petroleum jelly). Place them in and near infested plants. This will reduce the damage to a tolerable level. Use an insecticide as a last resort. Read and follow label directions.

Control mites and aphids with a strong blast of water followed by some insecticidal soap. Repeated applications may be necessary.

BULBS

Mold may develop on non-hardy bulbs in storage, due to too much moisture. They will rot and spoil others. Toss them. Be sure there is good ventilation and that temperatures remain cool.

EDIBLES

Watch for aphids, whiteflies, and spider mites on indoor herbs. Warm, dry indoor conditions favor these pests. Periodically rinsing foliage under the kitchen faucet will keep most of these pests at bay.

Fungus gnats do not damage the plants, but their larvae feed on organic matter in the potting soil and (rarely) on plant roots. Keep plant debris from accumulating on the soil surface, and allow the soil mix to dry out between waterings.

LAWNS

De-icing salts to melt snow and ice accumulations on the sidewalk and driveway are harmful to most lawn grasses. The runoff from sodium-based de-icing products or the spray from city snow removal plows may end up on your nearby lawn. When this dissolves and enters the soil, it is harmful to the grass roots, causing the plant cells to die.

Use non-salt de-icing products to melt snow and ice. Consider kitty litter, coarse sand, or wood ashes on your sidewalks and driveways.

PERENNIALS

If wind continues to blow mulch off exposed garden beds, consider anchoring it down with chicken wire. Use landscape pins to hold the wire down.

Alternative mulches may prove helpful. I like to use pine needles because they knit together nicely and are less likely to blow away.

ROSES

Wind and drought can be the nemesis of all roses in the Rockies. Add to that, periods of warm winter weather that trick the plants into premature growth, followed by temperatures below freezing. In some years, roses must endure extensive winterkill. Be sure that hardy climbers are securely tied to their supports if left upright. If the canes of shrub roses are becoming battered by frequent winds, tie extra twine around the plants to steady them.

Indoor miniature roses can become stressed from lack of sufficient light and humidity. Check them often. If necessary, increase artificial light, and consider placing them on a pebble tray to add humidity.

SHRUBS

This is the season that critters visit the yard to nibble on the tips and bark of shrubs. Every once in a awhile check for signs of rabbits, field mice, and voles feeding at the base of shrubs. You may need to pull away mulch if it touches the base of the stems. Deer and elk hoofprints in the snow or mud and gnawed bark on shrub stems will clue you in that these four-legged creatures are visiting your garden. You may need to put up deer fencing or other barriers. Repellents are only temporary.

TREES

Strong winter winds can threaten young and newly transplanted trees in some exposures. Either stake them or construct wind barriers of burlap to block the worst of the wind's force. Do not use plastic.

Be on the watch for critters that like to munch on the tender bark of trees. Wire cages may be needed to protect the trunks of trees if deer and rabbits are of concern. Try the homemade deer repellent on page 221 that will help to deter critters. Re-spray after a snow or every few weeks as the materials will break down when exposed to sunlight and moisture.

VINES, GROUNDCOVERS & ORNAMENTAL GRASSES

Critters known as voles are one drawback of persistent snow. They can tunnel under the snow to eat the roots and tender bark of vines and groundcovers. Be on the watch for them. Trapping may be needed or you can check out the homemade repellent recipe on page 221. If deer are a continual problem, consider investing in a deer-proof fence.

Beware of road salt that is spread on the street to melt ice and snow. If a snowplow splashes this onto your groundcovers or other plants, the soluble salts can damage the roots. Shovel salt-laden snow and ice off plants, and leach the soil with copious amounts of water as soon as the ground thaws.

Homemade Remedies and Techniques for Pest Control

Compiling this book of advice and personal observations has led me into closer contact with our horticultural past, which is a combination of science and art. It has added to my respect for the experience and wisdom of the Gardeners Who Have Gone Before, those who were willing to experiment with natural ways to combat pests and diseases. My Italian grandmother taught me that homemade bug sprays made with Castile soap could effectively control a wide range of garden pests. She wasn't squeamish about handpicking or squashing the bad bugs that infested the garden. These old-fashioned traditions can be not only quite effective but also less meddlesome and less destructive to our earth's resources.

I hope you find these homemade recipes and remedies useful in your gardening endeavors. You may be creative and discover some of your own safe, natural methods of dealing with the various pests that invade your yard. May your Rocky Mountain garden grow and prosper!

SOAP SPRAY FOR APHIDS, SPIDER MITES, AND OTHER SMALL INSECTS

Household dishwashing soaps, like Ivory, and liquid Castile soaps made with olive and other plant oils, have been used for generations to control insect pests in both indoor and outdoor gardens. Many are effective insecticides when used as a diluted spray.

Tip: As cleaning products change or are "improved," be cautious that they do not contain additives such as bleach, degreasers, or chemicals that may be more caustic to the plant foliage. The old-fashioned, biodegradable soaps or liquid detergents are generally the safest to use.

1 to 2 tablespoons liquid Castile soap
1 quart water

Pour the mixture into a spray bottle, combine, and apply to the undersides of foliage, on infested stems, or directly to the insect pest.

Used at a diluted rate, soap sprays are generally safe for most plants. Some plants with waxy leaves may be more sensitive to soap sprays, so test the dilution on a small amount of foliage first to check for damage. **Caution:** Do not apply to the foliage in the heat of the day. Always apply soap sprays in the coolest part of the day or on an overcast day.

SPIDER MITE SPOILER

¼ cup buttermilk
2 cups flour
2 gallons water

Combine, and pour this mixture into a spray bottle; shake the potion thoroughly and often, as you spray it on plants that are bothered by spider mites.

POWDERY MILDEW CONTROL

Powdery mildew infects a wide variety of plants, including roses, lilacs, honeysuckles, crabapples, woodbine, phlox, dahlias, beebalm, and zinnia. This fungus disease coats the leaves with a grayish white powdery substance that looks ugly, but seldom kills the plant. If you're growing plants that are susceptible to this fungus, here's an effective homemade remedy to keep the disease at bay.

1 gallon water
2 to 3 tablespoons baking soda
1 tablespoon Castile soap or mild
  dishwashing soap

Mix all ingredients together well. Place in a tank sprayer or spray bottle and start spraying when you spot the first signs of the disease. Apply to both sides of the leaves. You can spray every seven to ten days as a preventative treatment before any sign of the disease appears; reapply after a heavy rain.

Tip: Remove badly infected leaves and dispose of them. Prune or thin plants to increase air circulation around the foliage. Keep your plants growing healthy with good cultural techniques, as stressed plants are more susceptible to infection.

GARDEN SLUG TRAP

They hide during the day and make their sneak attacks at night. They munch on the new and succulent leaves of flowers, vegetables, even lawns, and they can demolish whole plants with their voracious appetites. They are slugs!

You've most likely heard that beer attracts slugs. It does. They crawl to containers filled with beer, glide down into the brew, and drown. But I'm not fond of sharing my beer with slugs. Here's a homemade remedy that works better than beer.

1 cup water
1 teaspoon raw sugar
¼ teaspoon yeast

Warm the water in a microwave for one to two minutes. Add 1 teaspoon sugar, and stir until dissolved. Add ¼ teaspoon yeast, and mix thoroughly. Put this liquid slug bait in shallow containers, like empty tuna cans or yogurt cups cut in half. Bury the containers in the ground to their rims. The slugs will crawl in and drown. Repeat as often as necessary.

Traps should be checked each morning, and any slugs collected should be destroyed.

EARWIG TRAPS

Earwigs, often called pincher bugs, feed on fruits, decomposing plants, vegetables, and flowers. They will invade gardens, and can find their way indoors. Here are some methods to get rid of earwigs without chemicals.

- Encourage natural predators like toads and birds. They will feed on these pests.

- Roll up an old newspaper, moisten, and place near the base of your plants at dusk. You can also use cut up sections of an old garden hose. Earwigs will crawl into these traps. Empty traps into a bucket of soapy water every morning.

- Set out a shoebox trap by poking several holes in the outer sides of a shoebox near the base. Spread a thin layer of oatmeal or wheat bran in the box. Place the lid on the box and set this trap in the garden. Check traps in the morning and shake the pests into a pail of soapy water.

DEER AND RABBIT REPELLENT

6 egg yolks
1 teaspoon liquid lemon-scented dishwashing soap
2 to 3 tablespoons hot pepper sauce
1 gallon warm water

Purée the egg yolks in your kitchen blender. Add the hot pepper sauce, and pour the mixture into the warm water. Add the dishwashing soap. Thoroughly mix the ingredients. Spray this homemade remedy on the bark of trees and shrubs, and around the bases of flowers and vegetables that are frequently visited by deer and rabbits.

The aroma stops most deer, rabbits, and other browsing wildlife in their tracks. Reapply after a heavy rain or as often as needed.

HOMEMADE HORTICULTURAL OIL

Make your own horticultural oil from familiar household products. Use this spray to reduce invasions of aphids, whiteflies, soft scale, and spider mites.

Stock Solution

1 tablespoon liquid dishwashing soap, preferably lemon-scented
1 cup corn, olive, peanut, safflower, soybean, or sunflower oil

(The soap is needed to emulsify the oil in water. Do not use detergents with bleach or other additives that will burn plant foliage.) Combine the ingredients in a bowl and mix well. Store in a tightly sealed bottle. Add 1 to 2½ teaspoons of the stock solution to 1 cup of water. Pour solution into a plastic pump-handled bottle. Agitate the mixture and spray onto the undersides and topsides of infested leaves.

APPLE WORM (CODLING MOTH) TRAP

Water
1 cup sugar
1 cup apple cider vinegar
1 banana peel

Combine the ingredients in a 1-gallon plastic milk jug, and fill the jug almost ¾ full with water. Place the cap on the jug and shake this brew vigorously to blend thoroughly. Hang the gallon jug of this homemade remedy in the middle of each apple or pear tree. Be sure to remove the cap after you've secured the jug to a branch. Soon this trap will be packed with codling moths, the mothers of those dreaded apple worms. Empty traps as needed. Clean and reset traps throughout the growing season.

WEED BUSTER

The natural way to get rid of weeds in your garden is the "cowboy way"—pulling by hand, hoeing, or digging. If you're getting tired of this method, you can thwart them with a shot of vinegar spray. Grandma used this to kill weeds in the driveway and cracks in the sidewalk. It has a short residual in the soil, too, and can keep weeds from coming back up for several months. Vinegar is a nonselective weed control meaning it kills *anything* to which it is applied. Don't use in your lawn.

Vinegar (5% acetic acid)
Dishwashing soap, such as Ivory or Joy

To 1 gallon of vinegar add 1 ounce dishwashing soap. Spot-spray weeds, dousing the weed's foliage and the crown (the area at the base of the weed). Vinegar does not kill the roots. The roots may die anyway, depending on the type of weed. If the weed grows back, repeat the application.

Tips: Cut the bottom out of a plastic milk jug, and use the jug as a shield to keep spray off desirable plants. Place the milk jug over the weed and spray through the top opening of the bottle. Note, if you use a metal tank sprayer, be sure to rinse the sprayer with water because vinegar is corrosive.

TIRED & ACHING ROSES? TRY EPSOM SALTS!

Did you know that rose bushes like Epsom salts? Epsom salts can be used as a supplemental fertilizer on your rose bushes. American Rose Society members in Portland, Oregon, found that applying Epsom salts led to higher growth rates, increased basal breaks, stronger stems, and improved color and foliage. Epsom salts are suggested for use on magnesium-deficient soils.

Use at the rate of 1 tablespoon per rose bush each month throughout the growing season. Stop applications by mid-August.

ROSE TONIC

One of my favorite and most effective fertilizers for all roses is this homemade rose tonic from the late and passionate rosarian, Jo Kendzerski.

5 tablespoons Epsom salts
½ cup fish emulsion
⅓ cup Sequestrene™ Chelated Iron
5 tablespoons bloom-promoting fertilizer
    (15-30-15 or 10-60-10) soluble plant food

Combine the ingredients in 5 gallons of warm water, and mix thoroughly.

This tried-and-true homemade fertilizer mixture will "perk up" your roses, flowering shrubs, perennials, and annual flowers. It is especially good to use after transplanting bedding plants and vegetables.

How to Apply Rose Tonic to Roses, Ornamental Trees, and Shrubs

- Start applications of this fertilizer to rose bushes soon after leaf emergence in mid- to late spring.

- Water the rose garden prior to the application of the Rose Tonic.

- Use 2 quarts of tonic for each rose bush.

- Water the fertilizer into the soil with an additional 2 quarts of plain water.

- You can apply fertilizer to the rose garden every four to six weeks throughout the growing season; stop applications after mid-August.

How to Apply Rose Tonic to Flowers

Apply this homemade plant fertilizer to annual and perennial flowers early in the spring to get them off to a happy and healthy start. Follow up with monthly applications throughout the growing season.

SOIL SOLARIZATION FOR SOILBORNE DISEASE AND PEST CONTROL

If you've been plagued by recurring soil-inhabiting pests or diseases, here's a simple and inexpensive way to sterilize the soil without chemicals. Cover moist soil with transparent polyethylene plastic for six to eight weeks during the late summer and early fall. The process, known as soil solarization, also improves yields and crop quality.

During the process, radiant heat from the sun raises soil temperatures to levels lethal to plant pathogens such as Verticillium and Fusarium, weed seeds and seedlings, nematodes, and some soil-inhabiting mites. For effective treatment, the area should be moist, level, and free of weeds, debris, or large clods. Air pockets will slow the heating process, so press the plastic to the soil surface, and anchor it by burying the edges under soil. Moisture conducts heat faster and makes organisms more sensitive. Irrigate the area before laying the plastic. Or, soak the area afterward by inserting hoses under one end of the tarp.

Polyethylene plastic of 1 mil thickness is the most efficient and economical for soil heating. Patch holes as they occur. Thicker plastic up to 2 mils can withstand higher winds, but it reflects more solar energy away, which results in lower soil temperatures.

Killing pathogens and pests is related to time and temperature. Although some pests and organisms are killed within days, allow at least four to six weeks of treatment in full sun during the summer and early fall for maximum effectiveness.

Research has shown that soil solarization can increase yields and result in earlier crops, possibly by promoting the presence of beneficial micro- and macroorganisims such as mycorrhiza and by destroying phytotoxic substances in the soil.

FUNGI KILLER TO CLEAN AND DISINFECT CONTAINERS

When I was a young boy, Grandma would periodically clean flower pots with a household solution prepared from liquid bleach. Even with today's technology of fungicides, this homemade remedy remains one of the most effective and least expensive ways to disinfect containers and gardening tools.

Caution: Wear rubber gloves to protect your hands.

1. Scrub dirty clay and plastic pots with a brush to remove caked on soil and other debris.

2. Soak them in a solution of 1 part liquid bleach to 9 parts water (this is a 10-percent solution).

3. Allow the pots to soak for twenty to thirty minutes, remove from solution and let dry.

4. If you clean garden tools with this solution, remember that bleach can hasten rust formation on metal parts. Rinse metal parts thoroughly, and dry with a cotton cloth.

PRESERVE WINTER SQUASH AND GOURDS

Bleach can make winter squash and gourds last longer. Add 1 tablespoon bleach to 1 quart water. Wash dirt and other solids from the squash and gourds with the bleach solution, then dry with cloth or paper towel. Now your squash and gourds are ready to be put into storage in a cool, dry storage area till you need them.

FOUNTAIN OF YOUTH FOR SEEDS

Heat and humidity will shorten the life span of seeds. Specialists gently dry bulk seeds and seal them in moisture-proof containers with a desiccant to absorb moisture and keep them dry. Next, the seeds are placed in cool, air-conditioned storage. These precautions prolong seed vigor for three to five years. Now you can utilize a similar but inexpensive method of storing leftover garden seeds, using powdered milk as a desiccant. Here's how:

1. Unfold and stack four facial tissues.

2. On one corner of the stack, place 2 heaping tablespoons powdered milk from a freshly opened pouch or box to guarantee dryness.

3. Fold and roll the facial tissue to make a small pouch. Secure with tape or a rubber band. The tissue will prevent the milk from sifting out and will prevent seed packets from touching the desiccant as it absorbs moisture.

4. Place the desiccant pouch in a wide-mouthed jar, and immediately drop in packets of leftover seeds.

5. Seal the jar tightly using a rubber ring to exclude moist air. Store the jar in the refrigerator, not the freezer.

6. Discard and replace the desiccant once or twice yearly. Dried milk is "hygroscopic" and will quickly soak up moisture from the air when you open the bottle. Therefore, be quick about it when you remove seed packets, and recap the jar quickly.

7. Use seeds as soon as possible.

CUT FLOWER COCKTAIL

When you buy a bouquet of flowers, the florist will usually include a packet of floral preservative. It's formulated with sugar to feed the rootless flowers, citric acid to lower the water's pH and disinfectant to inhibit microorganisms that will clog up the "plumbing system of the flower stem." You should already have most of these components to make your own floral preservative.

1 tablespoon light corn syrup
½ teaspoon liquid bleach
2 tablespoons lemon or lime juice
1 quart warm water

Combine ingredients in the water, and mix thoroughly. Before placing the flowers in the vase, strip off the lower leaves that would otherwise be underwater. Excessive foliage in the water increases bacteria, contaminates the water, and shortens the shelf life of your cut flowers.

How to Attract Birds to Your Landscape

Wild birds can add color and motion to the landscape in all seasons. Planting trees and shrubs that provide food and shelter is a great way to bring them into your yard. Nature takes care of stocking the feeder, allowing you more time to sit back, relax, and watch the birds. You can add bird feeders and a birdbath for even more visitors.

Following are some hardy (Zones 3 through 5) plants to consider adding to your landscape:

Arborvitae (*Thuja occidentalis*) BS
Chokecherry (*Aronia*) BF, BS
Coralberry (*Symphoricarpos orbiculatus*) BF, BS, HB
Dogwood (*Cornus*) B, BF
Elderberry (*Sambucus*) B, BF, BS
Flowering plums and cherries (*Prunus*) BF, BS, HB
Juniper (*Juniperus*) BS
Lilac (*Syringa*) B, HB
Rose (*Rosa*) B, BF
Serviceberry (*Amelanchier*) BF
Spirea (*Spiraea*) B, BF, BS
Viburnum (*Viburnum*) B, BF, BS
Yew (*Taxus*) BS

KEY: B-Butterflies; BF-Food for Birds; BS-Shelter for birds; HB-Hummingbirds

SUPPLYING WATER FOR THE BIRDS

If you have a wildlife-friendly garden, set up a winter-proof birdbath to provide a fresh supply of water. It is essential for them since natural water supplies may be frozen. Some birdbaths have built-in heaters that will keep the water from freezing.

Glossary

Alkaline soil: soil with a pH greater than 7.0. It lacks acidity, often because it has limestone in it.

All-purpose fertilizer: powdered, liquid, or granular fertilizer with a balanced proportion of the three key nutrients—nitrogen (N), phosphorus (P), and potassium (K). It is suitable for maintenance nutrition for most plants.

Annual: a plant that lives its entire life in one season. It is genetically determined to germinate, grow, flower, set seed, and die the same year.

Balled and burlapped: describes a tree or shrub grown in the field whose soilball was wrapped with protective burlap and twine when the plant was dug up to be sold or transplanted.

Bare root: describes plants that have been packaged without any soil around their roots. (Often young shrubs and trees purchased through the mail arrive with their exposed roots covered with moist peat or sphagnum moss, sawdust, or similar material, and wrapped in plastic.)

Barrier plant: a plant that has intimidating thorns or spines and is sited purposely to block foot traffic or other access to the home or yard.

Beneficial insects: insects or their larvae that prey on pest organisms and their eggs. They may be flying insects, such as ladybugs, parasitic wasps, praying mantids, and soldier bugs, or soil dwellers such as predatory nematodes, spiders, and ants.

Berm: a raised volume of soil created in the landscape, often as an island or distinct area, onto which plants are situated to accent the landscape and alleviate poor drainage conditions.

Bract: a leaf-like plant part, usually small, sometimes showy or brightly colored, and located just below a flower, flower stalk, or inflorescence. The bract usually differs from an ordinary leaf in size, form, or texture. For example, poinsettia and bougainvillea bracts are petal-like, highly colored, and conspicuous. Often, the bract is more visible than the actual flower, as in dogwood.

Bud union: the place where the top of a plant was grafted to the rootstock; usually refers to roses.

Canopy: the overhead branching area of a tree, usually referring to its extent including foliage.

Cold hardiness: the ability of a perennial plant to survive the winter cold in a particular area.

Chelate: metal ion bonded on to an organic molecule from which it can be released. For example, iron, only slightly available to plants growing in alkaline soils in its usual ferric hydroxide form, is readily absorbed when applied as a chelated form.

Composite: a flower that is actually composed of many tiny flowers. Typically, they are flat clusters of tiny, tight florets, sometimes surrounded by wider-petaled florets. Composite flowers are highly attractive to bees and beneficial insects.

Compost: organic matter that has undergone progressive decomposition by microbial and macrobial activity until it is reduced to a spongy, fluffy texture. Added to soil of any type, it improves the soil's ability to hold air and water and to drain well.

Corm: the swollen energy-storing structure, analogous to a bulb, under the soil at the base of the stem of plants such as crocus and gladiolus.

Crown: the base of a plant at, or just beneath, the surface of the soil where the roots meet the stems.

Cultivar: a (CULTIvated VARiety). It is a naturally occurring form of a plant that has been identified as special or superior and is purposely selected for propagation and production.

Deadhead: a pruning technique that removes faded flower heads from plants to improve their appearance, abort seed production, and stimulate flowering.

Deciduous plants: unlike evergreens, these trees and shrubs lose their leaves in the fall.

Desiccation: drying out of foliage tissues, usually due to drought or wind.

Division: the practice of splitting apart perennial plants to create several smaller-rooted segments. The practice is useful for controlling the plant's size and for acquiring more plants; it is also essential to the health and continued flowering of certain ones.

Dormancy: the period, usually the winter, when perennial plants temporarily cease active growth and rest. Dormant is the verb form, as used in this sentence: Some plants, like spring-blooming bulbs, go dormant in the summer.

Established: the point at which a newly planted tree, shrub, or flower begins to produce new growth, either foliage or stems. This is an indication that the roots have recovered from transplant shock and have begun to grow and spread.

Evergreen: perennial plants that do not lose their foliage annually with the onset of winter. Needled or broadleaf foliage will persist and continues to function on a plant through one or more winters, aging and dropping unobtrusively in cycles of three or four years or more.

Foliar: of or about foliage—usually refers to the practice of spraying foliage, as in fertilizing or treating with insecticide; leaf tissues absorb liquid directly for fast results, and the soil is not affected.

Floret: a tiny flower, usually one of many forming a cluster, which comprises a single blossom.

Frog-eye sprinkler: an old-fashioned, cast iron or metal sprinkler that resembles a "frog-eye" or "owl's eye;" used above ground to release water at a low arc in a circular pattern. Depending upon water pressure, this delivers water slowly and uniformly to the soil and is especially useful to water at the driplines of trees and shrubs.

Girdling: a ring or wound made by removing the bark around a tree's trunk or a plant's stem, which weakens and can kill the plant. Usually caused by a mower or string trimmer.

Germinate: to sprout. Germination is a fertile seed's first stage of development.

Graft (union): the point on the stem of a woody plant with sturdier roots where a stem from a highly ornamental plant is inserted so that it will join with it. Roses are commonly grafted.

Hardscape: the permanent, structural, nonplant part of a landscape, such as walls, sheds, pools, patios, and arbors.

Herbaceous: plants having fleshy or soft stems that die back with frost; the opposite of woody.

Hybrid: a plant that is the result of intentional or natural cross-pollination between two or more plants of the same species or genus.

Low water demand: describes plants that tolerate dry soil for varying periods of time. Typically, they have succulent, hairy, or silvery-gray foliage and tuberous roots or taproots.

Microclimate: local variations from the general or regional climate due to slight differences in elevation, direction of slope exposure, soil, density of vegetation, modified temperatures, etc. Such areas may allow growth of less hardy or tender plants.

Mulch: a layer of material over bare soil to protect it from erosion and compaction by rain, and to discourage weeds. It may be inorganic (gravel, fabric) or organic (wood chips, bark, pine needles, chopped leaves).

Naturalize: (a) to plant seeds, bulbs, or plants in a random, informal pattern as they would appear in their natural habitat; (b) to adapt to and spread throughout adopted habitats (a tendency of some nonnative plants).

Nectar: the sweet fluid produced by glands on flowers that attract pollinators such as hummingbirds and honeybees for whom it is a source of energy.

Node: the region of the stem where one or more leaves are attached. Buds are commonly borne at a node, in the axils of the leaves.

Nymph: the young stage of an insect with incomplete metamorphosis, differing is size from the adult form.

Organic material, organic matter: any material or debris that is derived from plants. It is carbon-based material capable of undergoing decomposition and decay.

Peat moss: organic matter from peat sedges (United States) or sphagnum mosses (Canada), often used to improve soil texture. The acidity of sphagnum peat moss makes it ideal for boosting or maintaining soil acidity while also improving its drainage.

Perennial: a flowering plant that lives over two or more seasons. Many die back with frost, but their roots survive the winter and generate new shoots in the spring.

Perlite: white and very porous volcanic mineral that is used as a medium for rooting cuttings, starting seeds, and as a soil amendment.

pH: a measurement of the relative acidity (low pH) or alkalinity (high pH) of soil or water based on a scale of 1 to 14, 7 being neutral. Individual plants require soil to be within a certain range so that nutrients can dissolve in moisture and be available to them.

Pinch: to remove tender stems and/or leaves by pressing them between thumb and forefinger. This pruning technique encourages branching, compactness, and flowering in plants, or it removes aphids clustered at growing tips.

Pollen: the yellow, powdery grains in the center of a flower. A plant's male sex cells, they are transferred to the female plant parts by means of wind or animal pollinators to fertilize them and create seeds.

Raceme: an arrangement of single stalked flowers along an elongated, unbranched axis.

Rhizome: a swollen energy-storing stem structure, similar to a bulb, that lies horizontally in the soil, with roots emerging from its lower surface and growth shoots from a growing point at or near its tip, as in bearded iris.

Rootbound (or potbound): the condition of a plant that has been confined in a container too long, its roots having been forced to wrap around themselves and even swell out of the container. Successful transplanting or repotting requires untangling and trimming away of some of the matted roots.

Root flare: the transition at the base of a tree trunk where the bark tissue begins to differentiate and roots begin to form just before entering the soil. This area should not be covered with soil when planting a tree.

Self-seeding: the tendency of some plants to sow their seeds freely around the yard. It creates many seedlings the following season that may or may not be welcome.

Semievergreen: tending to be evergreen in a mild climate but deciduous in a rigorous one.

Shearing: the pruning technique whereby plant stems and branches are cut uniformly with long-bladed pruning shears (hedge shears) or powered hedge trimmers. It is used when creating and maintaining hedges and topiary.

Slow-acting fertilizer: fertilizer that is water insoluble and therefore releases its nutrients gradually as a function of soil temperature, moisture, and related microbial activity. Typically granular, it may be organic or synthetic.

Succulent growth: the sometimes undesirable production of fleshy, water-storing leaves or stems that results from overfertilization.

Sucker: a new growing shoot. Underground plant roots produce suckers to form new stems and spread by means of these suckering roots to form large plantings, or colonies. Some plants produce root suckers or branch suckers as a result of pruning or wounding.

Sunscald: damage to the bark of trees, typically on the southwest side, when the bark splits and cracks. This happens when sunlight and heat on the southwest facing side heats up during the warm fall and winter days to make cells become active. When the temperatures plummet at night, the activated cells are killed, resulting in splits and frost cracks on the trunk.

Terminal bud: bud that develops at the end of a branch or stem.

Texture: relative proportion in a soil of the various size groups of individual soil particles. The coarseness or fineness of the soil depends on the predominance of one or the other of these groups, which are silt, clay, and sand.

Thatch: the dry layer of organic matter at the soil surface in a lawn.

Tilth: the physical ability of the soil to support the growth of a specific plant species; also, the state of being tilled, or prepared for a crop; for example, this land is good tilth.

Tuber: a type of underground storage structure in a plant stem, analogous to a bulb. It generates roots below and stems above ground (example: dahlia).

Variegated: having various colors or color patterns. The term usually refers to plant foliage that is streaked, edged, blotched, or mottled with a contrasting color, often green with yellow, cream, or white.

Vermiculite: a mineral, classified with the micas, which, with treatment at high temperatures, expand into wormlike scales and become a loose, absorbent mass. Commercial vermiculite is used as a mulch for seed beds, as a medium for rooting plant cuttings, and in potting soils.

White grubs: fat, off-white, wormlike larvae of various beetles. They reside in the soil and feed on plant (especially grass) roots until summer when they emerge as beetles to feed on plant foliage.

Wings: (a) the corky tissue that forms edges along the twigs of some woody plants such as winged euonymus; (b) the flat, dried extension of tissue on some seeds, such as maple, that catch the wind and help them disseminate.

Xeric or xeriscape plant: a plant that can withstand dry conditions most of the time. However, xeriscapes can have heavily irrigated areas as well as dry regions. Plants do not waste water, people do.

Xeriscape: A term used to describe a dry or desert-like (xeric) view, scene, or landscape; coined in 1981 by the Associated Landscape Contractors of Colorado to promote water conservation through water-efficient landscaping.

Index

Photo Credits

Bill Kersey: pp. 15, 19, 22, 62 (both), 67, 111 (right), 117, 124 (left), 135, 191 (right), 216 (right)

Candace Edwards: pp. 20 (both), 26 (all), 28, 29, 30, 34 (top), 40 (all), 56, 65, 73 (both), 74 (top), 78 (bottom), 79 (bottom), 90, 91, 97, 101 (right), 103, 111 (left), 113 (all), 114 (all), 116, 118, 119, 123 (left), 132 (all), 133 (left), 148 (all), 152, 153 (left), 155, 158, 160 (left), 164 (all), 172 (all), 175 (top)

Cool Springs Press: pp. 9, 10, 35, 57 (all), 58, 60, 76 (all), 77 (all), 78 (top), 79 (top), 80, 81, 82 (both), 86, 94 (all), 96 (all), 104, 120, 133 (right), 136, 165 (both), 168 (all), 169 (all), 170 (all), 171 (all), 184, 188 (all), 189 (both), 198, 204, 208

Heather Claus: p. 55

Jerry Pavia: p. 190

Lynn Steiner: pp. 37, 49

Neil Soderstrom: pp. 18, 25, 74 (bottom), 110, 149, 191 (left), 216 (left)

Shutterstock: pp. 6, 8, 16, 23, 24, 32, 34 (bottom), 36, 39, 42, 43, 45, 48 (both), 50, 66, 68, 72, 87, 88, 99, 100, 101 (left), 105, 106, 107, 108, 112, 123 (right), 124 (right), 126, 128, 129, 134 (both), 141 (all), 142, 144, 145 (bottom), 147, 150, 151 (both), 160 (right), 162, 167, 174, 175 (bottom), 176, 177, 178, 180, 182, 186, 187, 192, 194, 196, 200 (both), 202, 206, 212, 214, 225

Tom Eltzroth: pp. 54, 92, 145 (top)

Troy Marden: pp. 98, 153 (right)

Meet John Cretti

Regionally known gardening expert, radio and television host, author, columnist, and former horticulture specialist for Colorado State University Extension, John Cretti has more than forty years of horticulture experience. John hosted *Gardening with an Altitude* radio program for thirty years and provided expertise on *Rocky Mountain Gardening* for area TV and HGTV.

His down-to-earth approach broadens the horizons of gardeners dealing with the unique and challenging climates of the Rocky Mountain region, where temperature fluctuations, wind, hail, unpredictable storms, difficult soils, and cunning critters are the norm.

John has spent his life growing all kinds of plants, beginning as a child under the tutelage of his Italian grandmother, aunts, and uncle. This inspired his interest and passion for gardening while growing up in Western Colorado.

He has written hundreds of articles and features for newspapers and magazines including *Flower and Garden, Horticulture, Colorado and Boulder County Home & Garden, Green Thumb Extra, Garden Talk, Rocky Mountain News*, and *Post Independent*. He was columnist and contributing editor for the National Gardening Association and contributes to various other websites.

John's many accomplishments include various Garden Media Awards—Quill and Trowel Award for television and radio work from the Garden Writers Association, the Scotts' Horticultural Professional Improvement Award for lawn and garden communications, and the National Association of County Agricultural Agents Award of Excellence in Horticulture Communications. He also was recognized for outstanding community service for garden and education programs by Xeriscape Colorado. In addition to this book for Cool Springs Press, John is co-author of the *Rocky Mountain Gardener's Handbook* and author of the *Rocky Mountain Getting Started Gardener's Guide*.

Visit with John at his website:
www.gardeningwithanaltitude.com

CPSIA information can be obtained
at www.ICGtesting.com
Printed in the USA
LVHW02s1424270118
564201LV00007B/7/P